The NEW Adolescence

Also by Christine Carter, PhD

Raising Happiness: 10 Simple Steps for More
Joyful Kids and Happier Parents

The Sweet Spot: How to Accomplish More by Doing Less

The NEW Adolescence

Raising Happy and Successful Teens in an Age of Anxiety and Distraction

Christine Carter, PhD

BenBella Books, Inc.
Dallas, TX

The events and conversations in this book, while true, are recreated from the author's memory. In certain instances, names and places have been changed to protect an individual's privacy.

The New Adolescence copyright © 2020 by Christine Carter

BenBella Books, Inc.
10440 N. Central Expressway, Suite 800
Dallas, TX 75231
www.benbellabooks.com
Send feedback to feedback@benbellabooks.com

BenBella is a federally registered trademark.

Printed in the United States of America
10 9 8 7 6 5 4 3 2 1

Library of Congress Control Number: 2019031914
ISBN 9781948836548 (trade paper)
ISBN 9781948836791 (electronic)

Editing by Joe Rhatigan
Copyediting by Karen Wise
Proofreading by Lisa Story and Ashley Casteel
Indexing by Debra Bowman
Text design by Publishers' Design & Production Services, Inc.
Text composition by PerfecType, Nashville, TN
Cover design by Oceana Garceau
Cover images © iStock / nndanko (shoes), photopsist (glass), and alexey_boldin (phone)
Author photo by Blake Farrington
Printed by Lake Book Manufacturing

Distributed to the trade by Two Rivers Distribution, an Ingram brand
www.tworiversdistribution.com

Special discounts for bulk sales are available. Please contact bulkorders@benbellabooks.com.

For Macie, Fiona, Tanner, and Amalia—
I love you forever and ever no matter what.

Contents

Preface

This is a terrifying time to be a parent.

Teens today are suffering from an epidemic of anguish that cannot be ignored. Fewer than half of today's teens would rate their own mental health as "excellent" or "very good." Last year, almost one-third of high schoolers felt so sad or hopeless that they stopped doing their usual activities almost every day for two or more weeks in a row. Nearly 20 percent seriously considered suicide.

While we've always known that teenagers can be moody, this is *not* what we are seeing here. Nor are we now newly detecting problems that have been in our society all along. The number of American adolescents who reported having had major depression in the preceding year has increased 52 percent since 2005, with the largest increases coming after 2011. The number of teens who visited emergency rooms for suicidal thoughts and suicide attempts *doubled* between 2007 and 2015. This isn't a "phase" that teenagers are going to grow out of. Since 2008, there has been a *71 percent* increase in young adults ages eighteen to twenty-five experiencing serious psychological distress.

And yet, as a parent and a sociologist, I ignored the influx of alarming statistics for many years in order to quell my own anxiety . . . until I did the math. I have four teenagers, making it statistically likely that one of my children will be counted in one of those scary statistics. Instead of denying the odds, or continuing to ignore the data, I got to work on a sequel (of sorts) to my first parenting book, *Raising Happiness*, which was published in 2010.

I am not the same parent now that I was when I wrote *Raising Happiness*. I've remarried and gone from being a single mom to my creative, energetic, and compassionate girls—Molly and Fiona—to being a married mom in a blended family of six. I've gained an amazing, loving stepdaughter, Macie, and an affectionate, charming stepson, Tanner. As I write this preface, the kids are fifteen, sixteen, seventeen, and eighteen years old.

Our family is really different now than it was when I wrote *Raising Happiness,* but I've written *The New Adolescence* in the same spirit: as **a handbook for helping our kids thrive in an age of accelerated change**. Guided by research from neuroscience, psychology, and sociology, I've identified some best practices that are likely to be helpful to a wide range of families.

While I'd like to say that I did this purely for the benefit of the world, the truth is that I also did it for myself and my own family. Things are profoundly different from the way they were only a decade ago, and I realized only recently that I needed to take my own parenting up a notch. Like many authors, I write to figure out what I think and what I know, and I do research to fill in the gaps. I do hope that what I have written here helps you with the teenagers in your life as much as it has helped me with mine.

Take the strategies that work for you, and leave the ones that don't; there's no need to saddle yourself with unrealistic expectations that you'll do it all, and certainly not that you'll do it all perfectly. Raising teenagers takes courage. Our best bet, as my dear friend Susie Rinehart always says, is to choose "brave over perfect."

Here's what this book is *not*: It isn't a substitute for therapy or other professional help. It's not meant to guide you or your kids back from the throes of addiction, depression, or crippling anxiety. If you or someone in your family is really struggling, and especially if you think that they might hurt themselves, please talk to a professional—a licensed medical or mental health provider—right away.

And if your kids are struggling with mental health issues, your family isn't alone. Have compassion for yourself. What you are going through is hard. I hope that this book will help, and also that you will surround yourself with emotional support.

A note about who this book is for and how I'm protecting my kids' privacy: First, when I say "kids" or "teens" in this book, I'm technically talking about *adolescents*. Many researchers avoid the term "teenager" because it implies that all the action is happening between the ages of thirteen to eighteen. In truth, most girls are at the end of puberty by the age of thirteen. And the hormones that cause puberty—and the behavior we typically think of as teenagery—start changing the brain before they start changing the body.

Because, biologically speaking, a lot of adolescent growth happens between the ages of nine and thirteen (puberty typically lasts two to four years), this book is written for educators, caregivers, and parents of kids potentially as young as nine. Socially and culturally, as well as from a brain standpoint, adolescence lasts much longer than puberty . . . usually until kids (especially boys) are in their mid-twenties or later. So, even though I may refer to kids or teenagers throughout this book, I'm really talking about adolescents: preteens, teenagers, and young adults. I call them kids not because of their age, but because I'm writing from the perspective of a parent, and my kids will always be my kids, no matter how old they are.

Speaking of my kids, I've decided to protect their privacy in the following way: When I'm telling a story that is less than flattering, I will not use their names, opting instead for the less elegant but vaguer "my daughter." I'll always use female pronouns, so it won't be clear which of my children I'm talking about, and also so Tanner won't be singled out. (And if we are friends, and you are talking to my kids, please don't try to guess who is who!)

Finally, I'm grateful that my children are brave enough to be a part of this book at all. They know that it may open them up to some annoying questions, but they see how their generation is struggling, and they want to be a part of the solution. Their honest (and sometimes unconscious) feedback has made this book immeasurably better. I'm so happy to be on this great family adventure with them, with Molly and Fiona's dad, Mike, and with my unfailingly positive husband, Mark.

Molly, Tanner, Fiona, and Macie: Thank you for being on this great journey with me. Your courage inspires us all and makes the world a better place for teenagers everywhere.

Introduction

In January, our longtime family friend Sayra was totally fine. She stood in my kitchen beaming and radiant. A soon-to-graduate senior at a nearby college, she often came to our house for dinner. Over the last four years, she'd become a true role model for our kids.

At twenty-one years old, she was really coming into her own. She had just returned home from a semester abroad, and she was standing taller than I'd ever seen her before. Her straight, glossy, dark hair fell around her shoulders, swishing as she told us excitedly about her time away. Sayra was healthy and confident and beautiful. My four teenagers stood around her in rapt attention, a little starstruck.

By February, Sayra was back to her normal college routine, getting straight As, working on her senior thesis. She was starting to worry about what she would do after graduation, which seemed both normal and strange to me, as she'd just landed a plum internship with a prominent newspaper.

The next time we saw her, she hinted that she was struggling a little. She was spending three full days each week at the newspaper's San Francisco office, in addition to her full load of classes, her thesis, and a part-time job as a Spanish tutor. It was a lot.

The daughter of immigrants, Sayra grew up unconditionally loved and well cared for. Her parents believed she and her brother could do anything, be anything. They made sure Sayra went to great schools and played sports. They are active members of their church. They are the very definition of a tight-knit family.

But in some ways, Sayra misunderstood her parents' encouragement and support. When they said that she could be *anything* she
wanted to be, Sayra heard that she needed to be *great*. When they told
her she could do *anything*, Sayra heard that she needed to do *everything*.

Almost overnight, being great at everything became too much.

By March, Sayra was in a downward spiral of depression and anxiety. She wasn't sleeping. She'd gotten her first B–, the lowest grade she
could remember. She didn't know how to handle that kind of "failure." She felt she was falling behind on her thesis (although her professors didn't agree), and the newspaper was now sometimes asking for
three stories a week instead of two (because her work was so good). She
didn't know how to say no. She feared disappointing everyone.

She began to have panic attacks, which are terrifying. (A person
having a panic attack often feels like she's dying.) Some days, she was
unable to get out of bed. Five weeks before her magna cum laude college graduation, Sayra was contemplating suicide. Her inner world had
gotten so dark and fearful that she struggled to see a reason to live.
She began punching the insides of her arms until they were covered in
blue bruises—hurting herself on the outside so that she could see and
feel the pain that was tormenting her on the inside. Her bright future
seemed to be vanishing into thin air.

Fortunately, Sayra's parents were able to get her into treatment. She
started seeing a psychologist at her college several times a week. Her
professors helped her make a plan to get back on track academically.
The psychologist helped Sayra quit her job and her internship, to give
her time to recover. In June, Sayra graduated on time and with honors.

Unfortunately, Sayra's story is not uncommon. Sayra's cohort of
teenagers and college students (kids born between 1995 and 2012 are
often called Generation Z, or Gen Z) is on the brink of the most serious mental health crisis we've seen since we started measuring these
things. No matter what data we look at, mental illness in teenagers and
college students has skyrocketed in a very short period of time, zoom-
ing upward after 2011. And as I mentioned in the preface, this isn't just
a wave of mental illness that we're seeing, according to renowned psychologist and demographer Jean Twenge: "It's a tsunami."

I had seen the scary statistics before Sayra got sick. I'd carefully
read Twenge's book, *iGen: Why Today's Super-Connected Kids Are*

Growing Up Less Rebellious, More Tolerant, Less Happy—and Completely Unprepared for Adulthood—and What That Means for the Rest of Us. But it didn't totally register for me that **this was something that really could happen to one of my kids . . . that it really was happening all around me in families I knew and loved.** When Sayra got sick, it suddenly hit me that the tsunami of mental illness that is overwhelming today's teenagers was not something I could, in good conscience, look away from.

Like me, many parents turn away when they are confronted with super-scary and very depressing information, finding reasons that the data do not apply to their families. Often, we write off adolescent depression and anxiety as normal teenage angst. We consider teenage drug and alcohol abuse normal experimentation, just like the partying we did in high school. **Except that we know that this generation is different.** Make no mistake: the mental illness and addictions they are suffering from are not normal.

This means that it's time for us to take action. We need to understand what is happening so that we can course-correct. In the words of Marie Curie: "Nothing in life is to be feared, it is only to be understood. Now is the time to understand more, so that we may fear less."

The good news is that we *do* understand why this generation is different and why they are suffering, and this means that we understand what we can do to reverse and prevent the scary trends in mental illness.

Under Pressure

I often hear parents' laments about how much pressure their kids seem to be under from school—how much homework they get and how stiff the competition is in virtually everything from athletics and academics to leadership and the performing arts. And I also hear from teachers and school administrators about how unreasonable parents are these days, pressuring their kids to achieve, to get into an elite college. More than 60 percent of high school students today say they feel "a lot" of pressure to get good grades; another 27 percent say they feel "some" pressure to do so.

Kids today seem so much busier than previous generations—taking more Advanced Placement (AP) classes, doing more homework, volunteering more, playing more competitive sports, and so on—all as a means to get into a selective, brand-name college. Vicki Abeles, director of the film *Race to Nowhere*, has been sounding the alarm about academic stress for more than a decade. "In homes and classrooms across America, a silent epidemic is raging," she writes in her book, *Beyond Measure*.

> It afflicts the eight-year-old lying awake, pulling his hair with worry over tomorrow's test. The seventeen-year-old straining to keep up in AP chemistry on top of the three other AP classes and two sports and four clubs that she thought she needed on her résumé. And the thirteen-year-old still studying past one a.m., wondering in the back of her bleary mind if *this*—this never-ending contest for credentials, this exhaustion, this feeling of meaninglessness—is all life is.

Our education culture has clearly been warped by competition. College admissions scandals, where wealthy parents buy their children spots on elite college campuses, make it obvious that our supposedly meritocratic educational system has become dysfunctional as more and more students apply for admission to the same handful of elite universities.

But I don't think this narrative—that kids are cracking under the pressure to achieve—accurately represents everything that is really happening. If it were, you'd think that once the pressure of gaining acceptance to a college was off (because they were admitted and attending), students would begin to feel a little less overwhelmed. They don't, though. College students are not doing any better than younger teenagers.

In fact, the American Freshman Survey recently documented the highest levels of unhappiness ever recorded in first-year college students. Every single indicator of a mental health problem measured in the National College Health Assessment has reached an all-time high. More than 63 percent of undergraduate college students felt "overwhelming anxiety" in the last 12 months; 42 percent felt so depressed they could not function. And, like Sayra, 8 percent of college students intentionally injured themselves in the previous year, a 30 percent increase since 2011.

When we step back and look at the data, we can see that *all* segments of teens, not just college-bound ones, seem to be having a hard time coping. What's happening to the kids whose parents *aren't* pushing them to get into a selective college? What about the teens who *aren't* running faster and faster on a hamster wheel of APs and varsity sports? There must be something else at work besides, or in addition to, increasingly competitive college admissions. While it's true that our education culture has gone insane with competition, and while it's true that our society is fixated on one narrow definition of success, this is only part of the picture.

For starters, kids today aren't actually working themselves into the ground relative to past generations. The data show that my generation, Gen X, actually did more homework in the early 1990s than our Gen Z teenagers are doing. And while kids heading to four-year colleges might be obsessed with their college applications, today's teenagers aren't piling on more extracurricular activities than in generations past—time spent on student clubs and sports hasn't changed much over time.

In fact, teenagers today have more free time because they aren't working for pay as often. In the late 1970s, 78 percent of high school seniors worked for pay during the school year. By the early 2010s, only 56 percent had jobs.

A caveat: It's not that all segments of society are suffering at the same rates—it's that spiky increases in depression, anxiety, and suicidality are happening *throughout* society. It's true, for example, that teens with lower socioeconomic status suffer from higher rates of depressive symptoms than those with higher socioeconomic status. **And girls are suffering much more than boys.** One in five girls ages twelve to seventeen report experiencing a major depressive episode in the past year. Almost 40 percent of ninth- to twelfth-grade girls felt so sad or hopeless they stopped doing their usual activities . . . and *nearly one-quarter considered suicide.* About one-fifth made a plan to kill themselves, and more than 10 percent actually tried to do it.

The Perfect Storm

The pressure to achieve is not the only thing that is causing depression and anxiety in our kids. Teens today are growing up in a perfect storm of social change happening so fast that our schools and our parenting aren't keeping up.

Think about it: We are living and parenting through one of the greatest transformations in human history. The fourth industrial revolution—the relatively recent technological transformation in virtually every industry, from transportation and pharmaceuticals to communication and agriculture—has fostered parallel social and psychological revolutions. **In a single generation, how we all communicate, create, work, and think has fundamentally changed.**

But the technological revolution we are living through hasn't really *re*shaped the current generation of teenagers as much as it has *shaped* them to begin with.

Today's teenagers communicate with social media more than they see their friends in person. They binge-watch TV series alone in their rooms on personal devices instead of watching a sitcom in the family room. Many delay driving; affluent teens use Uber and Lyft. They shop online—clicking on ads that are served specifically to them—instead of hanging out at the mall with their peers.

Humans have endured big changes like this before. In the fifteenth century, for example, the invention of the printing press gave birth to mass communication, which led to social, cultural, political, religious, and artistic advancements affecting the way that people lived, learned, and built their communities. The resulting scientific revolution and the Renaissance paved the way for the Age of Reason and the Enlightenment. All of these things changed human society forever.

Few would argue in favor of reversing the period of growth and development that occurred as human society emerged from the Dark Ages. But let's not forget that these changes were probably not easy for the people adapting to them, who had to live through the massive institutional, societal, cultural, and religious upheaval as the new information era reshaped the human world. Humans, and human social structures, like families, schools, and businesses, need time to adapt to change, especially big change.

All of this is to say that the epidemic of anxiety and depression we are seeing comes not from the new technologies themselves, but from our lagging adaptations to this massive social change. Everything is changing so quickly that we can't keep up. We aren't teaching our kids how to manage their smartphones and social media, for example, in ways that won't hurt them. Why? Because most of us parents haven't adapted to all the new technologies ourselves, much less adapted our parenting. Eric "Astro" Teller, CEO of Google's X research and development lab, explains that when the rate of technological change exceeds our ability to adapt to it, as it now has, we human beings become "dislocated."

This means that our world is being reshaped faster—way faster—than we have yet been able to reshape our parenting. It's no surprise that the kids are feeling unmoored.

I am not hoping to slow or reverse technological change—that's not even possible, even if it were desirable. Nor is this book a social

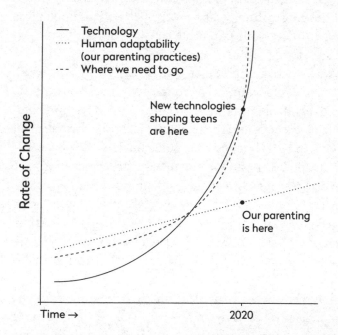

Adapted from Thomas L. Friedman's Thank You for Being Late *(London: Penguin UK, 2016).*

critique. I'm a sociologist, observing what is happening with acceptance and curiosity—if not resignation. And I'm a parent, determined to help my four kids adapt to this new world in ways that protect them. Adaptation isn't just about new digital technology; it's about all the ways that our world and our society have changed in just one generation.

For those reasons, this book is not about returning to a more analog world or trying to recreate what was good about *our* childhoods or *our* adolescence. This book offers adaptations for how we can integrate new ways of being, feeling, and doing into what we know produces health and happiness in humans—in both individuals and societies.

Parenting 2.0

There is good news here: We do understand, for the most part, what is causing the massive wave of depression, anxiety, and suicidality in our teenagers. And because we understand the causes, **the solutions are right in front of us**. We can adapt our parenting so that society transforms along with the new technologies—for the better. This book gives you concrete ways to adapt your parenting so that your kids are protected from these terrifying trends.

This book will help you upgrade to Parenting 2.0 in two ways. *The New Adolescence* offers adaptations to the two massive transformations that are likely happening in your family: the developmental transformation of adolescence and the technological transformation of the age we are living in. This book is your guide both to the new realities of parenting an adolescent and to the new technologies that have turned your tweener, teenager, or college student into a "screenager."

Once kids enter middle school, how we parent changes. What works for younger children doesn't work for teenagers. In addition, most of us are charting new ground here, because the ways that *we* were parented when we were teenagers certainly won't work for adolescents today.

You've probably heard that really skillful parents go from being their children's managers when they are in elementary school to being their coaches (or consultants) when they enter high school. **Part one** of this book will show you how and why to influence your teen *without* micromanaging them—even though you may be surrounded by heli-copter parents who have not made this shift.

To that end, chapters one, two, three, and four are science-based pep talks that will make parenting easier for you and life better for them.

In addition to adapting our parenting to our kids' developmental stage, we need to adapt our parenting to account for all the new technologies that have so dramatically changed our lives—and the lives of our teenagers. **Part two** will give you the three most important and character-building skills that parents can teach their teens for success and happiness in the digital age: **connection, focus, and rest**. You'll learn how and why new technologies like smartphones and social media are contributing to the largest mental health crisis we've ever seen—but more important, you'll learn simple, concrete strategies for protecting your kids' mental health.

Again, there is good news here, as there is a buy-one, get-one-free special running in part two of this book! As you teach your kids how to cope with their smartphones and social media so that the new technologies don't undermine their friendships, their ability to manage stress, and their focus, *you'll* also likely become happier, more productive, and less stressed-out.

Part three is your handbook for talking to your teen about topics that, if you are like me, you'd rather not talk about: **sex, drugs, and money**. All of these things have changed dramatically for today's teenagers, so our parental talking points need to change as well.

For example, we know that we need to talk to our kids about the birds and the bees, but thanks to internet porn, sexting, and social media, it's a whole new world out there. Want to know how to handle this? Your talking points are in chapter eight. Similarly, drug and alcohol abuse has changed dramatically since we were teens. Chapter nine will give you the skinny on vaping, today's super-potent marijuana, and binge-drinking trends.

Finally, chapter ten provides tips and talking points on raising teens who are financially responsible in an era of credit cards and high consumer spending. Did you know that 40 percent of Americans today have less than $400 cash in the bank that they could use in an emergency? While we can't make more money appear in the bank for them, we can help our kids develop a healthy and skillful relationship with their finances, including their spending and saving.

As you read this book, please remember that you don't have to get it all right. Legions of parents have been getting things wrong for eons, and somehow most of us turn out okay in the end. My great hope is that this book makes parenting your teenagers more joyful and less stressful. I hope it gives you the tools you need to know that you've done your best—and that your best is absolutely good enough.

The Foundation

CHAPTER ONE

This Is Going to Be Easier Than You Think

Parenting teens can be hard. And also, it can be much, much easier—and more fun!—than you've been led to believe.

"Wow. Ugh. That's amazing!"

This is the usual wide-eyed response when people hear that I have four teenagers. Sometimes people grimace, like the mere thought of it is a bitter pill. They are thinking, I know, that teenagers are *hard*, which, of course, they can be. Everyone assumes I must be insanely busy, or maybe just a little insane, and that raising four teenagers must be nearly impossible.

These thoughts occur because many teenagers tend to be either terribly disorganized, requiring constant nagging, or tightly wound, perfectionistic, and in need of constant therapy. There's also all that new neuroscience showing, unfortunately, that the brain regions that help humans make wise choices don't mature until kids are in their mid-twenties, and that many potentially life-threatening risks become more appealing during adolescence while the normal fear of danger is temporarily suppressed. Knowing these things can make it hard for us parents to relax.

Oh, and there's also that, at least in the United States, teenagers are more or less *expected* to be uncommunicative and rude. We parents understand, at least in theory, that developmentally, our teenagers need to differentiate themselves from us. The central tenet of adolescence is a drive for autonomy. This often sucks for us. When the children we've loved, sacrificed for, and doted on suddenly make it clear that they think we're lame through their eye-rolling and phubbing (phone snubbing) and straight-up verbal rejection, it can feel personal. It can hurt.

Yup, teenagers can be hard to parent; however, parenting teenagers is in many ways a hell of a lot easier than raising little kids. Teens can put on their own shoes without crying. They can pack their own bags for school or a trip, make their own lunches, change their own sheets, and bathe themselves. They can take the bus to practice. More than that, they can figure out which bus to take and get themselves on it! Many older teenagers drive themselves and even their siblings, greatly diminishing the time we spend as chauffeurs. So the good news is that the physical labor of taking care of little kids is done. Put your feet up while your adolescents fold their own laundry. Let this be a relief.

Our kids' adolescence is an opening, an invitation to shift how we spend our parenting time and energy. Almost overnight, we have a little more time to invest in ourselves. It's not just that they don't need us to tie their shoes, it's that they really do *need* time and space away from us. They need enough space so that when they make mistakes, they can't blame us for them (because we weren't involved). Similarly, they need us to back off enough that they can have successes they can definitely call their own.

Within this space we can reclaim the hobbies we gave up when our kids were infants, when we were too tired to do anything not survival related. It's time we can use to reconnect with our friends and our spouses (or to date if we're single). We can relaunch our careers; we can find meaning in communities of adults that we choose ourselves, rather than those that are chosen for us, through our kids.

And when we turn our attention back to taking care of ourselves, our teens truly benefit. Studies show that parents who are happy and fulfilled tend to be warmer and more responsive to their children. We know intuitively, of course, that our happiness affects our teens. Our emotions are contagious, and in families, moods can spread like wildfire. We most often think of how this goes when our moody teen is sulking in the kitchen, blaming others for their feelings of disappointment, frustration, or anxiety. But this works the other way, too.

When we are happy, we are less likely to get pulled into teenage moodiness, and when they are stressed or in crisis, we are more likely to be helpful to them.

Parenting Competencies

An interesting study demonstrates the importance of our own fulfillment as parents. Researchers compared the effectiveness of ten important parenting practices in terms of their influence on kids' health, happiness, and school success, as well as the quality of the parent's relationship with their children. (For example, they examined to what extent participants provided educational opportunities for their kids.) Here are the three parenting competencies that turned out to be most important:

1. **Love and affection.** Parents support and accept their child, are physically affectionate, and spend quality one-on-one time together.
2. **Stress management.** Parents take steps to reduce stress for themselves and their child, like practicing relaxation techniques and promoting positive interpretations of difficult events.
3. **Relationship skills.** Parents maintain a healthy relationship with their spouse, significant other, and/or co-parent, and model effective relationship skills with other people.

Here is what I think is amazing about this list of high-impact parenting practices: All of these things are free, all are possible for parents from all walks of life, and two of the three aren't even parenting skills, per se.

Most of us already know, from (unpleasant) experience, that when we parents are stressed out and our stress spills over, our kids can suffer, too. Similarly, we know that little is more important for our kids' well-being than maintaining and improving the relationships we have with our partners and co-parents. So it's not surprising that research demonstrates that our stress management and our adult relationships are really important for our *kids'* happiness and school success.

But when I suggest to the parents of teenagers that there are good reasons for them to spend more time on themselves and their own well-being during this life stage, I'm often met with resistance. "They need us more than ever, especially now that they are applying to college," parents argue. "I don't think this is the time to be selfish," others balk. Actually, I agree totally. Teenagers *do* need us more than ever, but **they need us in a different way**. This is definitely not the time to become more selfish and emotionally distant.

Self-Care Is Not Selfish

Fortunately, there is a world of difference between selfish parents and those who take time to practice good stress management and to nurture positive partnerships, romantic or otherwise.

Selfishness is an anxious focus on the self. Selfish people tend to refer back to themselves a lot by using words like *I, me,* and *mine.* They pursue extrinsic goals, such as preserving their own youthful beauty and cultivating an image of themselves on social media. They often hunger for more money, power, and approval from others, and they are often willing to pursue these things at the expense of other people or at the expense of their own integrity. Not coincidentally, this sort of self-focus is linked to stress, anxiety, depression, and health problems such as heart disease.

So I'm definitely not recommending selfishness. I'm suggesting *self-care* and personal growth. I'm suggesting that we parents invest newfound time, even if it's just the time we used to spend trying to get our kids to brush their teeth, in a renewed pursuit of meaning. It benefits our kids when we find fulfillment in realms outside of our parenting—particularly those realms that reduce our stress and deepen our relationships. This might mean volunteering for a cause you care deeply about, or seeing a best friend more regularly. It might be practicing yoga or learning meditation, if that is something you want to do.

If you're worried that you are being selfish or neglectful of your kids when you turn your focus back to your own well-being or as you take care of your own needs first, please repeat after me: **Stress-management is not selfish, particularly for parents.** Self-care is not for the unambitious or pampered. It will not be better for your career if you work to the point of exhaustion, and it won't be better for your teens if you hover over them, anxiously "helping." If you are worried about taking this mandate for self-care too far, or you're concerned that you might be neglecting your children, ask yourself: Are you extending yourself the same standard of basic care that you would your child? Or simply ask your kids: Do they want more time with you? Do they need more attention? Let them be the guide. **Consider this your permission slip to take care of yourself again.**

You Can't Fake It

Here's another reason we need to take care of ourselves more than ever when our kids are teenagers: We cannot lead where we do not go.

Teenagers can sniff hypocrisy a mile away. Developmentally, adolescence brings a new capacity for conceptual thinking and abstract reasoning, and this heightens their ability to think critically. Coupled with increased interest in the world beyond their immediate family, many teenagers develop a good nose for social injustice. They are able to analyze social systems in ways that younger children aren't able to, and as we all know, most teens will reject anything their analysis finds lacking, especially if it reeks of unfairness or pretense—tradition be damned. **Few things are more irritating to a teen than a person or institution that preaches one thing in public but does another behind closed doors.**

Learning how unfair and unjust the larger world is can make teens feel powerless, especially if they feel there is nothing they can do about the injustice. But when we, their parents, are hypocritical—when we make a rule for them, like not using phones while driving, and then we do that very thing ourselves—their reactions can become a source of righteous anger for them. Not behaving in the ways that we want our kids to behave gives them a perfect reason to reject our wise advice.

Live It to Give It

It's also true that teens learn the life skills they need to be happy and healthy by watching their role models, not from listening to us lecture them or by being forced to follow rules they feel are unjust and unfair. Like it or not, they are learning how to operate in the adult world by watching celebrities on Instagram and professional athletes on TV. Their teachers and coaches and ministers and older cousins and aunts and uncles can all be profoundly influential. And, **we parents are also their role models**. Most parents remain important influences on their teens' developing identities and behaviors. We just don't influence them as directly as we did when they were younger.

When I read through my high school journals, I am reminded that I had a lot of problems with my dad when I was a teenager. He was much stricter than my friends' dads, and he was prone to saying things that infuriated me, like "You don't know what you don't know" and "To those whom much is given, much is expected." At times, I wrote that I hated him. I judged everything he said and did.

The idea that I was ever critical and judgy of my dad is super surprising, to me and certainly to everyone who knows me and my dad now. There is no one in the world I admire more, or with whom I'd rather spend the day. Also, as an adult, *I'm just like my father.* I keep a nearly pathologically neat desk, just like my dad always did. I'm exceedingly wellness oriented, and my dad is, too. We both value all the same things: contributing to our communities, spending time with family and a wide circle of friends, helping at-risk youth.

Although as a teenager I saw my dad's many flaws, I don't think he was ever hypocritical. So, even as I balked when he insisted that the older boys I was dating come in to meet him, and I raged every time he told an offensive joke (think about the "dumb blonde" and ethnic jokes of the 1980s—why did anyone ever think they were okay?), I learned a lot about a life well-lived from my dad. I learned how to feel well-rested (track your sleep and try for a little more than eight hours). I learned how to be happy (keep your brother and best friends close by, and tease them a lot; practice the guitar every night; volunteer regularly, even when you're busy running a business and raising a family; tend to your marriage). And I learned how to manage stress (meditate and practice yoga; exercise every day). I don't remember my dad ever talking to me about any of these things, but he practiced them, and I saw that. I learned by osmosis.

As you read about the skills your kids need for lasting joy and success, you have my full permission—and the support of a trove of scientific research—to develop those skills in yourself first. This book is also a short guide to deepening *your own* relationships, to finding flow and focus in your work, and to managing your own stress.

Their Success Does Not Equal *Your* Success

Watching our teens develop into their own people can be a particular joy, especially when we release ourselves from the idea that our success can be measured through the success of our children. When we realize that our job as parents is to do our best, given our resources, to help our kids become the best version of themselves (rather than another version of ourselves), it shifts the burden of ownership from us to them. It can be exciting to witness our teenagers discovering their strengths and passions, particularly when we care for ourselves well during the stressful bits.

This is, of course, often easier said than done. As a professional advice giver, I have an opinion (science-based) about everything. When people seek out my coaching to improve their happiness, their productivity at work, or their parenting, I'm thrilled to tell them all the answers.

It hasn't been easy for Molly or Fiona to be the guinea pigs on whom I test my science-based parenting advice, in part because it is easy for me, and everyone around me, to see them as a "product" of my work. Once, dropping off the girls at sleepaway camp for the first time, I found myself suggesting to a nervous Fiona a particular way to breathe and specific things she might think about to manage her anxiety. In my own anxiety, I was telling her how to breathe and what to think. Jeez.

The irony, of course, is that trying to control our children is frequently futile and usually counterproductive.

That's the clear conclusion psychologist Wendy Grolnick has reached after over two decades of watching parents talk to their children. Here's the gist of her research: The children of controlling parents—those who tell their children exactly what to do and when to do it—don't do as well as kids whose parents are involved and supportive without being bossy. Children of "directive" parents tend to be less creative and resourceful, less persistent when faced with a challenge, and less successful at solving problems. They don't like school as much, and they don't achieve as much academically.

Enter my awesome stepchildren. They've been in my life for a decade now. I've loved and supported them, but at first from a distance—Mark and I didn't marry until 2013. It isn't that I haven't disciplined them, asked them to help out around the house, or offered an unpopular opinion. I've taken away devices, made and enforced rules, helped them address thank-you notes—just like I did with Molly and Fiona.

But I've not been as bossy with Macie and Tanner as I was with Molly and Fiona—more of a very involved aunt than helicopter mom. I don't criticize my stepkids, and I make a much bigger effort to hold my tongue when they do something I find irritating. The truth is, it was easier for me to be supportive of Macie and Tanner without being attached to the outcome. Instead of bossing my stepchildren around, I chose my requests carefully and tried to voice them respectfully.

When Macie was in tenth grade and Molly in seventh, I taught them both some new study skills. Subconsciously, I approached the "teaching" of each kid differently. With Molly, I told her what to do, sat next to her while she tried out my suggestions, and corrected her every move. The following day, she tried using the new technique for a little while, but like the kids in Grolnick's studies, she quickly got frustrated and gave up.

A few days later, when Macie needed help studying for a test, I offered to teach her the same study skills, but I made it clear that I wouldn't be offended if she declined. I was delighted that she took me up on my offer, but I wasn't attached to the outcome.

My emotional stance in these two situations was completely different. With Molly, I was an anxious mom, worried about her school performance. With Macie, I was just there, loving the opportunity to teach her something that might be useful. It dawned on me that I was much more respectful of my stepchildren's autonomy. I could support them without mistakenly thinking that their competence was my competence.

It is totally normal for parents to worry about how their children's success and failure reflects on them. Psychologists call this tendency ego-involvement. In her wonderful book *Pressured Parents, Stressed-Out Kids*, Grolnick and her co-author write:

Ego-involvement occurs when our protective and loving hard-wiring collides with the competition in our children's lives, prompting us to wrap our own self-esteem around our children's achievement. That gives us our own stake in how well our child performs.

However normal it may be, *my* ego-involvement wasn't helping anyone. Noticing how differently I was behaving with my stepchildren was a giant wake-up call. I learned that I needed to be more supportive of Molly and Fiona without being intrusive, to make requests without being so bossy.

After the study skills incident, I resolved to coach my children more like I coach my clients . . . and stepchildren: gently and without ego-attachment. Instead of dictating what I want when I want it ("Put that freaking device down! You should be helping me with dinner!"), I began using the methods outlined in part one of this book.

As I slowly let go of the ego-attachment that was hamstringing me as a parent, I also let go of the idea that I needed to wait to write this book. I had back-burnered this project, planning to return to it when my four teenagers had safely survived their adolescence. I realized that I was delaying because some part of me wanted to be sure my kids turned out okay. I'd built a reputation as a parenting expert, and I did not want a flawed teenage decision (anything my kids didn't do perfectly, basically) to cause people to call my credibility into question. Talk about ego-identification! I had hitched my career to my children's success and happiness. Yikes.

My ego-identification—the idea that my children needed to turn out well before I could write this book—was perfectionism rearing its ugly head. And my logic was flawed. We parents do not have total control over how our children "turn out," as much as we'd like to think we do. Please remember this when your children are struggling or suffering, when they make mistakes, if they do stupid and dangerous things. I often have to think to myself: *This is their journey. I am not the boss of them (anymore).*

The Three S's

Teens do, of course, still need time with their parents and families, even as they spend more and more time away from home. In fact, most psychologists believe that teens need the same type of basic attention they have always needed—the kind that promotes a secure attachment. According to UCLA's Dan Siegel, this means teens need to feel **seen, safe, and soothed**.

Seen

Teens feel **seen** when we are warm, affectionate, and supportive of them, even when we disagree with them. Research shows that warmth and support is associated with increased positive adolescent outcomes (like school success) and resilience in the face of difficulty. Parental warmth and support is so powerful that it affects the brain development of younger teens. Compared to those with parents who tended to be more argumentative and angrier with their teens, sixteen-year-olds who had warm and supportive mothers at age twelve showed brain changes related to less sadness and anxiety and increased self-control.

Safe

Helping kids feel **safe**, and indeed keeping kids safe, takes on a whole new meaning in adolescence. It turns out that risky teenage behavior is influenced by the emotional closeness teenagers feel with their parents. There's good news here: Even if you don't feel close to your teen right now, it's not too late. In one study, parents who grew closer to their teenagers—by practicing showing them respect, helping them talk through problems, and reducing their arguing and yelling—had teens who reduced their risk-taking behaviors.

Soothed

A lot of teens feel unsafe because they are stressed and anxious, and we parents play an enormous role in helping our teens learn how to **soothe** themselves. When they are babies we do it for them, and gradually, as they mature, they learn to calm their nervous systems down on their own. Family support is an important buffer against teenage stressors. Research shows that both family time and one-on-one time between parents and teens can help kids manage stress and become better at soothing themselves. One study even showed that just being at home when teens are at home, without being actively engaged with them, can help.

The rest of part one is about increasing the closeness your teen feels with you, which will help them feel seen, safe, and soothed. Chapters two and three, in particular, will give you simple, proven coaching tools that aim to increase the likelihood that your teens will feel seen and soothed, and that make it easier for us to be warm, affectionate, and supportive of our teens.

Rest assured, raising teenagers can be a lot easier than we have been led to believe. Teens do need us to be engaged, both physically and emotionally, but they don't need our direct help as often as they did as little kids. All the tactics I teach in the rest of part one will help you transition from being the directive parent of little kids toward a coaching model that is appropriate for older kids.

This doesn't mean that we parents of teenagers don't sometimes lie awake at night, processing their mistakes and emotional turmoil and carefully watching them navigate relationships and school challenges. I don't mean to suggest that having teenagers is always easy. But when we allow teenagers the space they need to develop their own identities, they move through the separation phase faster. In other words, they are no longer so rude, and they no longer seem to randomly reject even our best ideas. Our relationships with our teens change and become even better—potentially more interesting, possibly more rewarding, and almost certainly a whole lot easier.

CHAPTER TWO

Fortunately, Overparenting Doesn't Work

If you haven't already been fired by your teenager from your role as manager of their lives, you're about to be. Not to worry! Letting them manage their own lives (within limits!) is less work for you and more rewarding for everyone.

When one of our teens, who shall remain nameless, was fifteen, Mark and I got a surprising call from another parent I'll call Maureen. Our teen had decided to go to a concert with Maureen's daughter, Maddie, and Maureen was calling to let us know that she would be driving. The problem was that our daughter hadn't bothered to tell us about her plans with Maddie—because the concert conflicted with an important family dinner.

We have a huge extended family, and we are lucky enough to be able to get together regularly, including a few times a year for a big dinner. It's a long drive just for a mini-reunion, but we never even think about not going.

It wasn't that our daughter didn't want to go. She did. She loves her cousins and genuinely looks forward to seeing them. It was that she desperately wanted to go to the concert, too. How could she choose?

"You don't get to choose!" was my knee-jerk reaction. Still, she pushed it.

"Absolutely not!" I cried. "Family comes before friends! Family is the most important thing!"

Because my husband and I were refusing to even consider letting her out of the commitment, our teenager dug in. The conversation was over on our end, but she didn't let it go. We heard through Maureen that our daughter told Maddie she was still going to the concert, no matter what we said. We told Maureen that there was no chance (in hell!) that she'd be going, but thank you so much anyway.

When our daughter heard through Maureen that we'd overruled her yet again, she was livid. "It's *my* life!" she seethed. "You can make me go to dinner, but you can't make me have fun." And with that, she quietly left the room. Mark and I looked at each other, wide-eyed. She had a point. Our teenager had just fired her management team, this time for good. She had had it with our bossy and controlling ways.

Years ago, Mike Riera, the author of *Uncommon Sense for Parents with Teenagers* and an educator I respect a lot, had warned me that this would happen. But honestly, Mark and I just couldn't imagine it. We thought that we'd always get to manage our children's lives, at least while they were living under our roof. Personally, I think I'm pretty good at managing my family. I should be *promoted* as my kids get older, I used to think, not *fired*.

"You're Not the Boss of Me," Take 2

When our kids are little, we have to manage pretty much every aspect of their lives. We set bedtimes, plan meals, and make doctor's appointments. We arrange carpools and make all major decisions for our kids: where they will go to school, if they will go to camp, and where we'll go on vacation. And when our kids are little, for the most part, they appreciate having involved and loving parents. It's great having someone else manage your calendar and get you to your activities (mostly) on time.

But once kids reach adolescence, they need to start managing their own lives, and they do tend to fire us as their managers. **Parents who are too controlling—those who don't step down from their manager roles—breed rebellion.** Many kids with micromanaging parents will politely agree to the harsh limits their parents set with a "yes, sir" or a "yes, ma'am" attitude, but then will break those rules the first chance they get. They don't do this because they are bad kids, but because they need to regain a sense of control over their own lives.

This cannot be overstated: **Healthy, self-disciplined, motivated teenagers have a strong sense of control over their lives.** A mountain of research demonstrates that agency—having the power to affect your own life—is one of the most important factors for both success and happiness. Believing that we can influence our own lives through our own efforts predicts practically all of the positive outcomes that we want for our children: better health and longevity, lower use of drugs and alcohol, less stress, higher emotional well-being, greater intrinsic motivation and self-discipline, improved academic performance, and even career success.

Even teens who *don't* have a rebellious streak and who won't lie or hide their behavior suffer when parents micromanage them. These kids tend to expend emotional energy resisting advice from their parents that is clearly in their best interest, simply to regain a sense of control.

The answer, according to neuropsychologist William Stixrud and long-time educator Ned Johnson, authors of *The Self-Driven Child*, is to hand the decision-making reins over to our teens. You read that right: **By adolescence, we parents need to (take a deep breath and) let them make their own decisions about their lives. It's not that we never say no anymore. Nor do we stop enforcing our family rules. It's that we start to involve teens more in creating the rules, and we let them make their own decisions—which they are going to do anyway.**

Freedom Within Limits

Letting our teens become the decision makers doesn't mean that we become permissive, indulgent, or disengaged. Fifty years of research has consistently shown that authoritative (not to be confused with authoritarian) parenting is good for teens' health and well-being. Authoritative parents set and consistently enforce clear limits, and they are warm and engaged in their kids' lives. Authoritative parenting helps kids develop self-control—making them less likely to have problems with drugs, alcohol, or teen pregnancy. It also makes them far more likely to excel on many other measures of well-being. Teenagers with authoritative parents do better in school, have greater self-confidence, and have more friends.

WHAT KIND OF PARENT ARE YOU?

Authoritative parenting and authoritarian parenting sound similar in terms of their names, but the long-term outcomes of these parenting styles are very different. The good news is that you can always change your parenting style. It's all about practice!

- The **authoritarian** parent commands: "You're coming to the family dinner, and that's the end of the discussion."
- The **permissive** parent concedes: "Okay sweetie. Whatever you want to do."
- The **authoritative** parent empathizes and engages: "I understand that you really want to go to that concert. What is your plan for communicating to your cousins that you might not be at the dinner?"

In contrast to authoritative parenting, authoritarian parents are controlling, and they tend to be a bit cold or harsh in their dictates. Permissive parents, meanwhile, are very warm and often affectionate, but they are reluctant to say no to their kids or to upset them in any way.

Permissiveness is often predictable in this day and age. When we're all so busy, we don't want to spend our limited time with our kids arguing or nagging them to do chores. It's so much easier to let the rules slide, and so much more pleasurable to watch Netflix together. After all, it's so much easier to be their *friend* than it is to have them constantly railing against our authority. Or is it?

It's understandable that our generation of parents is saying no a lot less frequently than parents did in past generations—by one study's estimate, 50 percent less often—but how does this affect our kids? While our reasons for not wanting to say no vary, the research makes one thing clear: Teens need their parents to set limits, but in a positive way. They don't need us as friends, they need us as *parents*. When parents are firm *and* kind, when we are involved without being invasive, we are being authoritative.

How to Be Authoritative

So, how in the world are we supposed to be authoritative in our parenting once our kids have fired us as their managers, and once we are letting them make their own decisions? There are two equal parts to parenting without managing:

Part 1: We (the parents) establish and enforce age-appropriate family rules—like time limits on technology use and expectations about drug and alcohol use—in a warm and engaged way. We don't dictate the rules, we discuss them. This way, our teens have a safe space to operate in without becoming overwhelmed by everything they need to do and learn.

Part 2: We hand over further decision-making to our kids. They are free to operate autonomously within the limits we've set.

Teens who are given both limits *and* the freedom to make their own decisions tend to be both self-driven *and* self-disciplined. This means that they'll tell themselves no before we have to—and I probably don't have to tell you that that makes parenting a heck of a lot more fun.

Part 1: Setting Limits with Teenagers

When we set limits, we build the scaffolding that supports our teens as they grow and create their lives. We want them to grow up to be independent thinkers and to eventually be able to manage both the basics and the complexities of their lives . . . without us. We want them to manage things as simple and straightforward as their laundry, as well as things as complex and potentially confusing as their sexual relationships. For this to happen, **we must move away from using parental pressure to get them to do what *we* want them to do, and instead nurture their own ability both to *know* what they want for themselves and to *do* those things—for *themselves*, not for *us*.**

As our adolescents get older and more experienced, we gradually remove the scaffolding and reduce how much we monitor them. We already do this well for things like driving. New drivers (at least in California) start by taking lessons with an instructor. Then we let them drive a regular car with a permit and an adult in the passenger seat. Then they get a provisional license that allows them to drive alone with additional restrictions. It's only after they've had their provisional license for a year that they are free to drive like any other adult. Learning to drive is like a lot of other things that teenagers must learn to do. Eventually, they must learn to manage and monitor their own:

- screen time, social media, and devices
- sleeping, eating, and basic self-care
- homework and school attendance, including getting extra help when they need it
- calendars and appointments—and learning to manage their time in general
- all things money: budgeting, saving, spending, and, of course, earning
- dental and medical care
- contributions to the household, including cleaning their bedroom and the bathroom they use, doing their laundry, and helping with cooking, shopping, and cleaning
- transportation, including driving, biking, and navigating public transportation and airports
- social lives and free time (including how they spend their summers and vacations)
- relationships with their extended family
- relationships with friends and in their communities
- sexual relationships and family planning

They won't be able to do most of these things by themselves until they reach adulthood, but adolescence is the time when they start practicing doing all of these things on their own.

It can be tricky to know when to set limits and when to just let kids manage the things on the above list alone. **When we aren't sure how to set limits for our adolescents, we often just don't do it.** Middle schoolers, for example, do not tend to be developmentally ready to have total freedom online and on their phones, but many middle schoolers know so much more than their parents about their phones, the internet, and social media. And when this is the case, parents may let their kids navigate the new technology with little support and even less guidance.

But would the same parents hand that same middle schooler the keys to the family car and let them figure out how to drive it themselves while getting advice from their peers and learning through trial and error? Of course not. We recognize that before kids can "drive alone," they need to know a little more about how the world works. They need clear roads with bright lines painted for them to show them where to go—and where not to go. They need to practice, with supervision.

First, Build Temporary Scaffolding

So, how do we build the roads and paint the lines? We can start by envisioning a series of milestones—like passing the written learner's permit test, then taking driving lessons, then passing the behind-the-wheel driver's test—in any given arena. What do they need to accomplish in order for you to give them freedom?

When our kids first got phones, for example, we were very restrictive about their use and the amount of privacy they were allowed to have on them. But we could envision the day when they would monitor themselves entirely. By default this would occur by the time they left for college. Because we want them to have a year or so of practice monitoring themselves *before* they leave home—so that we can support them when they make mistakes—we aim to have our kids fully self-monitoring by their junior or senior year in high school.

Knowing this allows us to work backward, using the four or so years before they leave the nest to help them establish healthy habits. For example, one limit we set for our younger teens is that phones always, without exception, need to be charged outside of their bedrooms. We strictly enforce this until their seventeenth birthday. Our hope is that this becomes a habit. (While it is no longer possible for Fiona and Macie to charge their phones outside of their dorm rooms, they've certainly learned through experience the benefits of doing so.)

Each limit we set is part of the supportive scaffolding that will eventually be removed, piece by piece, before the kids leave home.

Remember, we don't want to set up so much scaffolding that they never have the chance to make mistakes, or so that it doesn't hurt a little when they fail. We *want* them to stretch and to be challenged.

When our kids were younger, we monitored their social media accounts and their texting very closely. Middle school was fraught with lots of phone drama. Our kids made mistakes, and their friends did, too. Because we were monitoring our kids' usage so closely, we saw a lot of things that shocked us, and we also had a lot of great conversations about what had gone wrong, how to repair it, and how to do better the next time.

Then, Make the Scaffolding Visible

Once we've more or less figured out what the milestones will be for our kids, it's important to engage them in a conversation about what we envision about the limits that we are going to set, and what our kids will need to do to earn their freedom from those limits. Set aside a time to meet with your teen individually—or have a family meeting if the limits you plan to set affect everyone—and share with them your vision. The idea isn't to start a negotiation, nor is it a time to let your kids dismantle the limits you've just set. Instead, you are sharing with them what you'd like them to eventually be fully responsible for, the skills they'll need to build, and how they'll do that. Then engage them in a conversation about your plan and get their feedback. Do they think the limits and milestones are fair? Achievable? What are their concerns?

Once you've presented your vision, just listen. Even if you disagree with what your teen is saying, don't voice your resistance. Instead, practice actively listening by repeating your teens' concerns back to them to make sure you are really hearing them correctly.

You might want to take some time to process their concerns if they have many, or if they are really resistant to the limit. It's great to let them influence you, *if* you think that they are probably right. If they are lobbying for more freedom, that's great. Let them show you they can handle that freedom, and make it clear what they need to do to reach the milestone. This is where time-dated milestones (as when we set a bedtime for, say, all of ninth grade) might not be the best, because time is out of teens' control. When your teens resist this sort of limit, see if you can find one that gives them back a sense of control (like setting a milestone of being well rested, with no telltale signs of sleep deprivation, for a full semester).

For instance, before every school year starts, we have a conversation with each of our kids about sleep and bedtimes. We briefly mention the science related to sleep, screens, and social media (they've heard it all before), and how it affects their learning, athletic performance, and happiness. (See chapter seven.) We share with them our family value that health and happiness come before homework (another thing they've heard from us before!), and how that means we expect them to plan their lives so that they can get their work done *and* get enough sleep.

Then we let them tell us about their experience and their plans. How much time will they need in the mornings to get dressed, eat breakfast, make their lunch, and be on time for the carpool or bus? How do they feel when they get the nine-plus hours of sleep per night recommended for teenagers, and how do they feel when they do not? We encourage them to do the basic math, because our kids tend to skip this step ("So if you go to bed at 10:30 PM and wake up at 6:00 AM, that's *how many* hours of sleep? Is that what you were shooting for?") We ask them what time they want to wake up on school mornings, and how much sleep they want to get on the weekends. And then we agree to a bedtime . . . and it's nearly always the one that Mark and I had envisioned before the conversation started.

That conversation, by the way, is what makes our parenting authoritative. If we were being authoritarian, we'd just announce the bedtime or other limit, end of story. And if we were permissive, we'd never bother to set the limit or have the conversation—we might suggest a bedtime, for example, but then never enforce it.

Don't Limit What You Won't Enforce

Once we set a limit, whatever it is, kids need to know that the limit is going to be enforced. Otherwise it's not a limit. At best it's merely a suggestion, and at worst, it's an opportunity for rebellion. Teens (and, in fact, people of all ages) feel less anxious and more secure when their choices are limited, which is why the scaffolding we provide as parents helps our kids commit to some things and let go of others. But for them to reap these benefits, it's not enough to just tell them about the limit we are (hypothetically) setting. **They need to truly feel that their choices are being limited, and that the line where the limit will be enforced is clear.**

Parents who are unwilling to enforce their family rules can unintentionally harm their kids. They end up raising kids who can't deal with disappointment or take no for an answer, because they have learned through experience that no is never, in the end, the real answer. Indulgent parents believe that they are fostering closeness and loyalty with their teens when they let them off the hook, or by being the cool parent who gives their kids what they think they want, but permissiveness makes teenagers insecure. It puts them in the position of having to parent themselves, something they know they aren't ready for yet. Ironically, it's very stressful for teens when parents don't set limits and consistently follow through on them.

WHAT IF YOU AND YOUR CO-PARENT DON'T AGREE?

People often ask me what to do if their spouse (or co-parent) is having a hard time getting on board with these authoritative practices. Similar problems include not being able to agree on a limit, or one parent being unwilling to enforce the limits agreed upon.

These are hard issues. We know it is much better for kids when parents collaborate, when we are all "on the same page" and we "present a united front." There are mountains of research that demonstrate that conflict between parents is bad for teens, and collaboration is good for them. We get it. And yet, many people struggle to get others to parent in the way they want them to. It's so frustrating to not be able to control other people! Especially when we are right! (Kidding . . . sort of.)

If you are in this camp, believe me, I feel you. I clearly have given a lot of thought to what best parenting practices are, and the strength of my convictions is pretty mammoth. But my husband is also very strong-willed (and not a big reader of parenting books). He was raised by an authoritarian father and permissive mother, so he has *no* natural authoritative leanings.

Not only that, but I have other parents to contend with. Mike (Molly and Fiona's dad) is an easy sell, fortunately. Mike seems genuinely grateful for whatever guidance I give him, and we are pretty naturally on the same page. Even so, there are multiple households and other siblings and stepparents involved—which means that there are lots of different rules and routines. It's a big team of parents to try to get on the same page.

So, yes, it's hard. And also: We must carry on. The first step is acceptance. We can't change our co-parents, tempting as that might be to try and do. Trying to change a grown human is a fool's errand— not because they don't change, but because we can't force change in other people. The only truly effective option is to practice what we preach ourselves and hope it rubs off.

What has happened for me (and what I hope happens for you) is that the other parents in my life notice that the way that I parent works, and they can see that what I'm doing is rewarding for everyone. The kids respond, so my co-parents tend to be more motivated to mimic what I'm doing.

However, I'm also prone to overhelping my co-parents, which kills their motivation. When we overhelp, we subconsciously send the message that we believe that they can't do it without us. This can make them feel like they're being criticized or like they need fixing, and that can hurt. People don't appreciate it when their spouse (or former spouse or former spouse's new spouse) don't accept them as they are. Often, overhelping others gives us a false sense of power that can distract us from our own problems. This is why Anne Lamott says that "help is the sunny side of control."

Fortunately, we can still help family members parent more authoritatively by supporting their three basic psychological needs related to self-motivation: **autonomy**, **competence**, and **relatedness**.

We can support their **autonomy** by backing off a little. Let them make their own decisions about how they'll parent, even when they parent differently from you. This means practicing acceptance, as they are probably already parenting differently, whether or not we "let them." We can ask questions that help them build a vision for success and help them focus on the outcomes that they want. What does good parenting look like to them? How are they hoping to feel? And what will they need to do to succeed? Where will they need to ask for help?

We can encourage their **competence** by helping them build the skills they need. Do they want you to teach them what you've learned? What you are reading about in this book? What you are practicing? No? Then take a deep breath and back off.

Finally, we can foster **relatedness** by building a sense of family. How can you find security in doing something together? Can you create common goals and common values? How can you make it fun to do together?

In the end, the best idea is to keep our own side of the street clean. When we feel frustrated that our co-parents aren't doing it right, we'll do well to turn our attention back to ourselves, and to the things that are within our control.

"What's Your Plan?"

All of this can be confusing. We are no longer our kids' managers, but we still must set and enforce limits. How can we enforce limits without being dictatorial? Without managing things?

Here's what we don't do: nag. It doesn't feel good to the person doing the nagging, and it certainly doesn't feel good to be nagged. Moreover, when kids know we are going to nag them, they don't monitor themselves—**they wait to be reminded**. Sometimes many, many times. Ironically, this makes them feel dependent, and so most teens will then further resist the limit in order to regain a sense of control and autonomy.

Now that our kids are older, Mark and I have been clear that we are not willing to nag them every night to get to sleep on time—it is their life and their agreement to keep. We don't want the nightly hassle of herding them toward bed as if they were still in grade school. Instead of nagging, we ask them questions when we need to. My all-time favorite question is this one: **What's your plan?**

As in, "What's your plan for getting to bed on time tonight?" or "What's your plan for getting your homework done this weekend?" or "Is there anything that I can do to help you get your room cleaned up before you leave for school tomorrow?" This makes it clear that they are still in control of their own behavior, and it helps put them in touch with their own motivations and intentions. Often kids simply need to make a plan, and sometimes if they aren't asked to articulate it, they won't do it—especially kids who are used to being nagged because they know their parents will eventually get frustrated and do their planning for them.

This not-making-a-plan thing is developmental, by the way, and it is often more about their executive function than their motivation. Our frontal lobe, which enables us to make plans for the future, doesn't typically develop until our mid-twenties. This doesn't mean that they *can't* plan, or that we should do it for them; it just means that they need a little more support *practicing* planning than might be obvious given their other capabilities.

Finally, Establish Cause and Effect

If asking them questions about their plans is not enough, you can also follow through on your limit-setting by reminding your teens about the effect their choices are having. **The key is that teens (and people of all ages) retain their sense of control.** This happens when they can see cause and effect. Ideally, they feel intrinsically the effects of their own behavior. If they aren't getting to bed on time, the intrinsic effect of this is exhaustion, which can lead to poor school and athletic performance, moodiness, and even depression and anxiety. It doesn't feel good to be tired, to do poorly in school, or to drag on the athletic field. As parents, our best work is when we help put kids in touch with the intrinsic effects of their behavior, and they self-correct.

Teenagers, especially younger ones, rarely learn to self-correct before they make a lot of mistakes. Most teens will first test the limit. Are we serious? Will we enforce it? Can they feel secure that the limit is actually a limit?

When we initially set a limit with our kids, we also need to articulate the consequences of venturing out of bounds. Hopefully, these consequences are logical, or intrinsic, to the teen and the limit itself. In our household, for example, tired teens (aka, those who stay up past their set bedtimes) aren't allowed to stay out late or have sleepovers on the weekends.

Other examples: If our kids don't keep their rooms clean, they know that I will eventually clean their room for them, which they *hate*, because I love organizing, and I will clean out their drawers, organize their clothing by type and color, and otherwise violate their privacy to the nth degree. All I have to do is casually glance around their room and say, "I see you are inviting me to organize your room this weekend! Do you have a Goodwill pile going yet?" This generally inspires them to rapidly embark on their own organizing binge, which, for the record, they all find as gratifying as I do. (I do realize that many kids would be very happy to have a parent go through their rooms and clean everything—maybe the privacy violation is a bummer, but the personal organizer makes it worth it. Sometimes the answer is in picking our battles and not setting a limit around cleanliness in the first place.)

My husband and I have tried to articulate logical consequences— those that make plain the cause and effect—for violating the limits in our household. Kids who don't set the table on time get stuck doing the dishes for whoever set the table for them. Those who leave me to clean out their gross lunch boxes know that they are passively choosing to clean the fish tank in my office over the weekend—a fair trade, if you ask me. Kids who Snapchat while driving lose their car privileges. When they choose not to follow state laws and the safe driving practices outlined explicitly in our family driving contract (page 211), they know that they are, in effect, choosing to take the bus to school and to be driven by their parents to parties. Teens who are rude to me can similarly find their own ride to their friends' houses or otherwise not count on me doing them any big favors. They know that their negative actions have negative consequences. Their agency is obvious, because our household is predictable.

A final caveat, worth repeating: **If you don't think you can follow through and consistently enforce a family rule, don't set it.** You don't want to risk sending the message that you don't actually care enough about your teens or their well-being to follow through, or that agreements aren't important to keep.

Part 2: Hand Over Decision-Making

After we have set our limits, we then hand over further decision-making to our kids. **They have full agency to operate independently within the limits that we've set. This is what it means to be socialized or civilized.**

And you know what? They can do it! Teenagers are fully capable of making decisions for themselves. They can decide what classes to take in high school and college, which kids to hang out with, whether to play a sport or an instrument, what other extracurricular activities to be involved in, how much time to dedicate to homework and studying, what to eat, who to hang out with, where to apply for a summer job, and on and on.

They're also *already* deciding, ultimately, how to spend their free time with their friends (and whether or not to lie to us about that), how to spend their time online, and, for many, whether or not to engage in a sexual relationship. And since all of these decisions can have an enormous impact on their future, we want teens to make these sorts of decisions *deliberately.* It's our job as parents to make sure they have the tools they need to be good decision makers.

Learning by Doing

Decision-making is a skill—one that teens must develop before they can be truly independent. When we require that they make their own decisions (instead of just making them for them, as Mark and I initially did when we told our daughter she had to come to the family dinner instead of the concert), we give them really valuable practice. **They learn to look within themselves to understand their often-conflicting motivations and feelings.** They can consider their own values and the values of their family. They gain experience feeling accountable for the consequences of their decision.

Parents often worry, though. Here's what they tell me they are thinking:

What if they don't know what they don't know?

What if they don't want what we want for them and know is best for them?

What if we know they will make the wrong decision?

Taking decision-making away won't help our kids become good decision makers, nor is it a particularly good way to influence them. To paraphrase the authors of *The Self-Driven Child* again, this is in part because of two inarguable truths:

1. We can't make our teens want something they don't want.
2. We can't make them *not* want something they do want.

And so it's true: Sometimes our kids will make really bad decisions. Teenagers are fairly famous for making bad decisions, thanks to the aforementioned unfinished brain development, and their poor decision-making tends to happen in predictable circumstances:

- when they are excited, anxious, or upset
- when they feel pressured or stressed (including when they are angry at their parents)
- when they are seeking attention from their peers

Knowing this, we can guide them to make their decisions when they are calm and out of their friends' purview. This means that we help them think through *beforehand* what they will do at an upcoming party if all of their friends are getting high and they are feeling left out or pressured. And once they have made their decision, by the way, we can encourage them to make specific alternative plans. Research shows that making specific plans dramatically increases follow-through.

Even under ideal conditions, decision-making can be challenging for adults and teens alike, and it's unrealistic to think our teens will do it perfectly. Adolescence gives kids a period of time when they have their "learner's permit," when they still have some support both in making the decisions and in recovering when they make mistakes.

Which, again, they will. Often, humans need to really struggle in order to learn and grow, and this means they need to make mistakes . . . sometimes big ones.

If it will help them make an informed decision, we can neutrally offer our opinion. The neutral part is hard for me, and I have to practice nonchalance. After we casually offer our opinion, we (take a deep breath and) say: "It's your call." This is Stixrud and Johnson's recommended phrasing, and with our kids, using it is like a waving a magic wand. We say, "It's your call," and their whole demeanor changes.

Another magic line from *The Self-Driven Child* that I've tried to make a mantra is: "I have confidence in your ability to make informed decisions about your own life and to learn from your mistakes." I use this when our kids try to get me to make hard decisions *for* them, which means that I would also have to take responsibility for the effects of those decisions.

We can also, of course, tell our kids when we feel uneasy with a decision they're making, as long as we are sharing our *feelings* and not our judgments. This might mean that we say something like, "It makes me feel sad to see you so tired and anxious. I'm worried that the cost of taking such a heavy course load might be too high. But it's your call."

Also, we don't need to enthusiastically (or financially) support all of our kids' decisions. This is ultimately how we handled the family dinner/concert conflict. Mark and I apologized for our knee-jerk reaction and told our daughter that while we really hoped she would be at our family dinner, it was her call. If she decided not to come to the dinner, we asked her to communicate her decision herself to the rest of the family. If she was going to make her own decisions, she could also practice communicating them herself.

Once the choice was truly hers, our daughter ultimately chose not to go to the concert, and she seemed happy with her decision. She came to the family dinner *and* she had fun.

When we allow kids to make their own decisions, they don't waste their limited energy resisting us just so they can still feel a modicum of control over their own lives. Suddenly they stop seeming so irrational and teenagery—opposing things that are in their own best interest—and they start acting like the mature young adults they are becoming.

THE SAD BUSINESS OF LETTING GO

There's a booby trap to watch for: If our kids are to gain the independence they need to survive without us, we need to be willing to let them be truly independent. Many parents today don't really, in their heart of hearts, want their kids to leave home. It's too sad. They've been so dedicated to them, and their departure would leave a significant emotional hole in their lives. While parents sometimes complain to me that their kids are living at home again as young adults, it seems to me that it isn't necessarily the kids who are refusing to individuate from their parents, but rather the parents who are hanging on to their kids' childhoods.

If you suspect this might be you, I can offer you this reassurance: As I've made an effort to be less controlling, my connections with my children have instantly deepened. Why? Jess Lahey, author of *The Gift of Failure*, explained to me that parental control kills connection. It takes courage, but the old adage is true: If you love someone, set them free.

When our teens don't have to fight for their independence, our emotional connection with them grows. And when our ultimate goal is to strengthen our teens' secure attachments, they are better able to thrive. As mentioned in chapter one, secure attachments require that teens feel **seen**, **safe**, and **soothed**. When we set limits, teens feel both seen and safe. And when we allow them to make their own decisions, they again feel seen. Finally, having decision-making power soothes teens' nervous systems: Because they retain a sense of control over their own lives, they feel empowered rather than stressed.

Once we step down from our managing roles in our kids' lives and give them full decision-making power, we have another important task: To get ourselves rehired as our kids' coaches. **And this new role—coach—is way more fun than being a manager.** Chapter three will give you the skinny on how best to influence your teen in your new role as their coach.

What to Do When They Are Struggling

Watching kids struggle is hard. If you're anything like me, you'll want to intervene—to end their misery by just stepping in and "fixing it." Here's what to do instead.

Even as I was talking, I knew I was making a mistake. Sometimes, I just can't help myself.

My daughter had called me from school, weeping. She was not feeling well . . . again. She'd been struggling with a minor but persistent health problem for the last six months, and it was starting to get the best of her. She was running a low fever. She felt too lousy to go to class, really, but she couldn't imagine missing more school, either.

I'd been fielding these sorts of calls almost daily for two weeks. She was frustrated and disappointed that she couldn't do all the things she wanted to. "I just want to go to class and do my work," she sobbed into the phone. "I can't be sick anymore, Mom. I just want to have a good year."

Instead of just listening, hearing her out, and letting her feel sick and frustrated, I leaped into action. I couldn't stand the thought of my sweet baby feeling so bad, so I started off with suggestions for how much sleep she should be getting and how exactly she could get it. I next instructed her what to eat and drink. Even though I could tell she wasn't listening, I then reviewed what supplements and medications she needed to be taking. "Just one more thing," I said, each time she tried to cut me off. "Just hear me out." I'm not sure why I couldn't stop myself. Why was I still vaguely hoping against hope that she was taking dictation when I knew that she was just trying to get me to shut up?

"Oh. My. God! *Mom!!*," she finally shrieked, crying even harder into the phone. "Why can't you just let me vent?! I don't need you to tell me what to say to the doctor. I know what is wrong with me. I'm not five years old. Why can't you just let me be sick and sad? Why can't I ever just feel sorry for myself for one second?!"

And then, before I could respond or correct course or even really register what she'd just said, I saw that a call from her doctor was coming in. "Um, the doctor is calling me. Should I take it?" I asked her, feebly. "Yes," she said, exasperated. "Give *her* all your good suggestions." And she hung up.

I spoke to the doctor and then called my daughter back, but she didn't pick up. I texted her and got no reply. Dying to repair my mistake, I tried to say all the right things in a text, but when the right thing to say would have been nothing, texts don't make for a good repair strategy.

The irony of all this was not lost on me for a single second. Once again, I'd been fired as managing mom. As discussed in chapter two, I'd fully and totally lost my job as her chief of staff when she was fourteen, and it wasn't going to work to try to refill that post, as much as I wanted to.

In addition, I was letting my own profound discomfort with my daughter's suffering get in the way of her growth. She had a problem she needed to solve herself. I couldn't actually solve it for her. It is normal and healthy to be deeply uncomfortable when our kids are suffering. And yes, it's our job to protect them and to stand by them when they are in pain, but when we try to prevent or eliminate our children's discomfort, it sets them up for failure, not recovery.

Discomfort in the Age of Comfort

To understand historically how and why our parenting has changed in terms of our kids' discomfort, and the impact that this has had on their adolescence, I want to give you a little sociological context. The fourth industrial revolution—the relatively recent technological transformation in virtually every industry—has fostered another social and psychological revolution: our ability to be *comfortable*, seemingly all the time. Although we are still living in the shadow of the Great Recession of the late 2000s and income inequality has been increasing dramatically since the 1970s, Americans are living in a time of unprecedented consumer consumption the likes of which were unimaginable before World War II.

Many consumer goods such as washing machines, televisions, and mobile phones are now things people feel they *need* rather than *want*. In the 1970s, only one-quarter of Americans felt that air-conditioning was something they truly needed at home. But by the mid-1990s, air-conditioning was no longer considered a luxury: half of Americans (presumably those in warmer regions) considered it a necessity.

Even though real wages for most American families have stagnated since the 1970s, the material stuff "necessary" for a comfortable life in the US is more accessible than ever before. IKEA brings us inexpensive furniture and uber-comfortable mattresses. Famous fashion designers partner with Target to mass-produce hip clothing for cheap sale.

I don't mean to imply that we are all living in the lap of luxury. We are not. For example, one in eight people struggle with hunger in America, one in five American children live in poor households, and more than 12 percent of Americans live below the poverty line. But even in low-income households, Americans have accumulated more consumer goods than they used to. About 80 percent have air-conditioning, three-quarters have access to at least one car or truck, and around half have a dishwasher. Being poor is materially different than it used to be.

It's easy to forget that the vast majority of our creature comforts became cheap and widely available only recently. The first IKEA store opened in the US in 1985; Target in 1983. In other words, these changes had just become ubiquitous when today's teenagers arrived on the scene, and as such, our kids have grown up with more conveniences and more access to pleasurable experiences than any generation before them.

At the same time, the majority of us haven't encountered as much hardship as in previous generations. We've not contended with a draft or a world war, for example, or a lasting economic depression. Even the recent and deadly flu outbreaks did not rival the 1918 influenza pandemic, one of the deadliest natural disasters in human history. That flu resulted in the death of 3 to 5 percent of the *world's* population.

So, given the unprecedented material comfort that we are currently living in, it is ironic that people talk about their stress and the stress of our teens and college students as though life is barely endurable.

The Happiness Paradox

The relentless pursuit (and easy availability) of pleasure steers us toward a single feeling state: happiness. Seduced by the obvious desirability of pleasure and the very real benefits of happiness, it's easy to sour on anything less than comfort and joy. This also means that "we increasingly view discomfort as toxic, unmanageable, and intolerable," write psychologists and researchers Todd Kashdan and Robert Biswas-Diener in their book *The Upside of Your Dark Side*. And this, ironically, makes us more uncomfortable.

Here's why: As the range of experiences we seek narrows to include fewer and fewer experiences that fall outside of our "comfort zone," we get out of the practice of dealing with the harder bits of life. Hardship—or even just uneasiness—requires a skillfulness that many teens aren't necessarily developing.

While it's true that a joyful life comes from positive emotions, it also comes from resilience—from having the tools we need to cope with life's inevitable difficulties and painful moments. **Like it or not, we tend to develop the skills we need to cope with difficulty and discomfort only when we need them: when we're dealing with difficulty and discomfort.**

For that reason, **a certain amount of stress can be healthy**. A mountain of research shows that we learn and grow when we are out of our comfort zone—when we are exposed to something new. This is important because stress can act like a vaccine for future stress. (Researchers even call it "stress inoculation.") People who are able to weather stressful circumstances frequently go on to demonstrate above-average resilience.

But as our kids deal with discomfort less and less, minor inconveniences (like a long line or unexpected traffic) start to feel difficult to navigate. Loss, even if it is just a high school soccer game, feels intolerable. Not getting what we want can feel humiliating and scary.

When we parents see that our kids are anxious or upset, we want to protect them from emotional pain. We want to take it away. We don't like to see their anguish, so we do anything we can to eliminate their discomfort and difficulty. It turns out that this is not so helpful.

More than any generation that has come before it, Gen Z has learned that it must be really awful to feel and experience difficult things, such as homesickness, a superhard class, or changing schools. This just isn't true. Difficulty is rarely awful if you have the skills you need to navigate it. Even if we only want to feel happy, life will still be full of "difficult" emotions like anger, sadness, and disappointment, and most will pass uneventfully. **The so-called negative emotions are not necessarily traumatic, scarring, unnatural—or to be avoided.**

We parents think we are helping our kids when we rush in to protect them from disappointment and difficulty, but when we do so, we are basically teaching them that they can't handle challenges on their own. This probably *is* true if they've never handled a difficulty independently. Teens who always have problems solved for them don't know how to solve problems themselves.

More than that, many kids in Gen Z have come (subconsciously) to believe that they are *entitled* to a life free from hassle and inconvenience, and perhaps even disappointment. This is a pernicious learned belief. No one is entitled to a life free from adversity. Discomfort—and difficulty, and even pain—are inevitable parts of life. No matter who you are or where you come from, life can be hard, and loss, conflict, and challenging emotions are inevitable.

But what happens when kids, usually privileged ones, feel that they are entitled to comfort and pleasure and then inevitably hit a bump in the road? Instead of dealing with whatever difficulty is before them, they tend to get even more upset. They feel disappointed and frustrated not just about what is going wrong, but because everything is not as comfortable and easy and gratifying as they expected it to be. They get anxious and stressed that things aren't the way they believe they "should" be. They blame their own difficulties on others, and they look for the easiest way out—because they are, after all, entitled to it.

Comfortably Numb

As we pursue comfort, pleasure, and happiness with increased vigor, we're also driven to avoid pain. In the past we might have just had to suck it up and deal with whatever physical or psychic pain we might be confronted with because we had no other option. In so doing, we would have likely become more skilled in overcoming difficulty and challenge, but these days we can easily just numb our pain. We have the technology.

Dozens of new medications to combat sadness and anxiety have been released in the last two decades—many of which do not work as well for most people as, say, exercise does, but are, of course, much more convenient. By the time they graduate from college, more than one-quarter of Gen Z will be taking (or will have taken) a prescription medication to help manage depression and anxiety. These medications may or may not make them feel better; there is surprisingly little evidence that they work better than a placebo in adults, and little research has been done on adolescents. But we do know that these medications do not solve the underlying problems that caused the sadness and stress in the first place.

Not coincidentally, America's opioid epidemic started in the early 2000s when doctors began prescribing opioids for pain outside of a hospital setting. Although opium, grown from poppies, has been used as a medicinal painkiller and recreational drug since 4000 BCE, it is now more potent (often twenty times stronger than the opium of the eighteenth century) and pervasive than ever before. In 2017, 191 million opioid prescriptions were dispensed by doctors in the US. For reference, there are 326 million people in the whole country.

And let's not forget that our smartphones and tablets are numbing devices themselves, with their social media feeds and endless diversions. They have the power to distract us from anything we might not want to feel at any time of the day or night. But again, they don't solve the "problem" of our bad feelings. Negative emotions don't go away when we distract ourselves from them. We just become less aware of how we are feeling, and we tend to feel worse later than we would have if we hadn't suppressed the feeling. A study of college students found that those who checked their phones frequently tended to experience

higher levels of distress during their leisure time (when they intended
to relax). Ironically, avoiding negative emotions and experiences is contributing to Gen Z's pain and suffering.

When teens are not willing or able to experience tough emotions,
such as disappointment, embarrassment, and frustration, they are not
able to persist toward their long-term goals. For this reason and many
others, we need to teach our kids how to tolerate discomfort and, more
than that, distress. When they have developed some distress tolerance,
they become able to take risks, have difficult conversations, and stay
true to what they know is right.

Fortunately, we *can* help them develop distress-tolerance. The
rest of this chapter is loaded with science-based tactics for soothing
your stressed or distressed teen *indirectly*. These will give you a way to
actively support your struggling teen *without* rescuing them. That
way, they can learn from the difficulty and discover that they have the
strength to handle it themselves.

Coaching Teens Through Difficulty

Your mission, should you choose to accept it, is to become your kids'
coach. The key difference between managing and coaching is that
parent-managers rescue their teens from pain, whereas parent-coaches
see their kids as capable of making choices and solving their own problems. As coaches, we can ask questions that help our teens see the possibilities for positive action. Instead of making their decisions for them,
we can help them make better decisions *for themselves*. We can help
them focus on what they *do* want instead of what they do not want.

A word of clarification: Parent-coaches are nothing like mediocre
athletic coaches, yelling instructions from the sidelines. As discussed
in chapter two, we're trying to be less bossy and certainly less controlling, but this doesn't mean that we step back so far that we become
permissive or neglectful. As coaches, we still create the scaffolding and
structure our kids need to keep them safe and healthy and to allow
them to develop the skills they need for health and happiness. We
might lead drills and enforce league rules, so to speak, but they are the
team captain.

When our kids are struggling, instead of trying to mask or take away their pain, we can help them feel more comfortable with discomfort. This way, kids learn to rise to new challenges and grow from difficult or painful experiences. (Or they can learn positive ways of coping when they aren't getting what they want.)

Another caveat: Some teens are so anxious or depressed that they clearly need professional psychological support. The tactics in this section are for kids who are feeling normal grief over a loss, normal stress because of academic pressure, normal sadness or insecurities in response to social difficulties, and so on. If you aren't sure if the difficult emotions your teen is experiencing are in the range of normal, please consult with a licensed therapist.

Confronting Stress and Distress

The most important thing to do when your teen is anxious or suffering is to help them confront the stressor or worry rather than avoid it. Why? Because **avoidance fuels anxiety**.

In the short run, avoidance doesn't seem to fuel anxiety; it seems to provide relief. We often feel better just by *thinking about avoiding* something that is stressing us out. But because avoidance doesn't actually help us cope with whatever has us so worried, it'll usually come back to bite us in relatively short order.

Avoiding worries, stressors, and problems prevents our teens from seeing that they have what it takes to deal with their fears and challenges—and this is an important thing for them to learn. Moreover, avoidance fuels future avoidance, which in turn increases the odds that our teens will become increasingly afraid of whatever it is that they are avoiding. All of this worsens anxiety over time.

Here are some strategies that help more than offering reassurance, giving direction, or distracting your teen from their issue.

1. Ask your kid to simply describe the difficult circumstance.

Maybe it is a problematic friendship or perhaps they didn't make a team they really wanted to be on. Maybe they are stressed about an upcoming test or feeling left out of a social scene. Maybe they embarrassed themselves in class or, like my daughter, perhaps they are physically sick and in pain.

As parents, we need to recognize that their difficulties are real— even if they sometimes seem to us to be dramatic, overblown, or irrational. **The key is not to deny what they are going through and how it is making them feel.** For example, when they say that they are lonely, we might be tempted to say, "But you have so many friends!" Instead, have them simply give you the facts of the hard place they are in, and in response, show genuine curiosity about their experience. You are not trying to take away their pain. The goal is for them to feel **seen** and **heard** by you.

2. Help them identify how they are feeling in response to the circumstance.

"I'm feeling anxious right now," they might say, or "I feel stressed and nervous." This is the "name it to tame it" technique, and research shows that when we label our emotions, we are better able to integrate them. If they start telling you a story that is making them more emotional, gently bring them back to what they are feeling. The task here is to identify *what* they are feeling, not necessarily *why* they are feeling that way. This can be difficult for parents and teenagers alike because we can get attached to our narratives about *why* we are upset. It's usually easier to stick to our story than to reveal how we are feeling. But again, the task here is to talk about the actual emotions, not the reasons for the emotions.

Encourage your teens to hang in there with unpleasant feelings. See if they can objectify their emotions. Ask, "Where in your body do you feel anxious/lonely/homesick/sad? Does the feeling have a color? A texture? A shape?" Don't let kids distract themselves from their difficult emotions before they've acknowledged them. You might need to remind them that avoiding their feelings—or the situations that make them feel that way—actually prolongs difficult emotions.

See if you can sum up their difficult experience or circumstance (the facts, not the story) and their feelings about the circumstance in a simple phrase or two. For example, "You ate lunch by yourself again today. You feel sad and lonely." Throw in a little empathy if you feel like you need to, such as, "That's so hard. I can remember eating lunch alone and feeling lonely when I was in high school, too. It's awful." **Kids and teens are much more likely to listen to us if they feel understood.**

A WORD ABOUT KIDS WHO ARE *VERY, VERY UPSET*

It's normal if teens seem to be trying to make you just as upset as they are. Kids often communicate what they are feeling by *inducing those same feelings* in other people. When this happens, try to hold up an emotional mirror between you two by verbally reflecting back to them what they seem to be feeling. For instance, say something like "I can see that you are really suffering" or "I can see that you are very, very upset right now." Let them see that you aren't afraid of their big emotions, and that you aren't trying to change or fix them. It's hard, but resist the urge to reassure them, tell them everything is going to be okay, or offer platitudes like "this too shall pass."

3. If they are stressed or anxious, encourage them to classify their stress.

I've taken a lot of advice on this topic from psychologist Lisa Damour, author of *Under Pressure: Confronting the Epidemic of Stress and Anxiety in Girls*. Damour's stance is that we parents are most useful to our teenagers when we help them ask themselves "*What* is the source of my stress?" and "*Why* am I anxious?" It might be obvious to you what is going on, but the task here isn't to hand them a diagnosis, but rather to help *them* see *for themselves* what is going on more clearly.

It can help to let kids know what stresses most people out. Sonia Lupien at the Centre for Studies on Human Stress has a convenient acronym, NUTS, for what makes life stressful:

Novelty

Unpredictability

Threat to the ego

Sense of control

According to Lupien, we can help our kids identify causes of stress by looking for what might be new or changing in their life, looking for sources of unpredictability, identifying ways that their competence or safety is being threatened, and asking about the things in their lives that feel out of their control.

In addition to searching for sources of stress, it can be helpful for teens to classify the particular strain of stress they are experiencing. Is it related to a negative life event? Is it the result of cumulative day-to-day difficulties that are beyond the teen's control?

Life event stressors are things such as mourning the death of a loved one, changing schools, or dealing with divorce. The more change a life event requires a teen to make, the more stressful it will be.

Chronic stress is when "basic life circumstances are persistently difficult," according to Damour. Chronic stress is caused by things like living in poverty or living with a severely depressed parent, or having a chronic illness like cancer. I also suspect that many of today's teens are experiencing a form of chronic stress caused by current events. Three-quarters of teenagers in the US say they are stressed about mass shootings and school shootings. More than half feel stressed about the current political climate, and more than two-thirds feel significantly stressed about our nation's future. About 60 percent are worried about the rise in suicide rates, about climate change and global warming, and about the separation and deportation of immigrant and migrant families. Although as adults we may have the skills we need to shield us from these chronic stressors, a majority of our teenagers do not yet have this ability. In addition, social media is a source of chronic stress for many teens; nearly half say social media makes them feel judged, and more than one-third report feeling bad about themselves as a result of social media use.

Surprisingly, one study found that the number of daily hassles a teen faces can predict their emotional distress over time, and that daily hassles have a greater impact on teens' well-being than other types of stress. In fact, daily hassles tend to be *more* distressing for teens than negative life events or chronic stress. Knowing this, we can often help kids solve some of their daily hassles, even if we can't change their circumstances.

For example, when one of my daughters was going through a hard time at school socially, she also had a daily hassle: getting home from school. She often had to wait forty minutes or longer for the bus to come at the end of the school day. This was precious homework time. She was super stressed and having a hard time keeping up in her classes. I couldn't ease her social pain (a chronic stressor), but we eliminated the daily hassle of getting her home from school—the straw that was breaking the camel's back—by creating a carpool.

4. Help them see that their stress or anxiety can be helpful or good.

Stress, according to Damour, is the tension or strain we feel when we are pushed outside of our comfort zones. Stress is healthy and helpful when it creates enough tension and strain to foster growth.

Think of a muscle that is stressed by weight training. It tenses up and even breaks down a little. The weight might be very hard to lift, and the muscle might be sore afterward, but the stress of a heavy weight—so long as it isn't *so* heavy that it causes a significant injury—strengthens the muscle.

Stress can work the same way. (School is *supposed* to be stressful in this way.) Anxiety, on the other hand, is **the fear, dread, and panic that can come up for us in the face of a stressor** (or even just the mere *thought* of a stressor).

Sometimes anxiety is an important warning system that we are in danger. It's appropriate for us to feel anxious when we are riding in a car if the driver is texting, for example. *Legitimate anxiety* makes us want to get the heck out of imminent danger. I once had a really nice-seeming neighbor who scared the bejeezus out of me. Every time he'd stop to chat, friendly and normal-seeming as he was, the hair on my neck would stand up and my heart would start racing and thudding in my chest. It was all I could do to not run and hide from him. It turns out that my anxiety was legitimate, as I later found out that he had spent a decade in a maximum-security prison for violent sex crimes.

Other times, anxiety is more about excitement than it is a sign of danger. As Maria Shriver writes in *And One More Thing Before You Go . . .*, "Anxiety is a glimpse of your own daring . . . part of your agitation is just excitement about what you're getting ready to accomplish. Whatever you're afraid of—that is the very thing you should try to do."

But more often than not, our anxiety isn't helpful. *Unhelpful anxiety* makes us hesitate rather than bolt. We are afraid of looking stupid, so we don't ask a burning question. We fear failing, so we don't even try.

We can help our teens figure out whether they are experiencing legitimate anxiety or unhelpful anxiety. Do they have the desire to get the heck out of an imminently dangerous situation? If so, their anxiety is likely legitimate. We can support them in getting out of that dangerous situation. But if their anxiety is paralyzing them, help them consider that their anxiety may be unfounded, and that it is holding them back.

5. Practice acceptance.

The goal here is to help kids *drop their resistance* to the difficult situation and accept that it exists. For teens to do that, it helps when we also allow whatever is happening to be as it is for the moment. Why? Because resisting the current reality doesn't help us recover, learn, grow, or feel better. It simply amplifies the difficult emotions we are feeling. There is real truth to the old aphorism that what we resist persists. Weirdly, resistance prolongs our pain and difficulty, and the more our kids resist reality, the more likely it is that they will start showing signs of a dysregulated stress response. In other words, **when kids *aren't* managing stressful or difficult situations effectively, they tend to start having larger and larger stress responses to smaller and smaller stimuli**.

But how do we even begin to stop resisting what hurts or what scares us? And how do we help our kids do this, too?

Behavioral science and great wisdom traditions both point us toward **acceptance**. Research psychologist Kristin Neff and her colleagues have shown definitively that resistance increases our suffering, while acceptance—particularly self-acceptance—is one of those counterintuitive secrets to happiness. It is strangely effective to simply accept that which we cannot control, especially if we are in a difficult or painful situation. To do this, we accept a difficult situation, and also our emotions about the situation. We can't *make* our kids practice acceptance, but we can model our own practice of acceptance around their situation—and their feelings about that situation.

For example, they might have a particularly difficult relationship with a teacher or classmate. We can show them that we calmly accept this difficult relationship, and even that difficult relationships are a part of life. We can also let them know that we don't expect *them* to feel calm about this—we don't expect them to feel anything other than the frustration that they are currently feeling. In turn, they too might accept the difficult relationship as their present reality and also that they feel frustrated by the situation.

This doesn't mean that the situation will never get better; **acceptance is not the same as resignation**. We don't accept that things are going to stay the same forever, just whatever is happening in the moment. Teens can work to make the relationship less difficult (or to do their best studying for the next test, or whatever the situation), while at the same time accepting the reality that *right now*, the relationship or the class or the situation is very difficult. Maybe it will get better, and maybe it won't. **Practicing acceptance in the face of difficulty is hard, and it's also the most effective way to move forward.**

This approach requires trust on the parent's part. Trust that if your teen is still here and still breathing, everything is actually okay. Trust that even if we don't give them specific instructions for solving their issue, if we back off from trying to control them, life will continue to unfold just as it's meant to. Trust that even if it all goes to hell, even if other people make mistakes or do things differently than we would do them, our kids can deal with the outcome. Trust that they (and we) can handle all the difficult emotions that come up in response to what does or does not happen. Trust that they can handle loss and grief should it come.

We parents need to trust that this approach—practicing acceptance rather than resistance—works. **When we accept the reality of a difficult or scary situation and our limited control, it allows our kids to do the same.** Importantly, acceptance also frees them up to move forward, rather than remaining paralyzed by difficulty and fear.

The Difference Between Pretending and Positivity

In addition to simply distracting ourselves from how we are feeling—by checking our Instagram feed or eating the whole pan of brownies—one of the most common forms of resistance to a difficult situation is to pretend that we are feeling something other than what we are actually feeling. This is the "fake it till you make it" technique, and I don't recommend it.

Research indicates that faking a positive emotion usually makes us feel worse. Consciously faking a smile, for example, or other pleasantries to cover our negative emotions (what researchers call "surface acting") will often *increase* our distress. This kind of toxic inauthenticity is known to be corrosive to our health (especially our cardiovascular system), and it damages our relationships with others.

Instead of faking it, we can instead foster a genuine positive emotion. Researchers call this "deep acting," and it is when we genuinely work to foster more positive emotions in our lives. When we make a genuine effort to cultivate happiness, gratitude, hope, and other positive emotions, we *do* reduce stress.

Anger, fear, and negative emotions increase activity in the part of our nervous system that increases our heart rate. Gratitude, compassion, awe, love, and other positive emotions, on the other hand, decrease our heart rate, among other healthy things. This is why Barbara Fredrickson, a positive psychology pioneer, has famously shown that positive emotions put the brakes on the part of our nervous system that creates the deleterious stress response—what she calls the "undoing effect" of positive emotions. When we're stressed, positive emotions return us to our natural state, unwinding the damage that stress does.

After Acceptance: Positivity

We parents want our struggling children to feel happier for lots of good reasons beyond just the happiness itself. Positive emotions can help teens become more creative and motivated, more productive, and more skilled socially. This is because positive emotions send blood to their prefrontal cortex, allowing them to make better decisions than they would if they relied on the more primitive, instinctive regions of

THE DOWNSIDE OF EMOTIONAL CLOSENESS

I was recently at lunch with several other mom friends, and the conversation turned to the things our kids tell us these days that we would have never told our own parents.

"My daughter called me this morning in a tizzy, upset because she'd missed her train," my friend Lisa said about her daughter, Sophie, a high-achieving sophomore at an Ivy League college. "It turns out that she went into New York City for the weekend, stayed out too late on Sunday night, overslept, missed her train, and was now going to miss an important test."

My friend listened to her daughter's freak-out and helped her calm down, but when Lisa hung up, she was a little angry and confused. *Why was her daughter telling her about her mistakes? Didn't she know that her mother would be upset to learn that her daughter was out late partying and otherwise behaving irresponsibly?* We all agreed that we would never in a million years have placed a call like that to our own mother when we were in college. We didn't want our parents to know when we were messing up.

My friend Carrie had a different complaint about her son, Duncan, a senior in high school. He was occasionally, and seemingly randomly, incredibly rude to her. She showed me a text thread from the day before:

Duncan

> Hey do you think I could join two of my classmates for an admitted students thing down at Pomona on Monday?

Carrie

> Sure, how will you get there?

Duncan

> I can hop on whatever transportation the other guys are taking

Carrie

> okay, sounds good let's talk before the trip

Duncan

> So you can tell me to make good decisions?

Carrie just wanted to know more about an overnight trip Duncan was about to embark on. She knew from a previous conversation that the transportation was going to be expensive, and that she was going to be expected to pay for it if she didn't help him brainstorm other options. In return, she got a cheeky text suggesting that she was being invasive.

Both of these conversations fell into the category of "things we would never have said to our own parents." In many ways, I was close to my parents, and I always knew how much they loved me. They were consistently supportive in loads of practical ways, but for the most part, as a teenager, I did not look to my parents for *emotional* support. Moreover, once I reached adolescence, I had a private life that my parents were more or less unaware of. Because they had no way of tracking my whereabouts, I had a lot of freedom to do what I wanted in the evenings and weekends. I didn't lie to my parents because I didn't have to: I could tell them that I was "spending the night at Robin's," and so long as that was true, that I would eventually end up back at Robin's, I had little guilt about omitting the fact that I was going to a raging party before that.

I wouldn't have called my parents if I'd been late to work after that party because I wouldn't want to risk getting in trouble, and I wouldn't have been cheeky to my parents on my way out the door. If I had been, I wouldn't have been allowed to go. When I made mistakes or got into trouble, I looked to my *friends* for emotional support. And because I had a life that I lived outside of my parents' purview, I had a much stronger sense of my own independence.

Both Sophie's and Duncan's behaviors, though very different, are symptoms of the same thing: the emotional closeness that our generation of parents has fostered with our children. Sophie knew that she could look to her mother when she was in trouble to soothe her and help her feel safe. She knew that Lisa would keep her own anger and disappointment in check in order to provide the comfort that Sophie needed at that time. As a result, Lisa and Sophie share a close emotional bond that Lisa never had with her own mother. The downside of this closeness is that we parents see the private lives of our children—sometimes when we'd rather not.

How Duncan's rudeness relates is less obvious. Right before the text exchange about the Pomona visit, Duncan had gone to his mom for advice about his girlfriend. Carrie gave him the advice he asked for, and *Duncan took that advice*. The downside of this sort of emotional support is that it hinders the natural separation between adolescents and their parents. So right after Duncan confided his deepest feelings to his mom and then took her sage advice, he found an opportunity to be rude to her—a subconscious move to reestablish his independence.

While painful for us parents, this hot/cold strategy works for teenagers. It's a way of having both emotional closeness with their parents *and* independence. So, the next time you find yourself supporting your teenager emotionally, you can feel good about the fact that you are building a strong foundation for emotional closeness with them for the rest of your life. And also, brace yourself, because in the next twenty-four hours, they are likely to be shockingly rude to you or otherwise push you away. Prepare for door slamming, eye rolling, and general snarkiness as they send the message that they are *not* dependent on you.

their brains that are activated when they are under stress. The prefrontal cortex is responsible for their executive function, so they tend to have more self-discipline and better self-control when they are happy than when they are stressed. They're also able to learn difficult things more quickly and better retain what they learn over the long haul. So *after* they've practiced acceptance, teens do really well to foster positive emotions—authentically.

Fostering Positive Emotions

Positive emotions come in a lot of different flavors, so when we seek to increase the quantity of the positive emotions and experiences we have in a given day, we need to think beyond happiness or pleasure. Think about contentment, bliss, engagement, frivolity, silliness—these are all positive emotions based in the present. We can also cultivate positive emotions about the past (like gratitude) and the future (like faith, hope, confidence, and optimism). A flourishing life is also fed by positive emotions that are global in nature, like awe, elevation, and inspiration. Positive emotions that connect us to other people, like love and compassion, are our most powerful positive emotions.

For example, one of the most powerful positive emotions we have is gratitude. Relative to many other positive emotions, we have reams of research indicating that gratitude is part of the happiness holy grail. Scientists have found that people who practice gratitude are considerably more enthusiastic, interested, and determined than people who don't. In fact, they feel 25 percent happier, and they are more likely to be both kind and helpful to others.

Like most positive emotions, gratitude can actually be thought of as a *skill*, like learning to speak a foreign language or play a new sport. It can be taught, and it needs to be practiced consciously and deliberately. Yet, unlike learning a language or a sport, practicing gratitude can be blissfully simple. Teens need only to count the things in their lives that they feel thankful for.

This can, however, be tricky for parents. We often see the many things in our teens' lives that they "should" be grateful for, and pointing out these things to them when they are suffering is not likely to foster any positive emotions. You'll just end up with an annoyed and angry teen.

However, if your teen has practiced the five steps above, and they seem ready to move on—meaning they've clearly gotten to a place of acceptance—you can ask them if they'd like suggestions for resetting their nervous system. If they say yes, ask them what has recently made them feel genuinely happy. Perhaps it's playing with the dog or seeing a friend. See if you can support them in doing something they *already know* fosters a positive emotion.

It's important to help teens distinguish between the experience of pleasure or gratification and the experience of an authentic positive emotion, as the two things are different physiologically. If they say that eating cake or playing a video game made them happy yesterday, that's pleasure and gratification—not positive emotion. Try pointing them in the direction of one of the following positive emotions.

Gratitude

Many teenagers, especially those who journal or write a lot already, get a great deal out of keeping a gratitude journal, either handwritten or online. (There are loads of web-based versions). Again, the benefits of gratitude are huge: People who jotted down something they were grateful for every day for just two weeks (using an app created by the Greater Good Science Center at the University of California–Berkeley) showed higher stress resilience and greater satisfaction with life and reported fewer headaches, less congestion, and a reduction in stomach pain, coughs, and sore throats.

Inspiration

Inspiration—along with its cousins elevation and awe—is a positive emotion that makes us feel more content, joyful, and satisfied with our lives. Teens can find awe by viewing a grand landscape, by reading about a mind-expanding theory, or by contemplating something that changes the way they think about the world. Researchers induce awe in volunteers fairly simply by showing them video clips of people facing awesome things like waterfalls and whales or by having them write about something that was vast and altered their perception of the world. And awe comes with a wonderful bonus: It can make you feel less pressed for time and less impatient.

Future-Based Positive Emotions

Optimism, hope, faith, and confidence are all positive emotions about the future that research has repeatedly shown make us happier. One way to foster hope is to have teens write about their "best possible future self." This is a research-tested way to build optimism about the future—something that tends to motivate people to work toward their desired future (and therefore make it more likely to become a reality). To do so, have them take a moment to write about their lives in the future. Where do they want to be living? What friends and family will be in their lives? What type of work do they imagine doing? What hobbies will they have? How would they like to be spending their time?

If your teen is finding that this exercise leads them to examine how their current life doesn't match the "best possible self" that they imagine or that they've written about, encourage them to just focus on the future, imagining a brighter future in which they are fulfilling their potential. Part of the exercise can be describing the challenges they will have had to overcome to make their best possible life happen. (You can find more detailed instructions for this exercise on the Greater Good in Action website.)

Love

As it turns out, all positive emotions are not created equal. Love and the similar emotions that we experience when we feel connected socially—like affection, warmth, care, fondness, and compassion—are more powerful than the others.

The longest-running study of human development, the Harvard Grant Study, makes it clear that "the most important influence, by far, on a flourishing life is love," as one of the researchers behind the study, George Vaillant, put it in his book *Triumphs of Experience.* For the parents of struggling teenagers, this means that sometimes all we need to do is shower love on our kids. (Which is good news, because sometimes it is all we *can* do.)

For the teens themselves, it means that usually they will feel better when they reach out to the people who give them the greatest sense of belonging. Research shows that even a tiny experience of belonging can be game-changing. For example, when college students feel a sense of belonging, their grades go up. In one study, African American college students were asked to read a short testimonial from older students about how they had been worried about fitting in but found that things had turned out well. They then had to make a short video testimonial about their own experience of fitting in. This one simple intervention "led to an enduring improvement in GPA in nearly every semester of about 0.2 GPA units (for example, a GPA of 3.6 instead of 3.4)," writes UCLA neuroscientist Matthew Lieberman.

Chapter five tackles this topic in more detail, but for now, it can be enough to ask a struggling teen: Where do you feel the greatest sense of belonging in your life? Where do your strongest and most positive social connections come from?

Peace

A terrific way to evoke feelings of peace and contentment is simple meditation. Scores of studies have shown the benefits of meditation to be
broad and profound. Meditation lowers stress and anxiety, helps focus,
and (somewhat ironically since it involves time dedicated to doing nothing) makes us more productive. Meditation even makes people healthier! After meditating daily for eight weeks, research subjects were 76
percent less likely than a nonmeditating control group to miss work due
to illness, and if they did get a cold or a flu, it lasted only five days on
average, whereas control group illness lasted an average of eight days.

Teens who are interested in meditation would do well to learn
from a teacher. Transcendental Meditation teachers, for example, do
free introductory classes in most cities around the world. There are
also loads of meditation apps geared specifically to teenagers.

File Under: Science of the Blazingly Obvious

Every teen already knows that certain types of music and—here's a
shocker—*comedy* induce positive moods. When my teens need the
undoing effect of happiness after a particularly difficult day, sometimes
all they really need to do is play some upbeat music. Now neuroscientists have shown that while mentally fatiguing activities, like thinking
and creating, induce physiological signs of stress (such as the cortisol
levels in our saliva), listening to music reduces these signs.

Physical activity is even better at inducing good moods than happy
music, and it is crucial to the way we think and feel. Exercise prepares
our brains to learn, improves our mood and attention, and lowers stress
and anxiety. So perhaps you can convince your teen to at least take a
walk. When we've been really angry or had a fight-or-flight response,
physical activity helps clear the adrenaline out of our system. Happiness researcher Sonja Lyubomirsky says that exercise may just be the
best short-term happiness booster there is.

Most obvious of all is laughter. When they aren't feeling low, it
can be fun to have kids bookmark a few videos that consistently make
them chuckle. Humor is not a waste of time or a luxury. Laughter
lowers stress hormones (even the expectation of laughter can do this)

and elevates the levels of feel-good beta-endorphins and the human growth hormone.

In the end, we parents can't take away our children's pain and discomfort, as much as we might want to—and usually, we'd do well not to try to. But by peacefully accepting that being human is often hard and uncomfortable and even painful, we open the door to compassion and wisdom—both theirs and ours.

CHAPTER FOUR

How to Influence Your Teen

*Even though we can no longer manage every detail
of our teens' lives, most teens still need our guidance.
Here's how to be influential without being bossy.*

I frequently hear complaints from parents that their teenagers are irrational and impossible to influence. Kids say they want to get into a good college, for example, but then they fall asleep in class because they've stayed up half the night watching movies. Or they say they'd like to keep taking guitar lessons so that they might be able to join their friends' rock band, but they refuse to practice regularly.

It is our adolescents' developmental *job* to take the irrational position, the one that they know we'll disagree with. **Teens are driven to individuate, or to gain autonomy and independence by differentiating themselves from *us*, their loving parents.** This is why they sometimes take positions *we just know they couldn't possibly believe.* (Except that they do really believe in their take on things, at least emotionally.) Even when we understand the psychological theory of adolescent separation, it can really suck. It's no fun when kids push us away, especially when we are so full of good intentions and great ideas.

I'm not going to pretend I don't find it really frustrating that I can't just give my teenagers lots of (important!) information and expect that new information to translate to positive behavior. Teenagers don't usually know what they don't know about lots of things that will affect their health over the long run. It'd be much easier if we parents could just download information to them—say, about sex and drugs—and know that they were going to use that information well.

But alas, as I think we all know from experience, giving teenagers a lot of information doesn't seem to be the key to influencing them. In fact, we know from some interesting research on this topic that what is somewhat effective for elementary school children—giving them information about their health or well-being that they can act on—tends to be mostly ineffective for teenagers. This is because adolescents are much more sensitive to whether or not they are being treated with respect. The hormonal changes that come with puberty conspire with adolescent social dynamics to make teenagers much more attuned to social status. More specifically, they become super touchy about whether or not they are being treated as though they are high status.

In the teenage brain, the part of themselves that is an autonomous young adult is *high* status. The part of them that is still a kid who needs our support is *low* status. They might be half independent young adult, half little kid, but they are hugely motivated to become 100 percent autonomous . . . even if they do know, on some level, that they still need our support and guidance.

When we give our adolescents a lot of information about an (important!) topic, especially when it is information that they don't really want or that they think they already have, it can feel infantilizing to them. Even if we deliver the information as we would to another adult, teenagers will often feel disrespected by the mere fact of our instruction.

Proven Strategies

Fortunately, there are ways for us to influence our teens without endangering their need for autonomy. The tactics below draw on several bodies of work, the most prominent of which is called motivational interviewing. I learned motivational interviewing from Ron Dahl, a highly acclaimed UC Berkeley researcher who specializes in adolescent brain development and the secret emotional life of teenagers. Research shows that motivational interviewing is effective for fostering behavior change in teens in difficult arenas, like drug and alcohol abuse, disordered eating, and risky sexual behavior.

This chapter also draws heavily on my own life coach training, which I did with the brilliant Martha Beck, a Harvard-trained sociologist and life coach to Oprah, Elizabeth Gilbert, and many other people who've got it going on. Remember that our goal here is still to be the best parent coaches that we can possibly be.

We don't need to use all of these tactics, or use them all at once, but I've found that I need to have a few in my back pocket so that I don't start offering suggestions or, worse, criticism. Using any of the following techniques will help; start with what feels easiest to you.

Accord Them High Status from the Get-Go

When it's time to bring up the topic you want to influence your teen about, speak as you would to someone with the highest possible social status—someone you really, really respect. (I have to literally imagine that person in my head, and then imagine both the tone and the words I would use with that person.) Remember, if your teen feels disrespected, nagged, spoken down to, pressed upon, or infantilized, all bets are off.

The goal is to give them enough information that they can make their own informed decision, hopefully one that benefits their health and well-being in the long term, in a way that allows them to feel respected and high-status in the short term. They'll also need to feel competent, so it can help to point out all the ways that you see them as already very competent in this arena. What do you admire about them?

One way to convey respect is to demonstrate their value to a group of other teenagers. Are there other kids that your teens can help? Could you have them write a letter to someone else struggling with the same decision, outlining their situation and all that they know about the decision they need to make? This helps teens engage in what researchers call self-persuasion, and it makes palpable the wisdom that they have to share and the way that they can help others.

Give Kids a Choice About What to Talk About

Instead of sitting them down for a Big Talk and using a tone that suggests you are going to lay down the law, wade in sloooowly. Raise a problem you'd like to discuss from a couple of very different angles. For example: "Do you want to talk about what it is like when you lose your temper at school?" or "Do you want to talk about what makes it difficult for you to eat a healthy lunch?" and "What happens when you feel hungry at school?" Dahl recommends that we always also throw in a super open-ended question like "Or maybe there is something else you would rather discuss? What do you think?"

If they say they don't want to talk, let it go temporarily. Force never works, but persistence does.

Tell Them How You Feel

Say, "I'm feeling worried about the emails I'm getting from your teachers." Don't tell them what you *think* ("I think you can do better"). Then ask them when they'd like to talk about it. Once they see that you aren't going to let it go, but that you are going to give them choice, teens usually stop resisting.

Ask Open-Ended Questions to Understand Their Position

We want to encourage our teens to share with us their innermost motivations. To do this, we can phrase our questions nonjudgmentally, in ways that prompt our adolescent to elaborate. (Note: "What the hell is wrong with you?" is not recommended, even though it is, indeed, open-ended.) Try "What have you already tried that worked, or maybe didn't work, in this situation?" or "What matters most to you about this right now?"

Once teens have dipped their toe in the water of their own motivations, my favorite two-word sentence is "**Say more**"—not "Tell me more," which might sound like the same phrase but, trust me, isn't to a teenager. When we say "Tell me more," we've inserted ourselves, their parents, into the equation again—and teens are quick to sniff that out and shut down. It can land emotionally as though we are begging. "Say more" is neutral, and it doesn't smack of neediness.

Reflect Back What They Are Saying, Not What You Wish They Were Saying

This can be a *simple restatement*:

> **Adolescent**: All teenagers drink at parties. I drank too much last night, but I do not have a drinking problem.
>
> **Parent**: You feel strongly that your drinking is normal, and it's not a problem.

Or you can reflect *what they mean* but use different words:

> **Adolescent**: I'm not an alcoholic!
>
> **Parent**: That label really doesn't fit you.

Or try reflecting what they are *feeling*:

> **Adolescent**: I'm not an alcoholic!
>
> **Parent**: It makes you angry when you think you are being labeled in that way.

If our teen clearly expresses some ambivalence, we can also try amplifying or even exaggerating—without sarcasm!—what they are saying:

> **Adolescent**: I'm really not sure that I need help or treatment dealing with this.
>
> **Parent**: Your life is fine right now, just the way it is. You're doing okay on your own.

My favorite way to reflect what my teens are saying is to preface my restatement with, "Tell me where I'm wrong." As in, "Okay, here is what I am understanding, tell me where I'm wrong: You feel like your life is just fine right now." Or "Tell me where I'm wrong: What is making you really angry about this situation is that you've been labeled as having a drinking problem."

Asking teens to tell us where we are wrong harnesses their strong impulse to make sure that they are right and we are wrong, while at the same time getting them to further clarify their motivations.

Show Them Their Inconsistencies—Gently

Using the above tactics, we can reflect back to our teens their conflicting motivations—the inconsistencies between what they say their goals or beliefs are and their current behavior.

What to say, then, to that teen who wants to join the garage band but has not been practicing regularly or learning the music? First, ask her permission to tell her what you see. If she says she's willing to listen to your perspective, gently point out in a nonjudgmental, factual way the discrepancy between what she says she wants and what she's doing to make that happen: "Tell me where I'm wrong. It seems like you really want to join Jack's band, but before they'll let you audition, you need to learn all the songs on their playlist. You haven't started learning those songs yet. It seems that when you get home from school, you often just want to chill out in your room."

Support Their Autonomy and Emphasize Their Personal Choice and Control

Teens are most likely to change when they recognize the problem themselves and when they are optimistic about their ability to solve the problem. We can help by expressing our confidence in their abilities and by emphasizing that we can't change them—that the choice about whether or not to change is the adolescent's alone. Dahl recommends saying something like this: "Whether or not you make any changes in your activities or your behavior is entirely up to you. I definitely would not want you to feel pressured to do anything against your will." Or, as discussed in chapter two, we can take a deep breath and use the mantras from *The Self-Driven Child*: "It's your call" and "I have confidence in your ability to make informed decisions about your own life and to learn from your mistakes."

Surf Their Resistance Like a Wave

In other words, practice acceptance again. Say you want your teens or tweeners to get to bed earlier or to spend more time on their homework. It's normal for adolescents to resist you on these things, especially if they are feeling pushed to do something they are not ready to do—even if they agree with you on some level. For example, they might recognize that they are not doing as well in school as they'd like, but they aren't ready yet to commit to spending more time on homework and less on video games.

Sometimes (often?) we parents cause kids to dig in their heels when we argue our own position more forcefully. This is like trying to be understood in a foreign country where we don't speak the language: When we ask a question to a local who doesn't understand English, we may get frustrated and ask again—but this time louder: "WHERE IS THE TRAIN STATION?" Similarly, with teens, it doesn't help to make the same argument again, but louder. We'll just annoy them. Instead of trying to persuade kids, we need to accept their resistance as normal and try a different tack.

Genuinely Appreciate Their Position and Participation in the Discussion

Used sparingly, affirmations build connections. You might be shocked (or depressed) by what your teen is telling you, and tempted to point out the mistakes that could ruin their lives forever. Instead, appreciate how hard the conversation might be for them and thank them for their honesty: "I can only imagine that this is an awkward conversation for you. I'm so grateful that you are willing to talk with me about your sex life. Thank you for explaining why you've been sneaking out with your girlfriend. Your honesty says a lot about who you are as a person."

Don't overdo this one, though, or say anything you don't actually mean. You'll just come off as inauthentic and manipulative.

Shift the Focus of Your Discussion

Offer a little relief by changing the topic ever so slightly. Perhaps you've been talking about how your daughter's boyfriend sometimes makes her feel unattractive by making jokes about her weight. You might temporarily shift the focus of your discussion by saying something like, "You're pretty confident that you're in love with Pete, though, and you say he's 'the one.' Say more about that."

Side with Their Negative Position

When my kids were toddlers, their dad and I used to laugh at how well reverse psychology worked, and if you are particularly skilled—that is, if you can do this without sounding critical or sarcastic—it might work with your teen or tweener, too.

For example, your teen might be ranting about how her other parent is really bugging her to try out for soccer, and she wants him to back off and let her do her own thing. You could agree with her negative position by saying something like "Maybe he should just leave you alone, even if it means that he isn't involved in your athletics, which is what he's trying to help you with." Or you could say, "Yes, you both might be better off if he focused his energy on your younger brother."

––––––––––

All of these techniques take practice. (At least for me. The only thing that seems to come naturally to me is bossiness.) The good news is that we parents of teenagers are generally presented with a lot of opportunities to practice these tactics! And if you don't think you've got any current practice opportunities, I recommend you work on the more mundane areas where you'd like to see growth, and then when you need these strategies for bigger issues, you'll know what you are doing.

As parents, I think we often forget that teenagers are motivated by totally different things than we are. We want them to do the things that are best for their health and well-being, and they want to do the things that bestow on them the highest social status. **But we are most influential when we are able to take advantage of teens'** *existing*

motivations, rather than trying to get them to feel motivated by *our* goals.

Fortunately, our motivations tend to turn out to be aligned already. Our adolescents want to feel like competent, well-respected, autonomous adults, and in the end, we want our children to be competent, autonomous adults who make choices we respect and admire. The big decisions that our kids need to make as teenagers can be a bridge between how they want to feel and the young adults they are becoming. Although they may not see it right now, they are so lucky to have us parents walking across that bridge beside—or perhaps a touch behind—them.

The Power of a Behavior Plan

Once our kids indicate that they are ready to make a change, one of the most powerful things they can do is come up with a behavior plan. We can help them with this if, and only if, they don't know how to do it on their own, and if they ask us for help. **The idea is to encourage teens to make their intentions more concrete and specific, which research shows dramatically increases the odds that their behavior really will change.**

Here's the thing: Intentions are never enough. Even full-blown goal setting isn't worth much if you don't do it right. Just vaguely wanting to do well in school, spend less time on their phones, get better at handling stress, make the team, develop closer friendships, feel happier, or be class president will not get teens where they want to go. But kids don't know this, and how could they? We parents need to teach our teens (and our college students) how to change their behavior in a way that helps them reach their goals. Here's how:

Ask Your Teen to Articulate What They Are Hoping For

What do they want to accomplish? Remember, a behavior plan will work only if it is what *they* want to accomplish for themselves, and not what you, their wise parent, want for them.

It isn't unusual for teens to seem stuck on what they *don't* want rather than what they *do* want. It is, after all, so much easier for kids to complain and wallow in their dissatisfaction than it is to create the life they want—especially if they can get a concerned adult to rescue them from their difficulty or pain (cue helicopter parent here). Good parent-coaches won't fall into that trap. They'll help their teens refocus on the outcomes that they *do* want rather than ruminating on what they *don't* want. Some coaching tips:

- Communicate clearly that you know they are capable of making their own choices and solving their own problems.
- Say, "I care about you, and I know how capable you are."
- Ask questions that help them see possibilities for positive action.

You will be right there on the sidelines supporting them, but you aren't going to rescue them. If they are really having trouble figuring out what they want, or they just can't stay focused on what they *do* want instead of what they *don't* want, invite them to imagine their "best possible future self," as discussed in chapter three.

Once kids know what they want, they can make a behavior plan. Don't be offended if they don't want to do this with you—the point is that they need to totally own this themselves. If they clearly need help but won't work with you, see if you can get an adult they respect to walk them through the steps. Aunts and uncles, family friends, therapists and school counselors, and older cousins have all helped out our family in the past.

For example, my daughter Macie was applying to colleges the fall of her senior year in high school and asked me for help managing her time better. Her ultimate goal was to get into her first choice, but I was able to get her to articulate what she was hoping for more specifically. She knew that she had a lot to do besides just filling out the application: She had to keep her grades up, improve her SAT scores, impress the college riding coach, and so on, all while continuing to lead in her community service and other activities.

She knew she needed more sleep than she was getting to be mentally and physically healthy and to do well academically and athletically. Specifically, she was hoping to avoid a cycle of exhaustion where she would oversleep and then rush out the door in the morning, skip-ping breakfast and generally not starting the day well. Her dream was to get eight or nine hours of sleep each night and get out of bed as soon as her alarm went off at 6:30 on weekday mornings.

Ask Them What Identity They Need to Assume

What do they need to believe about themselves so they're not creat-ing inner turmoil when making this behavior change? Kids who have a goal that involves an athletic accomplishment, like winning a tourna-ment, are more likely to succeed if they identify as athletes. Kids who want to go to an elite college need to identify as driven, high-achieving students. Kids who want to improve their grades need to identify as someone who works hard and has great study skills.

Macie wanted to be able to honestly say, "I am a person who is well rested and self-disciplined." When her sister Molly wanted to be accepted into a competitive art program, she needed to be able to say, "I am an artist"—not that she was hoping to *become* an artist, but that she already *was* one.

Why? Because behavior that conflicts with our identity will not last. The more deeply something is tied to our identity, the harder it is to change it—and, by the same token, the more a new behavior is aligned with our beliefs about ourselves, the more likely it is that we'll adopt it. So Macie would not be able to avoid exhaustion and the morn-ing rush if she identified as one of those frantically busy students who rushes into school with their coffee every morning—if the exhaustion and morning rush were in fact part of her persona (which, fortunately, they weren't). And Molly would never have been able to muster the dis-cipline it took to build her portfolio if she'd been committed to a belief about herself like "I can't draw" or "I'm not creative."

Help Them Create a System, Habit, or Process That Generates Evidence in Favor of Their New Identity

Macie wanted to get eight or nine hours of sleep each night and get out of bed within five minutes of her alarm going off in the morning. So she tracked the days she got into and out of bed on time so she could look back and see, "Yup, I'm on it!"

To do this, Macie needed to outline specific morning and evening routines (in 10-minute time increments). These two routines became the system, or habits, that generated evidence that she was disciplined and well rested. In addition, she needed to:

- Get an alarm that didn't bug her so she wouldn't resist setting it.
- Set her alarm for 6:30 AM.
- Ask a parent to enforce the family rule that phones are charged outside of bedrooms. (We had let that slip with her over the summer.)

These specific plans helped her see what she needed to do to get to bed by 10:00 or 10:30 PM and wake up on time. When she got an old-fashioned alarm clock, she was collecting evidence that she was "a person who is well rested and self-disciplined."

Our kids' accomplishments and achievements are actually a better reflection of their *habits* than their goals. For example, when kids study more than usual every day, their grades tend to improve. When they practice a musical instrument or sport skill a little more every day, their performance usually improves. When Macie got to bed by 10:30 every night, she was able to be more alert in class.

The more we can help kids collect evidence that supports their desired identity in a *habitual* way, the more likely it is that their behavior change will last. Habits put behaviors on autopilot, and this makes everything easier—we don't need much willpower to enact our habitual behaviors.

Kids can make their behaviors habitual by anchoring them in existing habits or routines, or even a schedule. To do this, use a "when/then" statement: "When I do x, then I will y." For Macie, her evening routine—which became a habit—actually started at 7:00 PM: "When it's 7:00, then I will put my phone in the charging station while I study." (This helped her be less distracted, which meant that she finished her homework much more quickly, which meant that she could get to bed on time.)

Helping Teens Set Up Good Systems

Once they have (1) articulated how they'd like to change or what they'd like to accomplish, (2) determined what aspect of their identity they are proud of that the change or goal is most closely aligned with, and (3) identified a routine or a habit that will generate evidence in favor of their positive identity, we can help in a handful of ways—if they want more help, that is! Here are some more ideas.

Help Them Set Up Their Environment to Make Things Easier

Our environment dramatically influences our behavior. We like to think our behavior is all a reflection of our personality and preferences, or that it's the strength of our ironclad will that determines our success. But actually, we are hugely influenced by the people, places, and technology that happen to be in close physical proximity to us.

This means that to be successful in reaching our goals, it's very helpful to set up our environment to make things easier, or to create what are called structural solutions. This usually means removing temptations. For Macie, that meant getting her phone out of her bedroom while she was studying and sleeping.

Help Them Identify Ways to Make the Behavior More Enticing

We humans pursue rewards: a pretty little cupcake, attention from a mentor, a sense of accomplishment. When our brains identify a potential reward, they release dopamine, a feel-good chemical messenger. Dopamine motivates us to pursue the reward, creating a real sense of craving, wanting, or desire for the carrot that is being dangled in front of us.

Rewards need to be immediate or, even better, built into the routine or system when possible. Macie loves her bed, and hitting snooze instead of getting up is its own reward, which makes getting out of bed much more difficult. So I worked with Macie to praise herself enthusiastically when she gets out of bed on her own using what B. J. Fogg at Stanford calls the "Yay me!" reward. Even something as small as a short mental victory dance can trigger a little hit of dopamine—enough to tell your brain to repeat whatever you just did. Macie was basically giving herself a pat on the back and noting how "disciplined" and "on it" she was, which reinforced the behavior.

Help Them Identify How They Want to Feel

Help kids think less about what they want to *achieve* and instead focus on how they want to *feel*.

We do better when we let go of our logical reasons for why we want to do something. Why? Because research shows that good, solid, logical reasons for doing something—like exercising because we want to lower our blood pressure or ward off cancer—don't actually provide lasting motivation. It turns out that emotions are far more motivating than achievement goals. For example, Macie wanted to get out of bed on time because she wanted to *feel* "on it," "well rested," and "disciplined." Molly wanted to be in the drawing and painting program because she *feels* happiest and most free when she is drawing and painting.

Help Them Make Plans for Obstacles

It is extremely important whenever teens establish a new behavior that they really think through all the seemingly minor details—especially the details that tend to hang them up in the end. They need to set themselves up to overcome the obstacles that they may face. People who plan for how they're going to react to different obstacles tend to be able to meet their goals more successfully.

In fact, a large meta-analysis of eighty-five studies found that when people make a specific plan for what they'd like to do or change, anticipating obstacles, they do better than 74 percent of people who don't make a specific plan for the same task. In other words, making a specific action plan dramatically increases the odds that your teen will follow through.

Parents can help teens think about these challenges and obstacles as they try to change their behavior.

Macie knew beyond a shadow of a doubt that she was going to be tempted to hit snooze in the morning, even if she did get to bed on time. So, after a brainstorming session with me, she decided to move her alarm clock to the far side of her room, where she couldn't reach it from her bed. This is an example of setting up the environment. Then, she made a plan: "When my alarm goes off, I will turn it off and walk into the hallway immediately, even if I want to lie back down on my bed." Once she was in the hallway, she would find herself habitually walking to the bathroom, and then she was on her way to start her morning.

What to Do When They Miss the Mark

Once we put together the behavior plan, Macie immediately started getting more sleep, and her grades started noticeably improving. That said, she was (of course!) not always successful in following her plan. She sometimes got distracted by social media and went to bed too late or failed to start her homework during her planned study hours. When I saw this happening, I did my best to respond with compassion rather than disappointment.

Here's why: **Criticism doesn't work. It doesn't motivate our kids over the long term. Expressing our disappointment or anger when our teens fall short causes stress and fear. And ironically, criticism is associated with decreased motivation and future improvement.**

I grew up believing that if we are really hard on ourselves (and the people around us) when we make mistakes, we'll do better the next time—we'll be more vigilant about not making the same mistake again, or we'll be more motivated to perform better in the future. But the research doesn't bear this out. When making mistakes is stressful—as it is when we disappoint our parents, make someone angry, or are punished for our mistake—we learn to disassociate our own behavior from the mistake. We blame others, we pretend it didn't happen, and we do our best to sweep it under the rug and hope no one notices. We avoid and ignore rather than learn and improve.

But when our mistakes are met with compassion—as when we actively soothe our teens after they make a mistake—we create an opportunity for learning. We allow them to sit with the discomfort of having made a mistake so that they can examine it closely, learn from it, and move on.

This applies when our kids violate our family limits and rules as well as when they fall short of their own goals. When we are harsh, angry, and critical, teens may internalize (often unconsciously) that their biggest mistake wasn't that they violated the limit or missed the mark, but rather that they *got caught*. We do well to calm down before talking to our teens about their mistakes.

So when Macie would flub it up, I'd express compassion. "Oh no," I might say. "Looks like it is going to be a late night, despite your best intentions. What a bummer." My goal was to help bring her awareness to the situation and to empathize. I was also helping to put her back in touch with her original goals and intentions. "Can I help you get back on track?" I might ask. "Is there anything you want to talk about before you start your homework?" My hope is that now that Macie is away at college, she will have a similar response to herself when she falls short of her own goals—that she will respond to herself with self-compassion rather than self-criticism. Research shows that self-compassionate students are less prone to depression and tend to be more satisfied with their social lives and major life choices.

Now you have some tools for supporting your kids when they encounter life's inevitable difficulties. In part two, we'll consider one of life's *new* difficulties: technology overuse (and addiction) and its consequences.

Three Core Skills for the Digital Age

CHAPTER FIVE

Connection

Real-life connection, which includes eye contact and physical touch, is a powerful key to both success and happiness; however, teens have less real-life connection with other people than ever. Here's how to reverse the trend.

We were all home when the doorbell rang. I was in the kitchen making meatballs for dinner, a messy process. "Can someone please get that?" I called out. Silence. "My hands are dirty." One of the kids was parked on a couch ten feet from the front door. Mark, at his desk engrossed in emails, was also closer to the front door than I was. Only Buster, our dog, moved. The doorbell rang again. This was not just our UPS guy dropping something off and leaving. A *person* was still standing there, waiting. Buster was barking madly, working himself into a full tizzy.

"Please?" I called again. Nothing.

"*Seriously?* Is anyone out there?" Nothing.

Frustrated, I washed my hands and opened the door. It was Mark's voice teacher, Rebecca, who is also the kids' teacher.

"It's Rebecca," I called. We all know and love Rebecca, but still no one made a move to greet her. I was surprised the nearby teen hadn't jumped up to give Rebecca a hug. I peeked into the TV room near the front door. Said teen was fully prone, under a blanket, iPhone inches from her face, headphones in. "Rebecca's here!" I whisper-shouted, waving my arms, hoping to rouse her.

I caught up with Rebecca while Mark "finished something" on his computer. We joked about how every member of the household was so spellbound by their screens they didn't even register the *live human being* who had entered our home. But it wasn't funny.

Parents constantly ask me whether I think smartphones, video games, and social media are evil—whether all the new technologies are *ruining* our kids. Are all the new devices *good* or *bad*?

On that particular day, I could see how profoundly antisocial technology was making my family. That doesn't mean technology is bad, but it did seem like it was something that needed to be addressed. I know I'm not alone. Half of parents surveyed in 2018 said that they were concerned that their "child's mobile device use is negatively affecting his or her mental health," and nearly half thought their child was addicted.

Here is what we know for sure: **The spike in the amount of time teenagers spend on screens is a likely cause of the ongoing surge in depression, anxiety, and suicide that began around 2012, shortly after smartphones and tablets became widespread among teenagers.** By analyzing multiple data sets—all from large-scale, long-term scientific studies—demographer and psychologist Jean Twenge has clearly shown that American teens who spend more time online are more likely to have at least one outcome related to suicide, such as depression or making a suicide plan.

The numbers are enormous: Nearly *half* of teens who indicated that they spend five or more hours a day on a device (like a phone or laptop) would be classified as at-risk for suicide by the Centers for Disease Control and Prevention ("at-risk" means they report having felt very sad and hopeless for two weeks or more, having seriously considered committing suicide, having made a plan to commit suicide, or having attempted suicide). This is compared to 28 percent of those who have less than an hour of screen time a day.

Twenge, who has analyzed the data more closely than anyone, writes, "The results could not be clearer: Teens who spend more time on screen activities are more likely to be unhappy, and those who spend more time on non-screen activities are more likely to be happy."

There is a toxicity to screen time—although not everyone agrees with this message.

The Smartphone Controversy

Even given these scary statistics, though, the technology itself is neither all good nor all bad. It just *is*. There is no turning back at this point; our kids' devices are not going away and there are many more coming down the pike for us to contend with. We need to understand what it is about screen time that affects our kids so dramatically so that we can adapt to these new technologies in a positive way.

An important first step is to stop resisting the notion that screen time can be, and often is, harmful to kids. All the research I've seen on new media and teens indicates, in one way or another, that there does in fact seem to be a "dosage effect." Some smartphone use, for example, is totally fine, but after a certain point it can become toxic.

And yet, sometimes, even the researchers themselves deny this toxicity. For example, Candice Odgers, a psychologist at the University of California–Irvine, wrote in *Greater Good Magazine*, "There is no compelling evidence that spending time online has a deleterious effect on teens' mental health." I was surprised by this, so I took a look at the large-scale study published in *Psychological Science* in 2017 that she references.

It was loaded with evidence that spending a lot of time online is correlated with lower well-being in fifteen-year-olds. As you can see from the graph on page 76, the more "daily digital screen engagement" (here, that's smartphone use), the lower the teen's "mental well-being" (which includes how happy, connected, resilient, and self-confident they feel). And the higher the number, the greater their mental well-being. The relationship is very clear and very linear: After a little less than an hour a day of time spent on a smartphone, their well-being begins to decrease.

Doubters are quick to suggest that depression may cause teens to spend more time online rather than the other way around, but Twenge and other researchers have considered that possibility, and they hold that it just isn't the case.

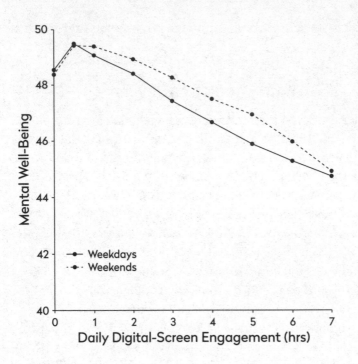

For one thing, a fair bit of research suggests that screen time (especially social media usage) leads to unhappiness. For example, there are several studies that have all found basically the same thing: The more time people spend using Facebook, the lower their happiness (and the higher their loneliness and depression) when researchers assess them again later. It wasn't that people who were feeling unhappy used social media more; it's that Facebook caused their unhappiness.

The other thing is the timing of it all. If feeling depressed causes people to spend more time on their devices and not the other way around, then why did depression and suicidality increase so suddenly after 2012, when smartphones became much more widespread? "Under that scenario," says Twenge, "more teens became depressed for an unknown reason and then started buying smartphones—an idea that defies logic."

When we resist the idea that new technologies can be harmful, we rule out a fuller understanding of their toxicity. **And if we don't**

understand how they are shaping us and our kids, we can't adapt to them in healthy ways.

Fortunately, not only do we know *that* technology overuse causes mental health problems, but we know *why* it does. Here is the really good news: When we understand what it is about the new media and devices that causes depression and anxiety, we can see solutions that are more constructive than "limit screen time" or "don't give your kids a smartphone"—which are not especially realistic or helpful solutions, in my opinion. In this chapter, we'll be looking at three significant ways that too much screen time and social media can make our kids depressed and anxious, and then we'll look at the powerful antidotes to technology toxins.

Why Technology Overuse Is Toxic

1. More Screen Time Usually Means More Time Alone

Teenagers make an interesting case study in loneliness. Although they seem fantastically connected socially (my teens are constantly communicating with literally hundreds of kids through text and social media and video chat), more teenagers now feel left out and lonely than ever before (or at least since we started measuring these things). A surprising 48 percent more girls and 27 percent more boys feel left out these days compared to how they felt in 2010.

Why are they so lonely, even though they're super-connected online? One reason may be that they have the ability to see what everyone else is doing at any given moment—so they know when they are being left out of something. When one of my kids was in eighth grade, she was invited to a lot of bat mitzvahs and thirteenth birthday parties—it seemed like there was one every weekend. But what our whole family remembers are not the parties she went to, but the very few she did not.

Every eighth-grade party played itself out on Instagram and Snapchat. All the kids in attendance documented who was hanging out with whom and posted it for public consumption. My daughter couldn't help but sit back and watch, compulsively checking her phone to see what she was missing. It wasn't a case of FOMO, or fear of missing out—she was feeling the pain of actual social exclusion. She'd been rejected . . . intentionally *left* out and she knew it. Brain studies show that this sort of social exclusion hurts in the same way that physical pain does.

Illustrating the blazingly obvious, research documents that the more time kids spend online and on their devices, the less time they tend to spend interacting with their peers (or adults, for that matter) in face-to-face encounters. Screen time is a zero-sum game: Social media, video games, online browsing, and other new media take the place of playing sports, going to parties, or just hanging out with friends . . . or, as proved to be the case in my family, simply answering the door and saying hello to a family friend.

So today's teenagers feel lonely because they are actually alone more. "The number of teens who get together with their friends every day has been cut in half in just fifteen years, with especially steep declines recently," writes Jean Twenge. Over the course of a week, they see their friends an hour less a day than their parents' generation or even the early millennials did. This means that each day they are spending one hour less developing their social skills and friendships, and navigating the inevitable emotions and conflicts that arise when they are with other people.

This hardly needs to be said, but loneliness and social isolation cause profound distress. Feeling lonely causes your cortisol, a stress hormone, to skyrocket. Experiments by neuroscientist John Cacioppo have shown that feeling acutely lonely is as stressful as experiencing a physical attack.

Moreover, people triggered to feel lonely (by a hypnotist, of all things) in Cacioppo's studies became radically more depressed. "The stunning thing was that loneliness is not merely the result of depression," Cacioppo told Johann Hari in his book *Lost Connections*. "Indeed, it *leads* to depression." On the flip side, **people who were triggered to feel connected became radically *less* depressed**—and therein lies the antidote, which we'll get to in a moment.

2. Social Media and Materialism Go Hand in Hand

Although we talk about the 1980s and 1990s as a time of extreme materialism, students entering college today are more likely than ever before to say it's important to be wealthy. They are also less likely to value intrinsic goals, like finding meaning.

New media and new technologies may be largely to blame here, too. The data show that teens who spend more time online during their free time are more likely to believe it is important to own expensive things. They are also less likely to think about or be engaged in social issues, even though social media can be a great way to spread ideas and information related to the issues teens care about.

This is not surprising. Social media (and media in general) lets kids peer into the lives of the rich and famous. Celebrity YouTubers display in exquisite detail what to covet, and they are teaching our kids values more explicitly than many parents, schools, and churches are. And that's saying nothing of the celebrities who are being paid by advertisers, or the actual advertisers themselves, who are, of course, intentionally and successfully cultivating materialism.

But is materialism really that bad? Psychologist Tim Kasser's work has shown that the more people think about acquiring wealth, stuff, or fame, the more unhappy, depressed, and anxious they will be. It's clear that spending a lot of time on smartphones predicts (and likely increases) materialism in teens, and when teens lose or fail to develop a meaningful set of values, they can easily become anxious, depressed, and lonely. With good reason, they feel empty inside.

3. Social Media Invites Insecurity and Comparison

Every peek at social media allows teenagers, subconsciously or otherwise, to compare themselves to others . . . and they rarely come out ahead. They open Snapchat and learn from the curated "stories" that the people who count are moneyed and beautiful. A one-minute scroll through Instagram—filled with photoshopped selfies taken painstakingly from an angle that makes someone look her thinnest—can easily make a secure and self-confident teen feel that her normal body is disgusting and aberrant. Uber-wealthy teens and young celebrities, who on some level seem like peers, post "wealthies" (selfies that display their wealth) while flying around the world in the family jet.

If teens were seeing people like them or worse off than them, they wouldn't feel so insecure. But they are seeing people who are thinner, richer, more popular, more successful, and more privileged. Even wealthy and middle-class kids often frequently feel, on some level, less-than. And beyond the bubble of social media, there is actually cause for their worry.

Before we dig in to that, I want to acknowledge that inequality, envy, and conspicuous consumption have always been a part of American culture, and TV certainly did a lot to expand our ability to compare ourselves to others. **But today's teenagers are experiencing far more media exposure—and they are living in conditions of far greater inequality.**

Right now in the United States, the median upper-income family has seventy-five times the wealth of the median low-income family. And the top *0.1 percent* of Americans take in as much income each year as the bottom 90 percent *combined*. This is the highest economic disparity ever recorded. In 2007, top earners were worth forty times as much as the median low-income family, while in 1989 they were worth twenty-eight times.

Here's how this is affecting our kids: Economic inequality heightens our social evaluation anxieties—essentially, our fear of being judged—and increases the emotional salience of our social status. So instead of seeing each other as equals, as we tend to do in more equal settings, we become more judgmental, comparing ourselves to others even more.

When researchers like Dacher Keltner at UC Berkeley's Greater Good Science Center study the effects of economic inequality, they do so with a simple exercise. Study participants are given a drawing of a twelve-rung ladder. Some participants are asked to "think for a minute about the people who have the most power, wealth, and prestige in the United States." Others spend a little time thinking about those with the least "wealth, education, and prestige—the impoverished and out of work and homeless."

Next, participants are asked to put an X on the ladder to indicate where they perceive their own social standing to be. Students who'd been thinking about the wealthiest and most esteemed, place their X lower on the ladder, and those who thought about people who are less fortunate place their X higher.

In other words, we inevitably end up comparing ourselves to the people we spend time thinking about. We do this without prompting, often subconsciously, and like the primates that came before us, we need to know where we are on the social status ladder. This is especially true for teenagers and college students, since social awareness is heightened during and immediately following puberty.

Where we place ourselves on that ladder is hugely consequential. Having a reduced sense of our own social status "gnaws at our nervous system," according to Keltner. It makes us hypervigilant to threats— perhaps more so than any other stressor. More than 200 studies indicate that threats related to social status, particularly when people feel they might be judged by others, tend to provoke larger and more reliable stress responses than any other stressful situations.

Feeling low in social status or feeling that you don't have the respect of others is a core cause of depression. And here's something surprising: Worse than having a low social status is feeling like your status is insecure or threatened, like you might be losing social status. Just a momentary shift in how we perceive our own social status—prompted by even a quick glance at Instagram or a friend's Snapchat story—can dramatically change how we function and feel. It can even change our brain chemistry, lowering serotonin levels. (Serotonin is the neurotransmitter that is targeted by our antidepressant drugs, like Prozac.)

Unfortunately, it's easy to imagine that teens today almost always feel like they are losing social status.

The Antidote: Real-Life Social Connection

Let's go back, briefly, to John Cacioppo's studies about loneliness and depression. Remember that people who were primed to feel connected socially became radically less depressed. Thank goodness, there's our antidote!

Do you know what the *best* predictor of a person's happiness and well-being is? It's the opposite of loneliness, materialism, and insecurity. It's having a large breadth and depth of real-life social connections. Not social *media* connections. Not a large network of online friends and family. Those things do not predict happiness. Feeling like we are a part of something larger than ourselves, feeling deeply embedded in a community of friends and family that we see face to face *does* predict well-being. Fortunately, this is something that we parents can foster for our kids.

Human beings evolved as a social species, dependent on eye contact and touch for communication and safety. As children, we develop psychologically and emotionally through our face-to-face interactions with others. Babies learn to smile—and express a whole host of other emotions—by mimicking the faces of their primary caregivers. Our ability to speak, regulate our emotions, and love simply does not develop if we don't have real-life social interactions and strong, positive connections to our "clan."

Although it is increasingly rare in today's day and age, eye contact is the foundation of all real-life social connection. And if eye contact isn't available, neither is touch, and absent these things, teens' nervous systems run amuck. They feel anxious, stressed, and insecure. Fortunately, there are many concrete things that we parents can do to provide them with the contact that their nervous systems need.

Tactic #1: Touch Your Teens

"But what about talking on the phone?" many a long-distance grandparent has asked me. "Or FaceTiming? Does that count?" Yes, of course. Technology *does* help us build and maintain our social connections, but unfortunately, phone and video calls can't replace in-person contact. The science of touch teaches us that physical contact is the primary way that primates, including humans, communicate compassion and other important positive emotions like love and gratitude. **Touch is fundamental for human bonding at any age.**

The benefits of touch start at birth. Preterm babies, for example, who received three fifteen-minute massages a day gained 47 percent more weight than those who received standard medical care. Touch promotes trust, signals safety, and soothes us when we are agitated. It has the power to activate the vagus nerve, which calms our cardiovascular stress. A single touch can trigger the release of oxytocin, a hormone that promotes bonding, love, and compassion.

There's a series of studies that demonstrate the power of touch when we feel threatened. Researchers have participants lie in an fMRI brain scanner and anticipate receiving an electric shock or painful blare of noise. Anticipation of pain heightens brain activity in regions related to threat and stress—unless someone they know is there, holding their hand. In those cases, participants don't tend to display neural activity indicating they are stressed or threatened. Their brains stay calm. The effects are strongest when it's a loved one that is doing the hand holding, and—get this—when the participant reports feeling a strong sense of social support from their wider social network in general!

Just for kicks, I asked two of my kids—the two most affectionate ones, coincidentally—what they thought of me advising parents to touch their teens more, particularly if they are feeling stressed or overwhelmed. "Oh my God, Mom, that is *so cringy*," one said, shuddering visibly. "Please, please don't touch me. Like ever," said the other. We had a good laugh.

I don't think most adolescents *consciously* crave more physical contact with their parents, or know that they benefit from it. In fact, just the thought of being hugged and held can make them feel dependent and babyish. But touch is not just for babies, and there is really good news here: extremely brief touches work wonders.

For example, one study showed that the brief touches of NBA basketball players—fist bumps, chest bumps, leaping shoulder bumps, head grabs, high fives, low fives, high tens, full hugs, half hugs, and team huddles—predict both individual and team success. And players don't actually touch each other that much. On average, a player touched his teammates for a little less than two seconds during the game, or about one-tenth of a second for every minute played.

So there's no need for us to accost our teens with hugs and kisses every time they enter a room, nor do we need to institute NBA head grabs and leaping shoulder bumps as forms of congratulations. Ironically, my teen who told me in jest not to touch him (ever), touches me so frequently in passing it's almost a game. When he passes me in the kitchen, he'll tap me on the shoulder with just a couple of fingers. If I say over dinner that I've had a good day, he'll humorously raise his hand for a high five. Little did I know that he was modeling the type of touch that teenagers need: quick confirmations that we are here, together, and we like it.

Tactic #2: Create Regular Family Routines and Rituals

As parents, we can create family routines and rituals—around the holidays, for example, or around dinnertime—that indirectly teach our kids about our values. This alone can effectively counter the materialism and other junk values they are constantly exposed to in the media. Rituals are any kind of routine that have symbolic or expressive meaning, and most of them foster social connection. They tangibly illustrate our values because teens know intuitively that we celebrate or ritualize the things we believe are most important.

Routines and rituals also provide the basis for kids to feel secure in their family connections, a security that can be profoundly anchoring when they feel like they are constantly being judged and compared to others in the rest of their lives. Predictable rituals help kids feel connected to something larger than themselves, and even though teens seem to be pushing us away, they still need to feel anchored in a family.

Dinnertime

In my family, dinnertime is really our only daily family ritual. I know that dinnertime is a tough topic for busy families that often really crave time together but can't seem to find it.

But as hard as it can be logistically, dinnertime is good for deepening our kids' social connections and for giving them that sense that they are a part of something larger than themselves. For that reason, it is important to fight for. We have to eat every day anyway, so why not eat together? Without our devices. Every family member doesn't have to be there every night, and we don't have to eat dinner together every night. Research shows that a majority of nights is enough.

Family meals foster many important social skills—the building blocks of social connection. The research is particularly compelling around language development and dinnertime—and language is the most important facet of social intelligence that we have.

For example, a team at the Harvard Ed School found that certain "rare words" were particularly good markers of literacy in children, and they wanted to know where kids learned those words. Of the two thousand words they were looking for, more than half were learned at the dinner table. This is one reason dinner loses its power when we isolate kid meals from adult meals. Although this study was with younger children, adolescence is also an important period for language development.

Similarly, manners are an important social skill, certainly more than our teenagers think. As a sociologist, I believe that certain social norms teach teens about the emotions that make up a happy life. When I say, "Please don't interrupt your sister," I'm teaching my kids about reciprocity and empathy. When they watch me offer a guest the biggest piece of cake, they learn generosity. And simple acts of gratitude, like saying thank you to someone for passing the salt, are connection building blocks.

Social skills, including language, are just that—they are *skills* that are built over time, better learned by example than explicit instruction. Teens develop any skill better if they learn it in a routine situation that feels safe.

Running out of things to talk about at dinnertime? Start telling your kids some family history. Research shows that telling stories about your shared past creates strong and secure emotional bonds, which directly impacts how socially connected they feel. Turns out this study also found that kids who knew a lot about their family history learned it at dinnertime.

My kids think this is corny, but I also think about what our dinnertime says symbolically about our family. We sit together at the table to literally create a family circle, and we try to get dinner on the table as a team. We try to prepare dinner as a team, even on the nights when the kids don't actually have time to help. Usually, only one kid has time to actually help Mark and me with food prep and cooking. But even on heavy-homework nights, our teens still come down for dinner a few minutes early to help get it on the table. Together they will set the table, toss the salad, get drinks, and feed the dog.

We try to clean up together, too, although again, it is often tempting to let the kids leave the table (as they lobby to do homework over dishes) while the adults hang around and talk. But we parents are not restaurant employees hired to bus tables and wash dishes, so we require that kids contribute to cleanup. This usually takes only a few minutes on their part.

Sometimes it is definitely easier to do the parent-as-waiter/personal chef routine, but when we wait on our children, the symbolic meaning is that they are passive actors who are entitled to our service, rather than lucky and active participants in a larger whole.

Kids who eat dinner with their families regularly are more emotionally stable and less likely to abuse drugs and alcohol. They get better grades. They have fewer depressive symptoms, particularly among adolescent girls. And they are less likely to become obese or have an eating disorder. And these associations hold even after researchers control for family connectedness, which means that the benefits of family meals go above and beyond being close-knit as a family.

I fear I'm really pouring on the pressure to have dinner together. I know personally how darn difficult this can be. Recently, Mark and I sat at the table with just one of our kids (the others were at school or practice), and I thought, *This doesn't feel symbolically meaningful.* No one wanted to tell me about their day. We didn't talk about current events. There was a lot of picking at the food and getting out of chairs "to get water." But while we were cleaning up, our daughter mentioned that her friends are jealous that we always manage to have dinner together as a family. Go figure.

Holidays

Even though they can also foster materialism, winter holidays like Hanukkah and Christmas are great opportunities to create family traditions that prioritize connection. We reconnect with our friends, neighbors, and coworkers through annual parties. And we reconnect with our extended family consistently throughout the season—our holiday rituals are what help make our family truly our family.

For example, the weekend before Christmas, my cousins always fly in from Massachusetts, Washington, and Florida for a big extended-family Christmas party, complete with a funny white elephant gift exchange. My mom always makes spritz cookies with the kids, a tradition started in Germany with her mother. We light the candles of the menorah and say prayers each night during Hanukkah, something my husband's Jewish family has been teaching me and my kids.

All of this is about renewing our sense that we are a part of something larger than ourselves. Again: **This sense that we are connected and part of a larger whole is the single strongest predictor of happiness that we have.** It is true that the holidays have become depressingly commercial in our culture, with a massive focus on what each individual will get and what kids want in terms of material gifts. It's true that every news report during the holidays seems to include something about how the economy is responding to the year's wave of massive collective consumption. But we can choose to focus on relationships instead of individual gift lists over the holiday season. Not surprisingly, people who focus on family or religion during the holidays report higher happiness than those who don't.

Birthdays

Birthdays are another great opportunity to foster connection through rituals and traditions, and you've likely already got a bunch that your family counts on. Traditions in our family include:

- Nana or Nonie (the grandmothers) make the cake, depending on whose birthday it is. Grandchildren get a homemade "Nanacake," a chocolate cake with chocolate frosting covered in jelly beans or Snickers pieces. Nonie brings an ice cream cake for the adult children.

- Birthdays begin at breakfast, with breakfast in bed, even on rushed school days, with whatever breakfast a child wants. I'm a health-food nut, but sugary cereal is not off-limits on birthdays!

- We go big, celebrating every birthday in our family with a dinner including all aunts, uncles, and grandparents who live in the Bay Area. Each family member typically has a favorite meal that we cook for them. The most important part? While we eat, we all go around the table and say what we appreciate about the birthday boy or girl.

- Before the birthday boy or girl opens their presents, the gift giver *pretends* to read a birthday card that doesn't exist by looking down at their hands held open to pantomime a card. They wax poetic, hamming up their most Hallmark-y self, "reading" the card they so lovingly would have written if they had bothered to buy a card and write it before coming. We call these virtual cards, and they are often the most fun or heartwarming part of the evening because sometimes people say the sort of really heartfelt things that are reserved for weddings and funerals.

These are just a few examples of birthday traditions that feel unique to our family and that bring us together as a group regularly, since we are a large, blended family. They wouldn't be right for many families, and I don't list them here because I think you need to institute them in yours. They are just meant to be examples of the quirky—and super simple—ways that families can establish traditions that make us feel connected and secure.

And I've found an additional benefit to these annual traditions: Routine makes them easy. We don't reinvent the wheel every time; we just do what we do for every single birthday celebration. And if I forget something, the kids remind me!

Tactic #3: Encourage Your Kids' Friends to Just Hang Out

As parents, we can sometimes make it easier for teens to spend time with their friends face to face. Sometimes all teens need is parental support to counter the trend of *not* seeing their friends. Although a lot of parents these days feel like letting kids just hang out is a waste of time, or even that they might be getting into trouble, remember that if the alternative is time spent alone on screens, that's usually riskier. It can be hard for teens who don't have access to a car to see their friends, especially if there isn't good public transportation where you live. This means that teens may need help figuring out how to stay at school a little later every day, for example, to hang out with their friends.

Invite teens who say they have no place to meet up with their friends to create a hangout space in your home or apartment. You may need to lure them, initially, with video games (ironically) and free junk food. I had a hard time with these things at first, but then I realized that during their leisure time, kids are gonna eat what they're gonna eat and find a place to play video games if that is what they want to do. My sister-in-law, who raised three very well-adjusted teenagers, showed me how to do it one day when she showed up at my house with two full grocery bags of junk food that was devoured in seconds by three teenage boys—who then started showing up at our house pretty regularly. I do buy crap food now, but the rule is that you have to have friends over if you want to eat it. (And then I put out baby carrots and hummus to make myself feel better.)

Tactic #4: Help them Connect to a Source of Meaning

Usually we think of connection as being to other people, but we humans also need to develop connections to sources of meaning, like purposeful work, nature, or a higher power, like God. Having a source of purpose or meaning imbues our day-to-day lives with significance.

Adolescence is the life stage when humans typically start to look for meaning, and teenagers are famous for asking big existential questions such as *What is the meaning of life?* For millennia, developing humans have found answers in the world's religions. Religious rituals and moral codes have traditionally illuminated a path that helps participants feel more connected to God—or something much larger and more powerful than the individual. This connectedness can endow a person's life with meaning and purpose.

But religion is no longer a clear path to meaning for Generation Z. Fewer people go to church, pray regularly, or have a religious affiliation. "If religion was once the default path to meaning," writes Emily Esfahani Smith in her book *The Power of Meaning*, "today it is one path among many, a cultural transformation that has left many people adrift."

College also used to be a place where educated people found a source of purpose and meaning. In the 1960s, the top priority of college freshmen was "developing a meaningful life philosophy." Almost 90 percent said this was an *essential* or *very important* life goal. But today, the top priority of first-year college students, by a landslide, is "being very well off financially." In 2016, fewer than half considered finding meaning an important life goal.

This is too bad, because finding meaning is essential if our kids are to lead fulfilling lives. People who find a reason for being tend to be more hopeful, resilient, and engaged. They get along better with others and report higher overall well-being. Moreover, they are less depressed, anxious, bored, and lonely. Teens who actively seek meaning report greater happiness and life satisfaction, and having a feeling of purpose is associated with better physical health. Unfortunately, many teenagers have "little to no sense of what makes life meaningful or of what greater purpose they might have beyond making money or landing a prestigious job," writes Smith.

So it's important for us to talk with our kids about the importance of finding meaning and purpose in life—at least as much as (or more than) we talk with them about the importance of achievement, getting good grades, or getting into college. We can start with a basic definition. I like this one, from the Purpose Challenge (purposechallenge .org), a website dedicated to helping teens find meaning:

> Having a sense of purpose means being committed to something that is meaningful to you but also makes a difference to something bigger than yourself. How you want to leave your mark on the world and make it a better place, how you want your life to have mattered . . . that's what purpose is.

Next, we can talk to them about why connecting to a source of meaning is important:

> People who have a strong sense of purpose in life tend to be happier, more motivated, and less stressed. Because they're working towards something they really care about, they find

studying and homework more meaningful, do better at school, enjoy their jobs more, and even live longer!

From there, we can encourage our teens to reflect on what is meaningful to them. Ask them:

- What really matters to you?
- What do you feel you are particularly good at?
- What do you care about?
- How can you use your skills to make a difference in the world?

Conversations like these can help teens connect to a source of meaning that may, in the end, come from connecting deeply with a spiritual practice, with nature, or by identifying a long-term goal related to work that serves something beyond themselves.

Tactic #5: Teach Them the Power of Being All-In

The opposite of loneliness is, in some ways, *commitment* as much as it is connection. In this age of instant gratification and Facebook friends, **it can be easy to forget that real connection requires commitment**. Meaningful work, for example, requires dedicated practice and persistence over time. This is true of all of our meaningful connections—our families, marriages, schools, and teams. They all require commitment to survive.

As parents, we can model commitment in our own lives by being really explicit about what we are committed to. We can also encourage commitment in our teens. Commitment requires, at a minimum, showing up. More than that, it requires effort, sacrifice, and, often, grit. It's sometimes uncomfortable to stick with our commitments, and in this age of comfort, it can be tempting to prioritize our own desires over the needs of the people and institutions that we are committed to.

It's important to show kids how to make sacrifices for the things and people we are committed to without acting like a martyr. We do this by making it clear that we don't expect anything in return when we are making an effort or sacrifice on behalf of a commitment. This is tricky, because usually we want at least a little gratitude, but when we are committed to something and we make an effort toward it, we make that effort in service to an outcome that is larger than ourselves. We do it to make our team better, our marriage more loving, or our family stronger.

Being all-in like this is a joyful and meaningful way to live. Our commitments center us and bring security, meaning, and purpose to our lives, and they are a fantastic antidote to the status insecurity and competition that social media invites.

I know that these tactics might seem a little obvious or old-school or even too simplistic to counter the effects of sophisticated new technologies, and yet, they are just what our kids need. The next chapter will give you more tactics for countering the addictiveness of social media so that our kids can regain another old-school skill: focus.

CHAPTER SIX

Focus

The most successful teens today—some would say the only truly successful teens—are able to command their own attention.

Having teenagers has unearthed all sorts of memories from my own adolescence. That said, my kids are having a very different adolescence than I had, especially when it comes to our school experiences. Even though one of my daughters and I both attended the same quirky boarding school, for example, little is the same about the way she and her peers study and the way *I* studied and learned.

Studying was easier when I was young. Even though I played sports, was active in theater, and was a part of many clubs and groups, there was less to distract me from my studies. Every evening, without fail, I could power through a lot of homework in a focused way, something I learned to do at the Thacher School, the school where Fiona now goes. Every school night after formal dinner, we went to a building called the Study Hall where we sat in silence from 7:30 PM to 9:30 PM and did a truly enormous amount of homework. We were helped by a faculty proctor, who monitored the quiet, curtailed the shenanigans of the ninth-grade boys, and managed all other potential distractions.

This was the 1980s, so there were no laptops or mobile phones. We handwrote drafts of our papers, and we made paper flashcards. We had to be super organized, bringing with us all the notes and books that we would need because once we got to the Study Hall, there was no leaving. For the most part, we didn't get up to get water or a snack or go to the bathroom. We did those things in the forty-five minutes of free time we had after dinner. We actually *focused* on one thing at a time for two hours straight. And then we were done. For the most part, we did it all in a relaxed way. While there were, of course, stressful exams and occasional late nights recopying our papers, for the most part, during Study Hall we were able to drop into a state of flow. Our normal routine did not require us to use stress and adrenaline to focus our minds because we were in the habit of thinking deeply on school nights, and this was both gratifying and effective. We did this as all Thacher students had done for 100 years before us.

After Study Hall, we'd run around outside and flirt with our classmates. We didn't have TVs or video games or social media to distract us from each other or from sleep. We took a real break from our studies to socialize or call our families (from pay phones), and then we simply went to bed.

Obviously, most people didn't go to boarding school where there was a structured Study Hall. Still, as I talk to my peers who went to the local public high school, they also have memories of sitting down at their desk and doing their homework without distractions—maybe with a radio or cassette player on in the background. What is exceptional about this now is that **it was totally routine for us to be able to command our own attention**.

Focus: A Twenty-First-Century Superpower

In a world where corporations now pay per view to rule teens' concentration and interest, and where social media and gaming empires depend on their ability to command kids' attention, focus has become the superpower of the twenty-first century—when it once was a routine commodity. Georgetown University professor Cal Newport writes, "The ability to perform deep work is becoming increasingly rare at exactly the same time it is becoming increasingly valuable in our economy. As a consequence, the few who cultivate this skill, and then make it the core of their working life, will thrive."

And yet, few teenagers these days seem to be cultivating this skill. Instead, more teens than ever are struggling to focus. The prevalence of children diagnosed with attention-deficit/hyperactivity disorder (ADD or ADHD) increased by 67 percent between 1996 and 2016.

ADD and ADHD are disorders marked by a person's inability to allocate their attention functionally. (Contrary to popular belief, many kids with ADD or ADHD *can* focus, especially on highly stimulating activities like video games, but they struggle to focus on things that aren't of particular interest to them . . . like school.)

Currently more than 6 million American children and adolescents between the ages of four and seventeen have been diagnosed with ADD or ADHD—more than 10 percent. Not surprisingly, there has also been a sharp rise in children and teenagers who take stimulant medications to treat their inability to focus.

Kids who have been diagnosed and are medicated for ADHD are at the extreme end of the spectrum, but I don't think it's an exaggeration to say that today, most people, including most teenagers, struggle to focus without also being stressed or under the pressure of a looming deadline. Instead of studying and learning in a relaxed way, as a society we now use stress and adrenaline to narrow our attention, to *force* ourselves to focus. This type of focus is driven by the fight-or-flight response, and it is better for surviving a life-threatening situation than it is for long-term learning.

The inability to focus and pay attention is a symptom of a larger problem: **inhibited dopamine function** in the brain. The cause of inhibited dopamine function is the overstimulation of the brain's reward system.

The Opioids in Your Brain

As a society, we have become oriented toward the pursuit of "happiness" at the same time that pleasure has become more readily available, historically speaking. New technologies and globalization have made rewarding substances that for millennia were rare and coveted—like sugar, alcohol, and potato chips—widely available.

For most of human history, if I wanted a drink at the end of a hard day, I would have had to ferment it myself, and I wouldn't have been able to get the alcohol content above 5 percent. Now, however, I can pop over to the local Trader Joe's and select from hundreds if not thousands of inexpensive options. I might settle for a delicious Belgian ale, with an alcohol content upwards of 12 percent.

Humans evolved having little access to pleasure in the ways that we now do, aside from sex and the occasional berry. "Prior to the eighteenth century, virtually every stimulus that generated reward was hard to come by, due to either its scarcity or its expense," writes neuroscientist Robert Lustig, in *The Hacking of the American Mind*. "There were no stores, no internet, and there was very little porn." It's hard to even fathom how much things have changed.

All of our new technologies add to the onslaught of pleasure in our daily experience. Both pleasurable substances (like sugar and alcohol) and new technologies (like social media and internet pornography) stimulate the reward system in the brain.

This means that today's teenagers live in a near constant state of reward-system stimulation. Social media, video games, YouTube, Netflix, and the internet—as well as processed foods like the chips, candy, gum, sodas, energy drinks, pretzels, and energy bars that they tend to have easy access to—all deliver a steady supply of pleasure to their brains, stimulating their reward centers. Teens think this is awesome, but that's because they've confused pleasure and actual happiness. "Pleasure and happiness, for all their apparent similarity, are separate phenomena, and in their extreme function as opposites," writes Lustig.

Why? When something activates the brain's reward center (like a video game or a social media ping), the brain gets a hit of the neurotransmitter dopamine. This is energizing, but that isn't the whole story. Dopamine functions in large part to create *desire and craving*, not pleasure. It motivates us toward a reward, but when we actually consume the reward—that is, when we actually see our "likes" on Instagram or eat a bowl of ice cream—we feel gratified because of a different class of neurotransmitters called endogenous opioid peptides (EOPs). It is these natural opioids that generate the feeling of pleasure.

We need both dopamine *and* EOPs to experience something as pleasurable. "Dopamine is the trigger," explains Lustig, "EOPs are the bullets. You need both to fire the gun, unless someone else fires the gun for you"—like a doctor might if you were recovering from surgery and she gave you a big hit of an opioid painkiller.

When Pleasure Is a Pain

This reward circuit in the brain doesn't just produce pleasure, however. Too much dopamine leads to aggression and irritability, reducing impulse control and making it less likely that we will be able to resist temptations— something I've noticed in myself and in my kids when we spend too much time binge-watching Netflix or scrolling through Instagram.

More than that, though, chronic dopamine overstimulation actually damages our brain cells. Because our neurons are at risk for damage and premature death when we flood our brains with dopamine, they protect themselves by reducing the number of dopamine receptors on their surfaces. All that excess dopamine then has nowhere to attach, and the neuron doesn't go into overdrive.

Every substance and behavior that floods the reward circuit in our brains with dopamine will cause a reduction in our dopamine receptors. **The more we indulge in a pleasure, the more immune to it we become.** So, with fewer dopamine receptors, we feel less pleasure. This causes us to need more and more stimulation to get the same hit of pleasure, and this, writes Lustig, "is a slippery slope to tolerance and addiction."*

But wait, there's more: Rewarding behavior and substances also decrease our body's ability to manufacture serotonin, the neurotransmitter we need to experience contentment and a sense of well-being. Serotonin is the neurotransmitter that popular antidepressant medications—called selective serotonin reuptake inhibitors (SSRIs)— like Prozac, work on. Serotonin is important because it decreases anxiety and helps mitigate depression. This means that overstimulation of the brain's reward circuit leads to more than just a decreased experience of pleasure—it also creates the conditions for depression and anxiety.

Why? The raw ingredients needed to transport dopamine and serotonin into the brain are the same, and they tend to be in short supply. If

---

*It is not a coincidence, by the way, that our nation is struggling with an opioid epidemic right now. Our natural EOPs bind to the same receptors as opioid drugs like morphine, Vicodin, and OxyContin—and produce the same pleasurable feelings. When the brain's reward circuit starts to break down due to overstimulation, we no longer experience the pleasure that comes from our natural opioids. If we then turn to external or synthetic sources, we are already primed not just for use but for addiction.

all the raw ingredients are being used up by reward-seeking behavior (for dopamine), there won't be enough left to make the serotonin we need to feel a sense of well-being—or to manage our depression and anxiety.

The Teenage Brain . . . on Dopamine

These brain changes occur in people of all ages, but the developing adolescent brain is particularly susceptible to addiction, in part because it tends to release more dopamine when the reward system is stimulated than an adult brain does. This means that rewarding substances (sugar, alcohol, and nicotine) and behaviors (playing video games) are more pleasurable for adolescents . . . at first. It also means that overindulgence more quickly leads to a greater decline in dopamine receptors— leaving teens wanting more, but feeling less pleasure.

To recap: All the reward-circuit stimulation our teens experience through their constant exposure to processed foods and by using new media is changing their brains at the cellular level, making them biologically prone to experience more depression and anxiety and less pleasure and happiness. And their inhibited dopamine function is leaving them struggling to focus.

The Trouble with Multitasking

It may seem improbable that teens are eating *that* much more sugar and spending *so* much time on their devices that their brains would actually be affected by this stimulation. And yet they are. By 2015, high school seniors were spending an average of six hours a day on new media, and by 2017 it was up to *nine* hours—texting, surfing the internet, Snapchatting, checking Instagram feeds, playing video games, video chatting, and so on. In addition, teens watch about two hours of television a day—often also from their phones or computers.

This seems, at first glance, impossible. If they are going to school, getting a decent amount of sleep, exercising or doing even a *single* activity after school, eating dinner in the evening, plus doing a couple of hours of homework . . . that would leave only an hour or so of leisure time. How in the world are they spending five to nine hours a day online and on social media?

They do it by **multitasking**. They are Snapchatting in class and watching TV while they eat. They scroll through Instagram while they ride to school; they text their friends and parents while they skim their homework. (And many *aren't* getting a decent amount of sleep—which I'll address in chapter seven.)

Multitasking is wildly inefficient, but it feels productive. Here's the thing: Our kids can be busy and stimulated all the time, and that's what we adults have been modeling for them. They have grown up with their parents working from home, checking their emails at the dinner table, and dialing into video conference calls from family vacations. Everyone seems too busy and important to ever take a break. **We have trained them through our own example never to focus on just one thing.** We've trained them to believe that multitasking is not just okay to do, but it's necessary to be productive, successful individuals. But multitasking is the enemy of focus. The human brain did not evolve to focus on many things at once; it evolved to focus on one thing at a time. **And so the brain does not actually ever multitask.** It can't actually run multiple apps at any one time. It can only switch rapidly between tasks. This is a giant energy drain for teens' brains in many ways:

1. Multitasking keeps students from learning easily and recalling what they need to know. When they constantly switch their attention from one thing to another, which they do super rapidly when they multitask, their overloaded brains stop using their hippocampus, which is the area of the brain responsible for learning and memory. This makes it nearly impossible to learn something new while multitasking, and it hinders students' ability to recall what they already know.

2. Multitasking makes it harder for teens to ignore irrelevant information. This, ironically, makes them feel more overwhelmed, which makes it harder for them to focus and learn.

3. Multitasking hinders their ability to organize their thoughts, which slows them down—especially when doing schoolwork— and makes them prone to spending time on unimportant and irrelevant work.

4. Multitasking cripples teens' ability to transition from one task or activity to another. Another irony, given that multitasking *is* rapid switching (from the brain's perspective).

5. Multitasking increases the odds that a person will suffer from anxiety and depression. It also makes it more likely that they will experience boredom and restlessness when they *aren't* multitasking.

6. Multitasking increases stress and tension levels, which is exhausting.

7. Multitasking slows down the speed of students' work but increases their error rate. Despite the widespread belief that multitasking is a productivity technique, wouldn't you say that anything that makes us slower and decreases the quality of our work is, um, not really a best practice?

Learning to Focus

When we teach kids to focus on one task at a time, they're actually more productive in the long run, and they're less exhausted at the end of the day. This is because multitasking exhausts more energy and time than single-tasking does. A quick shift in attention from one thing to another—stopping to open a new Snapchat, for instance—obviously increases the amount of time needed to finish whatever teens were working on before they checked their phones. In adults, multitasking slows the pace of work about 25 percent, a phenomenon known as "switching time."

Even though the benefits of single-tasking are huge, it is much harder for most kids to single-task than to multitask. True focus can require a lot of willpower in this day and age, but when we teach kids to set themselves up to focus—without needing a stress-induced shot of adrenaline to get them going—we teach them to access that unique brain state that allows them to do their best work: **flow**. Flow requires relaxed focus. It is not dependent on stress or adrenaline. **When we**

are in flow, time seems to stand still, and this is the very opposite of busyness.

How do we teach kids to find their flow so they can focus? How can we help them recover from the ways that their brains have changed to the constant reward-system stimulation of busyness and multitasking in this always-on world?

Focus Tactic #1: Make Technology Less Stimulating

Most kids don't actually want to be glued to their phones 24/7, but they can't help themselves. They check their phones constantly in part because our human brains have what researchers call a "novelty bias." According to cognitive neuroscientist Daniel Levitin, "This novelty bias is more powerful than some of our deepest survival drives: Humans will work just as hard to obtain a novel experience as we will to get a meal or a mate." Kids actually no longer have to work very hard to experience novelty. In fact, they need look no further than the screen in their hand.

This means that the new technology in all its various forms is much more gratifying for teens in the short term than buckling down and thinking deeply, or as we saw in chapter five, making eye contact with an actual human standing before them.

Key to the way that new media and our devices hijack our attention is that the novelty they provide is never predictable. We are drawn to our smartphones for the same reason that gamblers are drawn to slot machines: We never know when we'll get an affirming message on Instagram or a Snapchat with good gossip, so we simply keep checking. Researchers call this "variable ratio reinforcement." Sometimes, for example, the new social information our kids get through their devices is particularly gratifying—they took a quick peek at their phone during chemistry and hit the jackpot by learning of a sexting scandal unfolding in real time at school. But other times, their checking yields nothing except for a spammy promotional text from a teen furniture store. Ironically, research shows that the fact that our devices aren't *always* rewarding prompts us to become even more compulsive in our checking behaviors and less disciplined in our focus.

This means that it won't work to just *will* our kids to stop compulsively checking their phones through insistence and nagging or by threatening "consequences." Instead, **we need to help them configure both their devices and their online time so that they are less tempted to check compulsively**.

We can do this by providing **structural solutions**, which is basically anything that limits screen time that *doesn't depend on a teenager's self-control or your willpower as the enforcing parent*. It's not that I think that you (or your teens) don't have above-average discipline and follow-through. I do, but (no offense) even you (and certainly your kids) don't have the self-discipline it will take to resist the siren song of technology through the strength of your iron will. I've seen the research on this, and suffice it to say that our devices and the apps on them are designed to be addictive, and they are successful at this. Here are several simple strategies that limit technology's addictive power:

1. Help teens reorganize their phones so they are less addictive. For starters, have them turn off all alerts, which are a primary distraction. This will help prevent them from getting sucked in when they don't actually want to be on their phones. Next, have them move all the most addictive apps (like social media—and *anything they check compulsively or on a whim when they see it*) off their homepage. Put these apps in folders on back pages so that they have to search in order to launch them. They'll still be there, but they just won't be constantly seducing your teens with their siren songs.

If your teen wants to make their phone a *lot* less tempting, show them how to make their phones black and white. The bright and beautiful color LCD screens of today's phones are a huge part of what makes our brains so interested in them. This is thought to be evolutionary. In nature, bright colors indicate items of primary survival interest, like food and blood. When we take the color out of a tool, we make it much less pleasurable and therefore distracting and addictive to our brains. You may need to google how to turn your phone screen to grayscale, as most smartphones don't make this move intuitive. Be sure you also turn on the "accessibility shortcut" so your kids can easily toggle between a color and grayscale screen (so they can still see pictures in color, for instance).

2. Get your teen an old-fashioned alarm clock and banish all devices from bedrooms (yours included). Your teen's bed is not for working (or checking social media or watching Netflix). It is for sleeping and resting. Don't let their phones be the last thing they see before they go to sleep and the first thing they reach for when they wake up.

In fact, insist that your teens say goodnight to their phones and computers ideally *one hour* before they go to sleep. Do this so that they are able to sleep deeply and wake up rested. There is a mountain of research on the many ways that the blue light from devices disturbs sleep and the memory consolidation kids need for learning. Have them charge their phones outside their bedrooms and set the phones to automatically go into "do not disturb" mode an hour before their bedtime. Similarly, set their computers up to automatically shut themselves down at the same time every night.

At this point, most parents insist that they *can't* control their teens' smartphone and computer use. It is hard, but **yes, you can**. Unless your kids paid for the devices themselves and are on separate cell and data plans than you, it is *your* device. You wouldn't let them use your car in a way that caused brain damage and lowered their academic achievement, so why in the world would you enable device use in a way that inhibits their ability to learn and experience real happiness, and that causes anxiety, irritability, and aggression?

3. Get them an engaging printed book to read before bed. It's important for most kids to replace the time that they would have been on their phones with something that will capture their interest, but not keep them awake. Reading is also a great way to practice focusing.

Focus Tactic #2: Bring Back Study Hall

The most important step in helping teens focus and find their flow, especially when it comes to doing their schoolwork, is to teach them to build themselves a *fortress against interruption* that will enable them to focus instead of multitask. If they can't concentrate, they can't drop into flow. Period.

Teens need to buy into the idea that multitasking is a state of continual interruption, and that if they keep getting interrupted, they can't achieve the state of deep concentration that they need for flow—or to learn efficiently and effectively. Even if they like the interruptions (as when they get funny texts from a friend). Even if the interruptions are good for their work (as when a friend FaceTimes them help with a tricky homework problem).

THE TROUBLE WITH INTERRUPTIONS

Studies show that interruptions are costly and problematic. Here are three sometimes-hidden costs to interruptions:

1. They cost us a lot of time. On average, interruptions take about 23 minutes to recover from—even if the distraction itself lasts only a minute!

For example, say your teen is uber-focused, but then their sibling comes in for a minute or two to chitchat. Before they turn their attention back to their work, they are likely to take a quick peek at their social media, and while they're doing that, notice that they missed a bunch of posts and several DMs from Instagram. If they reply to just a few of those incoming communications, it may well be longer than 23 minutes before they actually get back to work. Some kids believe that if they try really hard, they really can get back on track faster, but that effort takes focus and energy that they could be putting toward their homework.

2. Interruptions lower the quality of their work. A mountain of research has demonstrated time and again that interruptions increase our error rate. For example, when college students are concentrating on a task that taxes their working memory and they are interrupted for 2.8 seconds, they make twice as many errors as those who are not interrupted. When they are interrupted for 4.4 seconds, their error rate triples.

Just being in a work situation where you can be interrupted by texts and emails can decrease your IQ by ten points. For teens working on a paper, the news here is even more depressing: Interruptions measurably lower both the quantity and the quality of writing a person can do in even a very short period of time (20 minutes).

3. Interruptions contribute to stress and overwhelm, making us feel conflicted and time-pressured. They make us feel busy—and thus important, because busyness is a sign of significance in most Western cultures. But as kids shift their focus between tasks, it increases their perception that they have too much to do in the time that they have to do it.

According to researchers who study interruption, when we are diverted from one task to another, we can pick up our work pace to make up for lost time, but this increased speed comes at a cost: People who've been interrupted report having a greater workload, more stress and frustration, a feeling of more time pressure, and a feeling of having to exert more effort.

And guess what? This makes a lot of people feel annoyed, anxious, and irritable. Behavioral scientist Alan Keen believes that the stress and overload that come from constantly being expected to multi-task is causing an "epidemic of rage." Interruption and task switching raises stress hormones and adrenaline, which tends to make us more aggressive and impulsive.

The takeaway: Interruption drains teens' energy and dampens their performance. The stress, inefficiency, inaccuracy, and time pressure that interruptions create are the very opposite of finding focus.

Study Hall—or a designated time each night dedicated to deep work—is an opportunity for our teens to train their brains to focus deeply. The key to an effective Study Hall is that it's **predictable** and **non-negotiable**. We want our kids to be able to count on an hour or two of quiet, uninterrupted time for deep thinking and learning each evening. This trains their brains to drop into that relaxed-but-highly-effective flow state.

Although we usually assume that a state of deep concentration is hard to achieve, the truth is that we can access this wonderful state much more easily than we might realize. Teens just need to create a little routine for themselves. Here are some things you can do to help your teen set up a high-functioning Study Hall:

1. Do some planning to get them set up. Ask kids what they need to build a virtual fortress against interruption. Take a minute to anticipate obstacles: What will distract or interrupt them? How can they prevent themselves from becoming sidetracked? Have them make a list of all the obvious things (turn off all alerts on the computer, use headphones, turn off the phone and move it to another room, etc.). Then have them make a list of not-so-obvious things: needing to charge their laptop, having to check a class website for an assignment, feeling too sleepy, or not being able to find the notes they need.

2. Create a habit or routine. When kids approach Study Hall ritualistically and habitually by taking the same steps to get themselves started every single time, eventually their brains will start focusing deeply without the same sort of herculean effort it can seem to take at first. For this to happen, though, they need a regular routine. This means that Study Hall happens at the same time on school nights or, at least, after the same trigger or anchor (for example, once dinner cleanup is finished, or as soon as they get home from school or sports).

They also need a little starting routine, similar to what athletes and actors do before games or performances. This starting routine gets them organized and charts the course for their study hall by pointing them in the right direction. And it signals to their brains that they are about to drop into a state of flow. Here are some things that might be included in a pre–Study Hall routine:

- **Clear off their desk or work area.** Remove yesterday's dishes, close books, put away pens, and stack papers into a (perhaps deceptively) neat pile.

- **Open their planner and spend a few minutes planning** out not just the next two hours, but schoolwork for the rest of the week.

- **Make a step-by-step plan for each block of work time.** For a two-hour Study Hall, middle and high schoolers do well with three half-hour blocks of study time, broken up by two fifteen-minute breaks (more on this below). Why make a step-by-step plan for this time? A precursor to deep focus is knowing where you are in your workflow. "That constant awareness of what is next is what keeps you focused," Mihaly Csikszentmihalyi, author of *Flow: The Psychology of Optimal Experience*, told *Entrepreneur* magazine. "That's where the engagement comes from."

- **Open any documents** on their computer that they'll need to use while doing focused work.

- **Quit email and other applications** and close any open browser windows that they won't need.

- **Put their smartphone into "do not disturb" mode or turn it off *and* move it out of the room.** Yes, it needs to be all the way out of the room. Research shows that proximity matters. Having it in their line of sight, even if it is off and facedown, is distracting and will lower their cognitive function. Really!

- **Have them use the bathroom and bring a glass of water and possibly a snack** to their work table.

- **Put on noise-canceling headphones and start a playlist** (if they focus better while listening to music).

3. Encourage them to take device-free study breaks. Have them use a tomato timer (there are zillions online) to buckle down and focus for 30 to 45 minutes, and then to take a 15- to 20-minute break. The key is that the break is screen-free (in order to enhance their learning and focus when they return to work). Encourage them to take a walk outside, preferably in nature. My teens usually play with the dog when they are taking a break. Make checking their phones less tempting by ensuring that they are powered all the way off at the beginning of Study Hall, and that they are out of sight at their charging station. I know this seems like a lot of break time for high achievers, but have them try it. If they don't get through their work faster and end up less stressed and exhausted, I'd be very surprised.

4. Memorize the routine. Ultimately, our teens need to memorize their get-into-the-flow routines or the routines won't become habits. And to make deep focus during Study Hall a *habit*, teens need to do the same activities in the same order each time, and they need to do these things automatically, without having to look at a list for reminders. Memorization can be done a step or two at a time. For instance, if they have ten steps, and they add one step to their memory every day, they'll have a routine in a couple of weeks.

They'll need to resist temptation to change the routines, however. Routines are, by definition, boring, and today's teens crave novelty. So remind them that Study Hall won't work if the format changes every week.

Once teens understand that they can train their brains like a muscle, they start to be able to focus with far more ease. Elite athletes, actors and musicians, and professionals of all kinds train themselves to drop into "the zone" unconsciously by performing little rituals. (Poet Maya Angelou said that she used her pre-writing routine to "enchant" herself.) Rituals like this make it possible for ordinary people to do extraordinary work; at a minimum, they can help teens work more efficiently and learn more effectively, which tends to give them both more free time and enough time to improve their academic performance.

———————————

Of course there is more to recovering from inhibited dopamine function than creating structure around study time and technology use, but learning how to focus again is the foundation for becoming successful in school without needless stress and anxiety. In the next chapter, we'll look at the other (major!) benefits to taking regular breaks, and learn how kids can improve both their well-being and their brain power when they *aren't* focusing.

CHAPTER SEVEN

Rest

We know there are benefits to downtime, but many teens feel like they don't have time to take a break. Here's how to show them that they can accomplish more by doing less.

How are you doing?!" I asked Sayra enthusiastically just before things started to really fall apart for her. I hadn't seen her for a while, and I was glad to have her back at our dinner table. Normally bright and cheerful, she smiled at me weakly, trying to muster a happiness that wasn't there. "I'm fine," she said, not meeting my eye. "Just really busy."

"What's wrong?" I whispered to her later when we were alone.

"I'm just so *slammed*," she said, "but I can't get anything done."

I'd never heard her say anything like this before. She was an organized student, a high achiever. She got stuff done. Little did I know that her feelings of overwhelm were starting to turn into bone-rattling anxiety, which was keeping her from sleeping. Soon, we would find out, her insomnia would spiral downward into total exhaustion and panic attacks.

Sayra is not alone. Nearly half of male college students and two-thirds of female ones said they felt "overwhelming anxiety" in the last year. And three-quarters of the boys and 87 percent of the girls said they felt "exhausted" (though not by physical activity).

Slammed

One significant cause of unhappiness for many teens is that, like the adults around them, they are so damn busy. We all ask each other, "How are you?" And everyone, our kids included, answers, "I am *so* busy." "We say this to one another with no small degree of pride," writes minister and therapist Wayne Muller in his treatise on rest. It's "as if our exhaustion were a trophy, our ability to withstand stress a real mark of character. The busier we are, the more important we seem to ourselves and, we imagine, to others."

But busyness does not make us happy. Muller reminds us that the Chinese symbol for busy is composed of two characters: heart and killing.

This trouble with busyness is best illuminated by a famous 1970s study by Mihaly Csikszentmihalyi, the author of *Flow: The Psychology of Optimal Experience.* Csikszentmihalyi unintentionally induced what looked like textbook cases of generalized anxiety disorder in his subjects simply by instructing them as follows: From the time you wake up until 9:00 PM, "we would like you to act in a normal way, doing all the things you have to do, but not doing anything that is 'play' or 'non-instrumental.'"

Research subjects could make their bed and pack their lunches, drive to work or school, come home and make dinner, do their homework . . . but had to skip all those moments of enjoyment in the day that bring flow or rest. For example, they were asked to refrain from doing anything at work or school that they'd normally do just for fun.

Following those instructions for just forty-eight hours produced symptoms of serious anxiety, including restlessness, fatigue, difficulty concentrating, irritability, muscle tension, and more. In other words, we humans get anxious and overwhelmed when we aren't having fun.

As Csikszentmihalyi wrote, "After just two days of deprivation (from fun, play, and downtime) . . . the general deterioration in mood was so advanced that prolonging the experiment would have been unadvisable." So it shouldn't be surprising that when we strip our kids' adolescence of play, flow, and downtime—as we so often do, in the name of fostering their success—their mood deteriorates.

It isn't just being busy that makes our kids anxious and unhappy, it's that they rarely rest. They are constantly entertained, but they aren't relaxed. Teenagers and young adults today have less true downtime than virtually all humans who have ever come before them. **By downtime I don't mean free time or leisure time, but rather time spent just doing nothing.** For example, they have less time daydreaming while staring out the car window or at the horizon or spacing out while waiting in line, eating, or walking to school.

And as I've said previously, this is not necessarily because they are doing or working so much more than we used to. In fact, on average, they are not doing more homework, working for pay more, or piling on more extracurricular activities than we did in the 1980s and 1990s. **They have less downtime because in every (possibly scarce) free moment, they are turning to their devices for stimulation.** They check their phones while walking down the street, while in the car, in class, while they eat, while watching TV—even when they go to the bathroom.

Fun, rest, relaxation, and flow have been squeezed out of their lives by the increased amount of time they are spending on their devices, by our society's relentless cultural pursuit of *more,* and our equally relentless fear of "wasting" time. We think they are doing more sports, more homework, more activities—and we want them to be spending less time slacking off, hanging around, chilling out—because this is our (broken) societal formula for gaining access to more-prestigious schools and higher-paying jobs. We are poisoned by the hypnotic belief, writes Muller, that "good things come only through unceasing determination and tireless effort," and so "we can never truly rest."

But this formula for success is faulty. When we don't rest, and when we ignore the regular cycle of life—the yin and yang of inhaling and exhaling—we do not become more productive and our kids do not become more successful. When we let plants, land, or hibernating animals rest, they are dramatically more productive, and the same is true for us human beings.

Cognitive Overload

All of us, our teenagers included, need rest and stillness—totally "nonproductive" time—in order to recharge our batteries. We need downtime in order to *function.* Constant busyness and never taking a break causes what neuroscientists call "cognitive overload." This state of feeling overwhelmed impairs our ability to think creatively, plan, organize, innovate, solve problems, make decisions, resist temptations, learn new things easily, speak fluently, remember important social information, and control our emotions. In other words, it impairs basically everything our teens need to function in a given day.

But we parents don't rest ourselves, and we don't encourage rest in our teens because we fear that downtime means that we aren't busy and important or that our kids will not be successful. Resting can make us feel unproductive in a world that values productivity. We feel panicky when we aren't getting anything done, even if all we are doing is checking our email. We feel guilty when we aren't working . . . or simply bored.

And so as a society, we have gotten really, really bad at just doing nothing. Look around: We can't even stand to wait in an elevator for ten seconds without checking our smartphones.

Death of a Daydream

Why is it so painful for us to be alone with our thoughts? We may think—mistakenly—that nothing much is happening in our brains when we aren't consciously doing something, but actually, our brain lights up like a Christmas tree when we're daydreaming. Many brain regions become active, far more than when we are focusing. This is because when we daydream, or relax our focus, our brain begins drawing connections between all the things that it previously didn't see as all that connected. Importantly, the brain networks that are responsible for creative insight come online.

There's a neurobiological story behind this. We have two primary attentional networks in our brain: task-positive and task-negative, and they function like a seesaw in that only one is active at a time. When we are focused on something, or using our willpower to do something, the task-positive attentional network is ON. (That means that the task-negative—mind wandering, daydreaming, "time wasting"—network is OFF.) We give credit to our task-positive attentional network for all the great work we do in the world. When we are focused, we write papers and study for tests. We build bridges. We raise children.

THE PAIN OF STILLNESS

I'm endlessly fascinated by a series of studies where the research subjects were put alone in a room, with nothing to do. The researchers describe their work:

> In 11 studies, we found that participants typically did not enjoy spending 6 to 15 minutes in a room by themselves with nothing to do but think, that they enjoyed doing mundane external activities much more, and that many preferred to administer electric shocks to themselves instead of being left alone with their thoughts. Most people seem to prefer to be doing something rather than nothing, even if that something is negative.

> You read that right: Many people (67 percent of men and 25 percent of women, to be exact) actually gave themselves painful electric shocks instead of just sitting there doing nothing, even after they had indicated to the researchers that they would pay money *not* to be shocked again. One guy shocked himself 190 times in 15 minutes.

Our culture tells us to focus, and that's the only way to get anything done around here.

But when we're staring out the window, out into space, relaxing, or driving but not listening to the radio, and we let our minds wander, the task-negative brain becomes active. All those neurons start making connections between things we didn't see before, usually at an unconscious level. This is where our creative insight comes from. We can't solve problems or do much of anything without the insights that come from that downtime. We certainly can't fulfill our potential without filling our need for creative insight, without nurturing our ability to draw connections. **This is why we often get our best ideas in the shower . . . it's the only remaining place in the world where we let ourselves do nothing!**

All of this has huge implications for our teens' academic performance as well as their health and well-being. They need to take screen-free breaks in order to allow their brains to transfer what they've learned into memory and to stave off exhaustion and overwhelm.

Radical Rest, aka Sleep

There's nothing more restful, of course, than sleep, and nothing we disparage more than unproductivity. Culturally, we don't value sleep because we see it as the polar opposite of busyness. But sleep deprivation is another core reason teenagers today often feel lonely, anxious, and overwhelmed. **Research indicates that most teenagers need nine hours and twenty minutes of sleep per night to feel and perform at their best.** Do you know *any* teenagers who get that much sleep regularly? (If yours do, you get an A+. Feel free to do a victory dance and skip to the end of this chapter.)

Very few teenagers regularly get even eight hours of sleep, because getting enough sleep is counterculture in a society where barely sleeping or "pulling an all-nighter" is not a sign of terrible time management but instead something to brag about. Americans hold up the ability to go without sleep as a sign of strength. We say things like, "I'll sleep when I'm dead," as though our inability and unwillingness to get enough sleep isn't already leading us closer to sickness and death. Indeed, the incidence of death from all causes goes up by 15 percent when we sleep five hours (or less) per night. **Some 40 percent of American adults—and 85 percent of teenagers, according to the National Sleep Foundation—live with daily sleep deprivation.**

In fact, research shows that close to half of American teenagers are *significantly* sleep deprived. Why? Again, it's probably mostly those dang devices. Here's a sign: 57 percent more teens were sleep deprived in 2015 than in 1991. More damning is that sleep deprivation in teens goes up after two or more hours a day of device use, and it shoots up dramatically from there.

Screen time at night interrupts kids' sleep and, as detailed in chapter six, we understand why. So it's not that surprising that teens who spend more than three hours a day on their devices are 28 percent more likely to get less than seven hours of sleep. Similarly, teens who use social media every day are nearly 20 percent more likely to not get enough sleep than those who don't.

It's well established that sleep deprivation alone increases depressive symptoms in teens. A poor night's sleep is the ultimate mood killer, and over the long haul, all those bad moods add up. **Teens who regularly get less than seven hours of sleep per night are 68 percent more likely to have at least one risk factor for suicide.**

But did you know that even modest reductions in sleep *quality*—simply not sleeping as deeply because of a blue-light-induced decrease in melatonin, for example—tend to make us feel lonely, and that it leads us to act in ways that increase our isolation? Interestingly, sleep-deprived people are less inclined to engage with others and are more likely to avoid contact with other people. Worse still, sleep-deprived teens tend to be judged as socially unattractive by others, and as if that isn't enough, the effect is contagious: Well-rested people feel lonelier after even a one-minute encounter with a sleep-deprived person.

The takeaway: Sleep deprivation *alone* is likely at the foundation of the mental health crisis in today's teenagers. In fact, little could be more important for teenagers than learning to embrace stillness, downtime, and sleep. Sleep is, arguably, their golden ticket to happiness as well as the true silver bullet to success.

Teaching Tranquility

There are two key ways to reverse the exhaustion and overwhelm that is hamstringing today's adolescents (and our whole society, if we're honest).

First: Teach kids how to slack off strategically by taking breaks at designated times and at regular intervals in ways that sharpen their focus when they get back to work.

Second: Structure and support teens' sleep more than most parents are typically doing today. Teens need to learn, through their own experience, that getting enough sleep and getting *high-quality* sleep can help them both feel better and accomplish their goals.

If we want our kids to be high-functioning and happy, they need to learn how to be still. Some of today's teens have had access to their parents' tablets and smartphones since they were babies, and they may have never been on a road trip or sat through a long dinner without electronic entertainment. They may not know how to be alone with their thoughts or how to deal with boredom or a lack of stimulation. But keeping themselves constantly occupied is exhausting, stressful, and ultimately overstimulating.

So when teens start feeling like there isn't enough time in the day for them to get everything done, when they feel overwhelmed and time-pressured, they don't actually need more time. **They need more stillness to recharge.** Stillness so that they can feel whatever it is that they feel. Stillness so that they can actually enjoy this life that they are living.

The best thing that we can teach them to do if they are feeling overwhelmed and time-starved is to *stop*. Remind them that what they need more than time is *downtime without stimulation*.

As a society and as families, we don't just need to learn to tolerate stillness, we need to actively cultivate it. Fortunately, it's not complicated. As parents, especially if we are paying for their devices and their phone plans, we still have the power to enforce a little device-free stillness in our households. This supports all that was recommended in chapter six on focus, because taking breaks from our devices decreases technology addiction, which, in addition to reducing overwhelm, also increases our ability to focus.

Rest Tactic #1: Create Technology-Free Time and Space

In addition to the ways that technology has become more and more addictive, it's the *constant access* to our devices that makes them a problem and keeps teens and parents alike from resting. So in order to rest, we need to be more strategic about when we access our technology. As described in chapter six, our best bet is to devise *structural* solutions so that we aren't relying on our (limited) willpower.

The best way to do this, I've found, is to designate device-free times and spaces in our lives. Just because our kids can physically take their computers into the bathroom these days does not mean that this is a sensible thing to do. (Fecal matter can be found on one in six cell phones. Need I note that this is disgusting?) Similarly, beds are for sleeping, not for checking Instagram. It isn't safe to text in the car while driving, nor is it polite to do so as a passenger, especially if the driver is a friend, a parent, or someone expecting conversation.

So we parents can set boundaries for when it is appropriate and when it is not appropriate for teens to be looking at a screen. For example, in our family, we've set the guidelines outlined below.

Places where phones are not allowed:

- bathrooms
- beds
- our dining room and kitchen
- the car, except for the passenger controlling the music

We all benefit from a little old-fashioned device-free staring into space. The **car** is a great place for this. Ban phones on your family drives, especially short or routine ones. Try driving in silence, with your radio off and phones in the trunk. Encourage your children to look out the window while you drive them, and notice where they are. If you want to go really old-school analog, teach them to navigate by using a paper *map*. (This is like a brain-teaser game in our family.)

Times when we expect everyone in the family to be *off* their devices:

- **Mealtimes.** Eat meals out of the sight and sound of all screens, including phones and televisions. If you or your teen is alone, practice eating mindfully and just being alone with your thoughts. Remember that this is far healthier and ultimately more productive than checking your phone while you eat. **Remember that kids may need reminding that boredom is not a health hazard, but technology overuse is.**

- **While someone else is helping you with something or while waiting.** This could be a clerk in a store or a parent helping with homework. Have kids practice staring into space while waiting in the lunch line, for class to start, or for the bus. As efficient as our society has become, there is still a lot of time every day when we all need to wait. Why not use this time strategically? Teens won't actually accomplish anything by checking their social media feed while they wait for the dog to finish eating (so they can take him out), but they will gain a lot from a little daydreaming!

- **At school.** This is a hard one, because often parents need to reach their kids on their smartphones, but it's important, because many teens turn to Instagram or Snapchat during lunch or recess instead of socializing with their friends. This is a great example of how screen time can easily replace real life social connections.

- **During Study Hall (see page 103).** Devices charge in another room while our kids study. Our kids do use their computers for their homework, of course, but apps for messaging, social media, and so on are closed.

- **After 9:00 PM or, ideally, an hour before bedtime.** Why an hour? Because the low-energy blue light emitted by tablets and smartphones makes us much more alert, and at the same time it suppresses melatonin, which is needed to fall asleep and sleep well. (Truth be told, in our household, we enforce thirty minutes before bed because our kids like to look at their phones when their homework is finished.)

- **Before breakfast.** We find that if our kids start checking their phones first thing in the morning, their morning routines are fully derailed. This then derails my morning routine, too, because they are likely to miss the bus, forget their lunch, or hold up the carpool when they are distracted.

The ultimate goal is for kids to check their devices *intentionally* at designated times and places. For example, they might check in the morning when they are all ready to go to school. And when they get home from school, before they start their homework. And maybe again before dinner. This intentional checking replaces the impulsive, compulsive checking most kids (and adults) do throughout the day just because their phone is always there with them, begging to be checked.

Carving out times and spaces when kids' devices are not there to check reopens the possibility that they will have face-to-face social interactions with their friends and family. Their devices are thus returned to their status as tools they use strategically—not slot machines that randomly demand their attention, often causing them to feel lonely and left out.

"But how in the world do you enforce all that?!" parents often ask me, despairing, sure that setting limits around screen time and device use is next to impossible.

It's hard, especially with older teenagers. But it isn't impossible. For starters, there are plenty of apps available that help us set limits on screen time. These are good examples of structural solutions, because you set them, and then they do all the hard work of limit setting. Each of my kids decided on their own limits for each of their apps (with guidance from us, of course, as unlimited screen time was not an option). When they reach their time limit for, say, social media in general or Instagram specifically, the app automatically shuts down the device (like the Xbox). There is no renegotiating time limits and no arguing about how long it has actually been. And their time limits accrue across devices, so if they are playing Fortnite on the Xbox, for example, they can't just switch to a computer or iPhone when their time on the Xbox is up.

In my experience, even though they aren't perfect, apps like these make our kids' devices much less addictive. Older teenagers (and tech-savvy younger ones) can easily disable them, but not without our knowledge. (The app we use sends me an alert that says one of the devices "may have been intentionally disabled.")

When my kids were younger, we ruled the devices in our household with a very heavy hand. There were hard limits, and disabling the limits we set (or using the phone in bed, or bringing it to the dinner table) would result in loss of a device or screen time. Now that our kids are older, though, I see breaches as conversation starters and not an invitation to lie or hide. "I saw that you disabled the app that limits social media," I might say, as casually as possible, even if I really want to scream. "Want to tell me why?" These apps are like speed bumps: They make technology overuse much harder and a much bigger hassle.

Once my kids turn sixteen, we stop placing such hard time limits on their phones, and we stop acting as the primary limit-setters. We do this because we want them to learn to manage the devices on their own. I've found that they tend to set more stringent limits for themselves than even I set! For example, once I told Fiona that I wasn't going to monitor her phone use anymore, she deleted all the social media apps from her phone and tablet. Now that she has to use a browser to access Instagram, she doesn't easily get sucked into spending hours and hours just scrolling.

Without email, social media, and messages as our constant companion, we do find ourselves waiting in line at the grocery store just standing and staring into space. Perhaps dying to check our phones. This may be uncomfortable. Resist the temptation to numb this discomfort by, say, eating that whole box of cookies in your cart.

If you or your teen feel like you'd rather be doing anything other than staring into space, practice bringing your attention back to the present moment. This is what the famous Harvard psychologist Ellen Langer termed being "mindful" more than twenty-five years ago. To Langer, mindfulness is the "simple act of actively noticing things," and she and others have shown that it results in increased health, intelligence, and happiness. So wherever you are, whatever you are doing, look around and really notice things. What is different in your environment? In the people you are with? In your own body?

Teach your kids not to be afraid of the emotions that arise when they are still. If uncomfortable emotions come up, that's okay. Feel what you are feeling. Remember that when we numb unpleasant feelings, we numb everything that we are feeling. So to honestly feel the positive things in life—to truly feel love, joy, or profound gratitude—we must also let ourselves feel fear, grief, and frustration. And boredom. So if you are feeling anxious or excited or bored, let yourself *feel* that emotion. We can surf our emotions like waves.

Rest Tactic #2: Sleep

I know, I know, your teens don't have time to sleep more. They're very busy and important. Or you think that they are the exception to the rule and that they really do feel rested with less than the nine-plus hours of sleep that doctors and sleep experts prescribe during adolescence. Maybe you wish they could get more sleep, but you just can't find a way to get them to put sleep above their other priorities.

So ask them: What are their other priorities? Their health? Their happiness? Good grades? Getting into a good college? Winning the big game? The truth here is that they will not fulfill their potential in any of these realms unless they get the sleep their body, brain, and spirit need. A mountain of research supports this claim.

So help your teens make a plan to get more sleep. If it feels totally impossible to them to just get to bed earlier, suggest they increase their sleep by four or five minutes a night until they've adjusted their schedule enough that they are getting eight and a half or, even better, nine-plus hours of shut-eye. For example, it might feel totally impossible to them to get to bed before midnight, but surely they can hit the hay by 11:56. If they go to bed every night just four minutes earlier every day for two weeks, they'll gain nearly an hour—and all the increased productivity, creativity, and happiness that comes with it.

At the time I started working on this issue with my children, our oldest daughter, then a high-achieving sophomore in high school, saw her sleep deprivation as a given. One morning at breakfast she told me that it was "a train that's left the station." She saw it as an inevitable and necessary cost in a culture that prioritizes adolescent achievement over health and happiness.

But here's the thing: As a family, we absolutely do not prioritize achievement (or success in school) over our children's mental and physical health or their happiness. We don't see their ability to hold up under the stress of sleep deprivation as a sign of strength, nor do we see their inability to cope while tired as a sign of weakness. And given that I've studied peak performance, happiness, and productivity since before my kids were born, we certainly don't see sleep deprivation as a given. We're clear that all human beings do better on all fronts when they get enough sleep. So I believe that train can be stopped. But how?

My original instinct was to provide our teens with the facts. If they just knew, for example, that sleep is the ultimate performance enhancer, they'd sleep more before tests. I wanted to explain all the specific neuroscience details, again and again. I wanted to show them the studies on school and athletic success that point to the benefits of extending sleep well beyond the standard eight hours. But explaining the science to teens over and over presumes that they think rationally about all of this. None of us think rationally about sleep these days, especially not teenagers.

Remember, it is totally normal for teens to take stances on things that are seemingly irrational to us from an intellectual or "economic" perspective, but that make perfect sense to them socially and emotionally. This issue offers a great opportunity to practice the coaching techniques you used in part one of this book. As a reminder, here are some tactics you might try:

Express Empathy

Kids and teens are much more likely to listen to us if they feel understood. Resist the urge to give advice or to finger-wag about getting more sleep. These two things tend to create defensiveness and resistance to our great ideas. Instead, reflect back to them their position on things.

We need to show our kids, for example, that we understand that everyone in their class is sleep-deprived, especially the ones who seem to be doing the best. We need to show them that we understand how hard it is to fit everything in, and that it's hard to balance school and work and friends and volunteering and athletics and family demands. It's hard to fight the natural urge to stay up later that comes during adolescence. No one is saying this is easy.

In our family, we still mandate the bedtimes of our younger teens, and so they need a different type of empathy: It's hard to have parents who are still enforcing bedtime when so many of their peers are staying up much later (which we know from the activity on their phones). This makes them feel excluded socially and like they're being treated like a little kid. The most obvious way to express empathy is to mirror what they are saying (see page 59).

Show Them Their Inconsistencies—Gently

It often helps if we can get teens to see their conflicting motivations and the inconsistencies between what they've told us they want and their current behavior.

What to say, then, to that teen who wants to do well in school but seems too tired to do her homework at night? First, ask her permission to tell her what you see. If she says she's willing to listen to your perspective, gently point out the discrepancy between what she says she wants and what she's doing to make that happen in a nonjudgmental, factual way. For example:

- "You really want to raise your GPA, and to do that you're going to need to improve your grades on tests and quizzes."
- "It seems like you might not have enough time to spend most of your weekends playing video games during the day and staying out late with your friends on Friday and Saturday nights."
- "The last few Sundays, you haven't started your weekend homework until after dinner. It seems like you've begun the week so tired that you probably aren't studying very efficiently."

SO. MANY. WORDS.

My weakness is that I talk too much. I learned this the hard way once while I was trying to make an important point to one of my kids, and she didn't seem to be getting it. I plowed on, with more examples. "Are you hearing me?" I finally asked. She looked up, eyes glazed over. "Yes," she said. "I hear your words. So. Many. Words."

So don't be like me: More information is not better. (Even the examples I give, like the one above, are long.) Use as few words as possible to make your point, and then shut up and watch for a response. Awkward silences are okay, as teens will often want to fill the silence and, in so doing, will actually contribute to the conversation.

Side with Their Negative Position

For this tactic to work, we need to do it without sarcasm. I've found it works best when their negative position is that they don't need our help. For example, your teen might be stonewalling because he believes you are wrong that he needs to go to bed earlier. He clearly wants you to back off and let him go to bed "when he feels tired." This is the negative position for you to side with. Agree with his negative position by saying something like, "Okay. I see that I should just let you go to bed when you feel tired. I am going to work on not worrying about your health and well-being, and I'm going to try to stop concerning myself with how well you do in school. All right. I'm going to refocus my energy on my own work."

This is hard to follow through on, but it will only work if you do. They need to feel that you are really seeing and hearing them. Once they see that you have joined them in their belief, teens often want to individuate away from you again, and they will take a different tack. Don't be surprised if the next day they ask for help. If they do this, be sure to let it be all their idea. For crying out loud, don't say, "Well if you'd just let me help you last week, you wouldn't be in this position," as tempting as that might be.

Help Them Make a Sleep (or Screen-Free Downtime) Plan

If your teen indicates that they are ready to make a change, ask them if they'd like your help making a plan. Do this only if you suspect that they won't be able to make a plan on their own and if they indicate that they would like your help. Use the three steps beginning on page 63, or if they aren't into a full-on planning session, simply have them list:

- the changes they would like to make
- how they want to feel when they've made the changes
- what the behaviors say about who they are (e.g., an athlete, a top student, organized, etc.)
- the specific steps they plan to take
- the people who can support them—and precisely how those people can help
- the challenges or potential barriers to their success and, importantly, what they will do when they encounter these difficulties

Have them tell you their vision for their success—how will they (and you) know that the plan is working?

Remember, human beings change their habits slowly, and that's okay. It is enough to take baby steps. When we are consistent, those baby steps can take us as far as we need to go.

Please remember that rest—the ability to just sit there and do nothing or to get enough sleep—is a skill, and as a culture, we're not practicing this skill much these days. When we can't tolerate stillness, we feel uncomfortable with downtime, so we cancel it out by seeking external stimulation, which is usually readily available in our purse or pocket. These screens don't make the discomfort go away. In fact, difficult emotions tend to become amplified in our bodies physiologically when we aren't conscious of what we are feeling. That means our body's stress response is likely to get bigger if we distract ourselves from it.

It turns out that we humans experience big joy and real gratitude and the dozens of other positive emotions that make our lives worth living only by being in touch with our emotions and by giving ourselves space to actually feel what it is we are feeling. This means that in our effort to avoid the uncomfortable feelings that downtime can produce, we also tend to unintentionally numb ourselves to the good feelings in our lives. We need to slow down and let ourselves feel. We need to be able to simply stare into space without needing to constantly check our phones. Once you've mastered strategic slacking and sleep, you can move on to sex. And drugs. And money. There's never a dull moment with teenagers in the house, and so part three will give you some tips and talking points to navigate through the racier issues!

PART THREE

Talking Points for a New Era

CHAPTER EIGHT

The New Sex Talk

This is your guide to the new sex talk, because everything has changed.

The summer before I started high school, unbeknownst to me, my mother tasked my father with giving me the sex talk during a seven-hour road trip.

I had never kissed a boy or even seen an R-rated movie. The internet didn't exist yet. I didn't know that people had sex for pleasure—that would be weird and gross. I honestly thought that sex was something adults did only a couple of times in their lives in order to have children.

About twenty minutes before we arrived at our destination, my dad said something like this: "Now that you are going to high school, boys are going to try to get you on the rack. Especially the older boys. Just say no."

I gazed out at Highway 33, near Ojai, California, where ugly oil derricks were dunking their heads below the earth. Our old white Jeep Wagoneer was making a weird noise. I had no idea what my dad was talking about. Drugs, maybe?

"Don't worry, Dad. I'll say no," I replied, still looking out the window.

At Thanksgiving dinner twenty-two years later, my dad used the phrase, "he's going to try to get her on the rack" again. The memory of that road trip when I was fourteen came flooding back, and I finally realized what he was talking about all those years ago. I threw my head back and guffawed. My mother, usually highly composed, came undone when I told her why I was laughing. Two decades late, she was furious that no one had ever really talked to me about sex.

Needless to say, I've tried to be a bit clearer in discussing the birds and the bees with my own teens, but what was once an awkward conversation is now awkward *and* incredibly complex. Sex is another area where there has been a true transformation and where we have not really seen an accompanying transformation in our parenting or sexual education. The goal of this chapter is not to invade our children's privacy or helicopter-parent their sex lives, but instead to provide them with the information they need to navigate the new world of sex.

Mom, I'm Queer

For starters, gender and sexuality are no longer binary concepts for much of Gen Z. The black-or-white categories of male/female and gay/straight have given way to a more complex understanding of gender and sexuality as existing on spectrums. This is understandably mind-blowing to many people in my generation and older; never before in history have we seen such radical social change in such a short period of time. If you are confused, you aren't alone.

You've probably noticed that the generic term "gay" has been replaced by the term LGBTQ+, which stands for lesbian, gay, bisexual, transgender, and queer or questioning—plus all the people who don't fit into these categories. The term has changed because many people now self-identify as gender-fluid or nonbinary rather than as within the binaries of either male or female, gay or straight. If LGBTQ+ doesn't yet roll off your tongue, you might want to say it ten times fast again and again until it does, because the term LGBTQ+ is here to stay.

More people in Gen Z identify as trans (short for transgender) than ever before. This means that their gender identity, or *how they see themselves*, is incongruent with their physical body and the sex organs they were born with. (Cis, or cisgender, people *do* see their gender identity as congruent with their physical body.) Being trans has no correlation with being straight, bisexual, or gay—for example, a trans man could be attracted to men, women, or both. In addition, many people identify as genderqueer or questioning. This means that they are questioning what their gender or their sexual orientation is. They may also be questioning or simply not identify with the gender-binary terms that have traditionally been used, such as male/female or man/woman.

One of my daughters identifies as queer, and this has been particularly confusing to my husband, in part because as far as he knows, she has only had boyfriends and seems very traditionally feminine. He continually presses her: "What does it really mean to be queer? Are you bisexual?" He can't seem to grasp that her experience of her gender and her sexuality is not binary.

Although Mark's constant questioning is very annoying—after all, it isn't very respectful to grill someone about their sexual choices and attractions—I think our daughter sort of forgives him because she can see that he is trying to understand, and that it is a very confusing concept to someone who was born in the 1950s. It's hard for him to fathom that the social or cultural meanings assigned to someone's perceived biological sex could ever shift, but shifted they have! Someday Mark will better understand that our daughter feels no need to define herself as gay, straight, or bisexual, or even as only female or only male, and he will understand that she experiences both her gender and her sexuality as fluid.

The Dating Apocalypse

Justin Garcia, the research director at the Kinsey Institute at Indiana University, explains that there have been only two major transitions in heterosexual mating in the last four million years. The first transformation was more than ten thousand years ago, during the agricultural revolution, when marriage became a thing.

The second major transformation in human heterosexual mating is happening right now. People used to meet their partners through their friends and especially their family members. Now they can also meet potential partners online, through websites like Match.com and OkCupid, and through mobile hookup apps, like Tinder, Grindr, Bumble, and many others. At the time I'm writing this, Tinder is the most downloaded lifestyle app in America. Even if our teenagers are not yet using it (we can hope they're not, but the reality is that many are), it is rapidly changing sexual attitudes and behaviors.

"Sex has become so easy," a twenty-six-year-old marketing executive in New York told journalist Nancy Jo Sales for a now-famous article called "Tinder and the Dawn of the Dating Apocalypse" in *Vanity*

Fair. "I can go on my phone right now and no doubt I can find someone I can have sex with this evening, probably before midnight."

"I'll get a text that says, 'Wanna fuck?'" Jennifer, twenty-two, a senior at Indiana University Southeast, told Sales. "They'll tell you, 'Come over and sit on my face,'" says her nineteen-year-old friend, Ashley.

I'm sure I don't need to tell you, dear fellow parent, that that sort of easy, fast, and frequent sex—without commitment or romance, or even basic respect—isn't helping our young people lead fulfilling lives rich with meaningful connections.

Tinder users, for example, are more likely to report being deceived by people they met through the app, and they were less satisfied with their last "first date" (although only the researchers call it that, as Tinder users meet to "hook up"—that is, have sex—not to date) than people who used online dating websites like Match.com, or those who don't use technology to meet dates at all.

"It's changing so much about the way we act both romantically and sexually," writes Garcia. "It is unprecedented from an evolutionary standpoint." Ironically, this is another shift away from in-person interactions—away from eye contact and touch, from true intimate connection to other people. In some extreme cases, it even represents a *total* shift away from human interaction altogether.

For example, research by the Japanese government shows that about 30 percent of single women and 15 percent of single men in Japan in their twenties have fallen in love with a *virtual* girlfriend or boyfriend—essentially, a character in a game that they can "date" online. According to Masahiro Yamada, a sociologist at Tokyo Gakugei University, this rise in virtual romance is accompanied by a twin rise in the lack of interest in having a real relationship.

And then there is all the internet pornography, which also fosters sexual behavior that doesn't involve real partners. Research shows that:

- 12 percent of all internet websites are pornographic.
- 25 percent of all online search engine requests are related to sex—that's about 68 million requests per day.
- 35 percent of all internet downloads are pornographic.

- 40 million Americans are regular visitors (in their own estimation) to porn sites.

- 70 percent of men aged eighteen to twenty-four visit porn sites regularly.

- The average age of first exposure to internet porn is *eleven years old*, although most experts believe that this number has already drifted younger, and is now more accurately nine years old.

Today's teens are accessing pornography at very high rates. According to the American College of Pediatricians, "Pornography exposure for children and adolescents has become almost ubiquitous." Research shows that kids *younger than ten years old* now account for 22 percent of online porn consumption among people under the age of eighteen.

Like social media and other forms of device use, internet porn and dating apps like Tinder are addictive, and as such they are changing the brains of heavy users and, in turn, their ability to form satisfying and stable partnerships. And, as we saw in part two, this undermines the very foundation of their health and happiness.

The sexual transformation—this shift from in-person to digital sexual and romantic behavior—is dramatically affecting the sexual attitudes and behaviors of today's teenagers, although it is probably too early to tell what the lasting effects will be.

For example: As late as 2006, about half of eighteen- to twenty-nine-year-olds believed that sex before marriage was "not wrong at all," a statistic that had remained pretty stable since the 1970s. But then in 2016, the number of young adults that approve of premarital sex shot up to 65 percent. Similarly, sex between teens younger than sixteen is now more accepted, and five times as many teens think it is "not wrong at all" for young teens to have sex than believed this in 2006.

Sexting

We are in the midst of a sexual transformation that has introduced entirely new sexual behaviors among teenagers in the form of sexting. A sext is a nude or pornographic selfie sent via text. If you think this is something your kids would never do, perhaps don't be so sure. A large meta-analysis of research on sexting showed that a sizable minority of youth between the ages of twelve and seventeen are engaging in sexting. One in seven teens sends sexts; one in four receives them. (These are averages, and the numbers go up dramatically as teens get older.)

Most concerningly, 12.5 percent of teens report that they have forwarded a sext without getting permission from the sender, and the same number report receiving a "nonconsensual sext," meaning, someone sent them a sext meant for another receiver.

Most parents I know assume that it is boys who are requesting nudes from girls—and then, upon receipt, often share with their friends and pass around school. But **the research finds no significant gender differences in the rate of sending or receiving sexts**. At least among teens, both boys and girls report sending naked photos of themselves at the same rates. That said, there probably *is* a gender difference here that isn't being picked up in the research. For example, anecdotally, young women say that young men seem to think that they are interested in "dick pics," which boys and men reportedly send girls and women, often unsolicited and unappreciated. (For the record, photos of men's penises are not something women report being interested in.)

Given that so many of our kids are receiving sexts, it's important that they know that the law has not developed a good way to distinguish between consensual sexts between teens and child pornography. My good friend Laura Beth Nielsen, a sociologist and law professor, says sexts are potentially the riskiest thing teens will deal with in their lives. For example, if there is a picture on your kid's phone—whether they asked for it or not—of an underage person's genitals or breasts, they can be put on the sex offender registry for life. If they do get a sext sent to their phone, they should delete it immediately. It's one of those things that is so common that kids will roll their eyes, but the reality is that if they mess it up, they can end up labeled a child sex offender.

Less Sex . . . But Why?

Does all this mean that teens and young adults are having more sex than in previous generations? Actually, no, most of them are not. Today, the number of sexually active ninth graders, for example, is *half* what it was in the 1990s. Among all grades of high school students, more than half (54 percent) had lost their virginity in 1991. Now it's 41 percent (43 percent of boys and 39 percent of girls). It's not that today's teens are having more oral sex, either. They are simply less sexually active in high school and are losing their virginities later.

I find it surprising that in today's hypersexualized media climate, kids are less sexually active. As a mother, I can't help but think that, finally, we have a positive trend on our hands here. Less-frequent high school sex means fewer teenage pregnancies and lower incidence of STDs—both good things. But **the delay in teen sex is also an indication of Gen Z's broader withdrawal from physical intimacy and face-to-face interactions with their peers**, and that is not a good thing.

Teens today sext each other because they are online together. But they have in-person sex less (even though attitudinally, they are more positive about it) because they don't spend as much time in person together. Increasingly, they say they don't go on dates at all. This shift is most pronounced for high school seniors, as twice as many reported not dating in 2013 as didn't date in 2001 (38 percent versus 17 percent). In the same period, the proportion of tenth graders who never date increased from 28 to 44 percent, and the proportion of eighth graders increased from 48 to 60 percent. That is a massive shift in social behavior; in 2001, more eighth graders dated than tenth graders do now.

The New Sex Talk

So, we've entered some uncharted territory here, which leaves us with a lot to talk about with our kids. Thinking back to my dad and his failed sex talk with me, it's hard to imagine what his goals were with that one talk. I think his main message was probably something along the lines of "Don't let upperclassmen boys pressure you into sex," but I'll never really know. I can't even imagine what he'd have said if he had to talk to me or my brother about sexting, pornography, or complex issues like gender roles, consent, sexual orientation, or gender identity.

Given all of this, it's clear that the new sex talk won't work as a single lecture, though it never really has. We need to have a series of conversations with our kids, with our sons *and* daughters, starting when they are young, given that they are being exposed to pornography so young. And we need to continue talking to our kids all the way through college. (It is never too late to begin talking about sex, even if your kids are already in college. In fact, college students are legally required to receive some sex ed online or in person as a part of their orientation, so that can be a good opener. As in, "So, what did the university tell you about sex and consent?")

I know, this is a bummer. There's just no way to let us parents off the hook here. Personally, I would love it if we could just have one sex talk with our kids and be done with it. I also think it would be great if they could just learn what they need to know about sex from their school's puberty unit in science class. But no such luck. Experts recommend that we talk to our teens regularly about uncomfortable topics such as masturbation, pornography, and the dangers (and, perhaps even more awkwardly, the pleasures) of sex.

Kids need our wisdom about how to know when they are ready for sex and our advice on birth control. They need to talk to us about what they are seeing in the media and how they experience their own sexuality. We need to talk to them about the pornography they've been exposed to. And they can benefit from hearing about our own experiences, both good and bad.

The stakes are high. There are, of course, risks related to rape, unplanned pregnancy, and sexually transmitted diseases, and our kids need information about how to avoid these risks. And there are the subtler risks to their well-being and identities that can come from feeling used and objectified. **Hookup culture promises sexual liberation, at least in theory, but in practice, it tends to reinforce the traditional gender roles that give boys more power.**

Not surprisingly, teenage sexual activity can directly affect emotional well-being by increasing risk of mental health problems, especially when it occurs early in adolescence and especially when it is "casual" or uncommitted sexual activity. For both boys and girls, teenage sexual activity is associated with significantly increased odds of depression, suicidal ideation, and suicide attempts. And no, it's not that depressed teenagers are not more likely to be sexually active; sexual activity predicts later depression, but depression does not predict sexual activity.

The scary statistics suggest that having sex early in adolescence can be harmful emotionally to both boys and girls. We can't say exactly why, but it is likely that sex early in adolescence doesn't lead to the type of connection, love, pleasure, or acceptance that it does later in life, and that it often leads to the opposite: feelings of disconnection, rejection, dissatisfaction, shame, and isolation.

And of course, we also want more for our kids than to just avoid the bad stuff. When the timing is right for sex, we want it to be a positive part of their lives—one that brings more love, connection, and pleasure than regret, pain, and embarrassment. This means we must muster the courage to talk to our kids about sex and sexuality. At least more than my parents talked to me about it!

You've Got This

I know I've just made the new sex talk seem impossibly complex and fraught with all kinds of issues we never had to deal with as teens, but if you've read this far, you already have the skills you need to talk to your kids about sex. Let's back up and take it one step at a time.

Some kids will learn about puberty, pregnancy, birth control, and sexually transmitted diseases from their school's sex ed program, but since only twenty-one US states teach sex and HIV education—and only twenty states require that if provided, sex and/or HIV education must be medically, factually, or technically accurate—you might want to start with the traditional birds and the bees stuff. But even kids who get sex ed in school know that there's a lot more to adult—and adolescent—sexuality than is taught formally at school. Part of the trick as a parent these days, I think, is knowing what our kids are being exposed to at any given age. So start by finding out.

Ask Questions

Remember that you don't have to have all the answers to all their questions right off the bat. The idea is to start an ongoing dialog, not to run a sex ed class from your kitchen table. Here are some starter questions, which you'll obviously have to modify based on the age and experience of your child:

- Do you know anyone who has watched porn? Where did they see it? How do you think it affected them?
- Among your friends, what does it mean to hook up?
- How many of your friends are sexually active? Or: Do you think any of your friends are sexually active yet? (You could also ask if any of your child's friends have kissed a boy or girl.)

Brace yourself, and keep your best poker face on. Instead of instructing, just keep asking follow-up questions, such as "What do you think of that?" and "How does that make you feel?" If they tell you something concerning about a friend, inquire further: "Are you worried about her?" "Do you think he needs help?"

Deal with discomfort by breathing deeply and slowly—not by preaching or avoiding the conversation. (Maybe reread part one if you find yourself lecturing or freaking out.) If we don't stay relaxed, our kids will only remember that we nearly choked every time we tried to talk to them about sex. This will not make them likely to come to us when they have a pressing question or, heaven forbid, a serious problem in the sex department.

Foster Closeness

Research shows that adolescents who have better relationships with their parents tend to have a lower likelihood of early sexual intercourse initiation. On the other hand, the same study shows that lower relationship quality and less parental monitoring increased the odds that a teen would initiate sex.

You can foster closeness with your kids in whatever ways sound fun to you. I like to read and so do my daughters, so we read on the same couch together a lot. Ditto with movies. My daughters and I *love* movies, but my husband and stepson don't, so I watch a lot of movies with the girls. Having a "thing" together draws us closer. (And occasionally watching movies together can be a great way to open up a conversation afterward about sex, as there is plenty of sexual content in movies these days.)

Fostering closeness doesn't need to take a lot of time. I try to create space, maybe ten minutes a day when I know we won't be interrupted, alone with each of my kids. It's often as they are going to bed or while I'm in the kitchen making dinner. That way there is always room for them to talk to me about their lives. We also have same-gender "date nights" when the opportunity arises for me to take one of our daughters out to dinner and/or my husband to take our son out. This opens up a longer stretch of time for deeper conversations.

Don't Rely on Abstinence Education

As parents we do well to refrain from trying to keep teens in the dark about birth control and protection against sexually transmitted diseases, even when we believe abstinence is the best thing for our kids.

Many parents fear sending a mixed message, so the only message they send is that sex before marriage is not okay, but research clearly shows that teens in abstinence-only education programs are no more likely than those not in an abstinence-only program to delay sexual initiation, have fewer sexual partners, or abstain entirely from sex.

In other words, telling our children to remain abstinent doesn't increase the odds that they will delay becoming sexually active, but it does deprive them of our guidance about sex. It makes them sneak around and hide their behavior, which means we can't support them if they need help. They go to strangers at clinics for birth control and health care instead of our family doctor—or they go without. So instead of "just say no," we can give our kids guidelines for their sexual behavior while still giving them the information they need.

What do you most want your teen to know about sex? What are your expectations for them? We can give them information and still send a very clear message about what we think is best for them. Here is what I said to my kids once they got into high school: "I feel strongly that having sex while you are still a teenager is not likely to be in your best interest. That said, I want you to have a lot of information, so that someday, when you are ready to have sex, you will be better prepared both to prevent an unplanned pregnancy or disease *and* to have a meaningful and enjoyable sex life."

Talk to Boys the Same Way We Talk to Girls—and Vice Versa

As a society, we expect—and in some ways openly encourage—boys to have sex once they've gone through puberty. Our cultural and societal norms are such that boys will pursue girls sexually, both offline and online. At the same time, our culture and society send girls the message that we'd prefer it if they looked sexy but didn't actually have sex. Girls who are openly sexual are shamed, called ho's and sluts. Both directly and indirectly, society insists that girls resist both their own sexuality and the advances of boys.

The often-unspoken message is that it's normal and healthy for boys to have a strong desire to have sex—but that girls don't naturally have that same desire, and it's dangerous when they do. This is a fundamentally flawed and terrifically outdated assumption. **Teenage girls are, of course, just as curious about sex as boys are, and just as sexually active.**

Not only do we expect girls to deny their natural drive and curiosity, as a society we expect them to regulate (and often, to deny) boys' sexuality. As a culture, boys are rarely, if ever, asked to deny or regulate their own or girls' natural desire to have sex. This is a profoundly unfair double standard that hurts both our boys and our girls, and one that we should not continue to propagate.

Instead, we can approach sex ed in a more equitable way, by talking to girls and boys similarly. We can educate both boys and girls about the risks of sex and, more than that, we can acknowledge and accept that sexual feelings and erotic leanings are a normal and healthy part of adolescence for both girls and boys.

We can share with both boys and girls that we want them to (eventually) develop healthy and satisfying sex lives. We can help both boys and girls understand that if they are reckless with their sexual activity as teenagers and young adults, they will likely hinder their ability to form intimate bonds as adults. In other words, we want them to be capable of loving, connected, fulfilling sexual intimacy as adults, and in order for that to happen, they will need a little honest guidance now.

The Specifics

There's still a lot to talk about. Below is a list of topics my husband and I are trying to cover with our kids, along with some approaches to use.

Pornography

We can ask kids how prevalent they think porn viewing is among their friends (few will fess up to their parents about viewing it themselves). Use "their friends" as a cover to see if they understand that although it can be very hard to look away from, pornography can really hurt them. For example:

- According to the American College of Pediatricians, pornography use among adolescents "is associated with many negative emotional, psychological, and physical health outcomes. These include increased rates of depression, anxiety, acting out and violent behavior, younger age of sexual debut, sexual promiscuity, increased risk of teen pregnancy, and a distorted view of relationships between men and women."

- Research catalogued in the book *Your Brain on Porn* finds that in the last fifteen years, the rate of sexual dysfunction, including erectile dysfunction, has increased nearly 1,000 percent in young men under the age of twenty-five, and that this is related to pornography usage.

- In the UK, the ChildLine counseling service recently released a report that found 10 percent of children in the *seventh grade* think they are watching so much porn that they are concerned they are addicted and may not be able to stop.

- A Dutch study found that pornography has the highest addictive potential of all device or technology use. Boys in particular can easily become addicted to masturbating to internet pornography, and when they do, it decreases their normal sexual function. Regular use of pornography often leads to a lack of interest in sex with a real partner, which can spiral downward into lone-liness and depression in adulthood.

- Access to pornography is changing sexual behavior among older teenagers. For example, in 1991, about one in ten adolescents between the ages of sixteen and twenty-one had tried hetero-sexual anal sex. In 2012, more than one-third had. Why? Anal sex is both common and glorified in pornography. It's important that our kids know that anal sex as depicted in pornography dif-fers dramatically from how it plays out in reality. Fantasy: Anal sex is as easy and enjoyable as vaginal sex. Reality: Many (if not most) women on the receiving end of anal sex report discom-fort, pain, and bleeding due to tearing in the anus.

We can help our teens understand that pornography use makes real sex less fun and exciting (and sometimes impossible when it causes erectile dysfunction). More than that, we need teens to understand that pornography can really hurt their ability to have a healthy long-term relationship with a real person—and that without healthy rela-tionships, it's hard to be happy in life.

Hooking Up

Many high school and college girls will claim that hooking up—casual and disconnected sexual activity (which may or may not include inter-course) with unfamiliar partners—is empowering. But experts such as Cindy Pierce, who has interviewed thousands of teenagers and young women about sex, consistently find that the idea that hooking up is empowering doesn't hold up in practice. "Many recent college gradu-ates cringe as they describe being disrespected, objectified, or even used by guys when they were younger, and regret their claims that the choice was empowering," Pierce writes in her book *Sex, College, and Social Media*. "A prevailing sentiment among these women is that they regret getting caught up in the random hookup scene, and they insist that I encourage younger women and men to make the choice to avoid it."

No matter how convincing the justifications and theories might be about why hooking up is empowering, in practice, disconnected sexual experiences are rarely satisfying and often leave girls, in particular, feeling degraded. The notion that someone needs to engage in sexual activity to prove they are sexually empowered is absurd. Girls who feel pressured by social norms to hook up are not liberated. Taking this stance might lead our kids to label us as anti-sex buzzkillers, but we can surprise them by becoming advocates for their healthy sexuality.

The Upside of Sexual Activity

Kids often learn about the risks related to early or unprotected sexual activity at school, but they don't tend to learn much about the joys of human sexuality, particularly the joys of sex with another living human being that they love. But they know that there is something awesome about sex, and we parents lose credibility when we make it seem like sex is nothing but dangerous. **When we talk to them about the upside of sexual activity, we prompt a process of weighing the benefits of sexual activity against the risks.** We want kids to think critically about sex rather than just acting emotionally and impulsively. We can ask our kids, "What do you think the benefits are to being sexually active as a teenager?" Similarly, you might ask what they think the benefits of being sexually active are for college students as well as for adults.

Not Everyone Is Doing It

In fact, more teens aren't than are. Teenagers need to feel that they are with the majority and that they aren't being left out. So it's important for them to understand that, surprisingly, hookup culture isn't as big a thing as they think.

Here's a conversation starter: According to the Pew Research Center, two-thirds of high schoolers have never dated, hooked up, or had a romantic relationship with someone. Other research shows that 59 to 84 percent of teens aged fifteen to seventeen have never had sex. At age twenty, one-quarter of young adults are still virgins.

What You Want Your Child to Learn from Your Own Experiences

This one is personal. My kids have listened with rapt attention when I've spilled the beans on myself. For example, I was date-raped on a graduation trip after I'd been drinking. (This happened to so many of my friends that we wrote a book about it called *The Other Side of Silence.*)

LGBTQ+

If you've ever made derogatory comments about LGBTQ+ people in the past, you might want to consider broadening your views before talking with your kids again about it. When parents disrespect people in the LGBTQ+ community or even just use disrespectful language by calling something they don't like "gay" or saying someone is a "fag," they send the message to their teens that they may not unconditionally support and accept their children as they are. **Fearing rejection and abandonment from family members dramatically increases an adolescent or young adult's risk of severe mental illness and suicide.**

No matter what our political or religious views are, when our first priority is the health and well-being of our kids, we need to bring openness and acceptance to our kids' experience of their own sexuality and gender. When teens feel that they need to hide who they really are from their parents, our relationship with them falters. But when we accept our kids as they are, we build a strong connection for them to lean on.

It's never too late to become more open-minded about changing social norms related to gender and sexual identity. When we demonstrate that we're rethinking some of our more narrow (or even bigoted) views, we model growth for our teens, and we open a line of communication between ourselves and our kids. We can even give our teens the opportunity to educate *us* if they seem more knowledgeable!

What Do They Want Sexually and Romantically?

Personally, I've found this conversation to be easier in the hypothetical, and my advice is to start having this conversation before your kids have boyfriends or girlfriends, if possible. The point is not to get teens to tell you their sexual desires (um, yuck), but to get them to think about it on their own and to define it for themselves and, later, for their partner. We want them to understand that not knowing what they like or not being able to tell their partner what they like is a clear sign that they should slow down and figure it out.

Here's a starter question: "I'm not asking you to tell me, but do you know yet what you want to feel or do when you become sexually active?" Or, if your teen is sexually active: "Without giving me the details, have you asked what your partner wants sexually? How do your partner's desires line up with your own?"

Consent Is the Wrong Criterion for Sexuality

Although it is, of course, essential to understand that consent is mandatory, I'm with psychologist Lisa Damour in thinking that **mere consent is an exceptionally low bar**. Ask your kids if they've talked with their partner about pursuing only those activities where you have common desire—or "enthusiastic agreement," as Damour calls it.

The real secret to good sex is communication, and **open and honest communication should be the most basic criteria for any sexual activity**. Asking questions, including for consent, is the foundation of good communication. Arm your teens with good questions, such as these:

- Does this feel good?
- Do you like this?
- I'd love to do [named sex act] with you. How do you feel about that?
- What would you like to do?
- Where would you like me to touch you?

The goal is ongoing, enthusiastic, verbal communication. Teens or young adults who are not asking or answering these questions are in dangerous territory. What they are doing is likely to leave them feeling unfulfilled and degraded, and they are at risk of committing a sexual assault. Cindy Pierce says this to the college students she educates: "If you think it would be awkward to actually *talk* with your partner, take a step back—that's a clear indicator that getting naked with that person isn't a good idea."

Help your teen establish general guidelines. You might start by asserting that if a person is too embarrassed to ask their partner intimate questions about what they want out of a relationship or about their sexual desires, they aren't ready for the intimacy of sexual activity. A general guideline might be, therefore, that if you can't talk with your partner intimately about sex, you aren't ready to be sexually intimate with them. Then ask if your teen agrees, and even has ideas of some other good general guidelines to keep in mind regarding sexual activity.

Another general guideline: Don't forgo your own sexual satisfaction (or safety or health and well-being) in order to please a partner. If sex is, at the barest of minimums, about experiencing sexual pleasure, then do not knowingly give that up.

Good Reasons and Bad Reasons to Become Sexually Active

One-quarter of young women regret losing their virginity to the "wrong" partner, and one-fifth have significant regrets about having unprotected sex or progressing too quickly sexually in a relationship. Ask your teen, "What do you think about those statistics?" "What do you think are some good reasons and bad reasons to become sexually active?"

How to Be "Good in Bed"

Although most teens won't come right out and tell you this, most of them don't just want to (eventually) *have* sex, they also want to be *good* at it. As parents, we can acknowledge that most people aren't out just to have sloppy or drunken or unsatisfying sexual experiences, but would rather have sexual experiences that are pleasurable for both partners (at a minimum). We can point out that sexual experiences can, in addition to being pleasurable, help us learn about ourselves and help us feel more connected to other people, particularly people we love.

But to accomplish these goals, most teens need more explicit information. For example, boys and girls alike wonder: How do women have orgasms? Unfortunately, most teens today learn about sex from porn or from their friends (who probably don't have any actual experience with truly good sex).

Most teens don't realize that the information they glean from porn isn't accurate, and the sex acts they learn online won't often (or maybe even ever) translate into sexual pleasure for their partners. For example, one study showed that nearly 90 percent of popular porn videos depicted physical aggression by men against women like spanking, gagging, choking, and slapping. Nearly half showed verbal aggression, like degrading name-calling. None of the sex experts I know would recommend these tactics for anyone who is relatively inexperienced or anyone wanting to pleasure a new partner. Nor do we have any evidence whatsoever that, in general, teenage girls and young women enjoy being hit, choked, and degraded during sexual encounters. But teenage boys and young men are, for the most part, *very* confused about this. For example, many college men believe women like it when they are physically aggressive during sex.

We can give our kids more accurate information. For girls, this often means reinforcing that their pleasure is nonnegotiable if they want to be "good in bed." Many girls need to hear that good sex is not a performance, and that their authentic sexual responsiveness is more important than the size of their thighs. Faking an orgasm is not hot; being really turned on is. Being insecure about your body and hiding it is not hot; really getting naked with someone is.

But how are our kids to know what type of touch is sexually pleasurable to them? This is extra awkward to talk about as a parent, but the best way to get good in bed is to **masturbate without pornography**. Learners can focus on themselves and the physical sensations that they enjoy. This is particularly important for girls, because the truth is that female pleasure is different for everyone, and it can be elusive.

Teens can be encouraged to use their own imaginations to develop their own unique sexual fantasies (also awkward encouragement coming from a parent). This is a particularly important strategy for boys, who often don't realize how much masturbating to pornography is making them bad in bed. According to Alexandra Katehakis, founder and clinical director of the Center for Healthy Sex, "While masturbating to porn, the adolescent brain is being shaped around a sexual experience that is isolating, visceral, and completely void of any love or compassion." This obviously affects their performance with live partners. Or as one of my most brilliant friends recently told her sons: "If you keep thinking porn is exciting, you will only be able to orgasm when the sex is porn-like . . . but porn is *not real*. So watching porn is *reducing* your chances of having a good sex life."

Another time-tested way to be good at sex is to **communicate well with your partner**. We need to teach this generation (again and again) that the basic ingredients for good sex are **connection**, **communication**, **trust**, and **respect**. In the age of Tinder and hooking up, much of Gen Z missed the memo that the best sex is loving and connected, which is why we old people call it "making love."

Giving Good No

When our teens want to delay sexual activity, we know that they often don't have the skills they need to do so. For peer- and status-oriented teenagers, rebuffing a sexual advance can be incredibly difficult. In addition, our cultural expectation that girls will say no at first even when they really mean yes can make it hard for boys to hear a no. These dynamics make "just say no" bad advice.

Both boys and girls alike may hesitate to issue a straight-up rejection to a sexual advance, especially when they don't want to reject the *person* they are with, but instead they just want to turn down the *act* being pursued. Teens know that saying no to any invitation, sexual or not, can be experienced as a rejection, which can cause anger, embarrassment, or humiliation.

We parents can talk to our kids, both boys and girls, about preparing easy outs. For example, they can say that they aren't feeling well (which they certainly aren't if they are uncomfortable with what is happening). Girls can hint that it's the wrong time of the month. Boys (and girls) can suddenly remember they made a prior commitment.

Teens sometimes need us to point out that there is a difference between rejecting a person and slowing down sexual activity, and they can make this distinction with their partners using a technique my dad called the "shit sandwich." This is where first we say something positive that is true. Next we deliver the disappointing news, and then we wrap up with something else that is positive. It might go something like this: "I really like you and I've had so much fun tonight. I'd like to slow things down a little right now and head home for the evening, but I'd love to see you tomorrow if you are interested."

The shit sandwich won't work if we have nothing that is both positive and truthful to say—we are *not* having fun, for example, and we don't want to be with a person again later. That's a red flag, and a sign that the relationship doesn't have a future. That is not the time to worry about letting someone down easy. In life, sometimes other people are going to be frustrated and disappointed when we don't do what they want us to do. That's okay. Other people's disappointment is not our responsibility, and it's okay if not everyone likes us all the time.

Safe Sex Specifics

No, I am not going to tell you that it's your job to teach your kids how to put on a condom correctly. This is actually where the internet can be our friend. There are great YouTube videos about using condoms correctly. Find one you like and direct your child to it. My kids and I have also agreed that our family doctor will aid me in providing them with advice and instruction about birth control when they are ready. We all agree that our family doctor is better suited to take care of their sexual and reproductive health than someone they don't know well at a clinic. Our doctor agrees and participates in these "new sex talks" every year at their annual exams.

Drugs and Sex Don't Mix

Sex is obviously much riskier, and also less pleasurable, while under the influence of drugs or alcohol, and hopefully our kids know that we don't approve of underage drinking or drug use, ever. But most kids need this spelled out for them repeatedly. Ask your teen in the hypothetical about peers who engage in sexual activity while under the influence. What do they think about using "liquid courage" to do something they'd be too anxious or uncomfortable to do sober? Show them their inconsistencies, gently. For example, your teen may say it's normal for college kids to have sex while under the influence. After asking if you could share your perspective, you might respond by saying, "You've decided that you only want to be with someone who you know actually likes you as a person, and isn't just using you for sex. It seems like that might be hard to actually know if there is drinking involved."

In Case of Sexual Assault or Sexual Harassment

Even in this time of #metoo, a shockingly high share of our daughters will have to cope with sexual harassment and assault. We might assume that girls are safer today because rape and harassment are being taken more seriously in the media and because we now have consent laws. But, unfortunately, we are not seeing declines in sexual harassment and sexual assault compared to previous generations.

In fact, things are worse for girls today. Why? Many think it is because pornography makes violent sex seem normal, and many boys and young men watch it without realizing that most women aren't interested in being roughed up. Moreover, social media and sexting provide a whole new avenue for humiliation, harassment, and unwanted advances. A national survey from the Harvard Graduate School of Education found that nearly 90 percent of today's eighteen- to twenty-five-year-old women have already been the victim of one or more forms of sexual harassment. This included:

- being touched without permission by a stranger (41 percent)
- being insulted with sexualized words by a man (47 percent)
- having a stranger say something sexual to them (52 percent)

In addition, research shows that more than 44 percent of our daughters are likely to experience attempted or completed sexual assault by the time they graduate from college. Here's how that looks:

- experiencing unwanted sexual touching (31 percent)
- being taken advantage of sexually when unable to give consent (22 percent)
- being forced to perform a sexual act (19 percent) or forced to do something sexual under threat (5 percent)

- being raped vaginally (18 percent), orally (6 percent), or anally (5 percent)
- being gang-raped (2 percent)

LGBTQ+ young people are the most likely to experience harassment and sexual assault. Transgender youth are at the highest risk; 64 percent will experience a sexual assault at some point in their lives.

Assault and harassment can easily shape the way our daughters think about themselves. Many don't tell anyone about their experiences because they think they must have done something to deserve such awful treatment or because they think it reflects poorly on them. They don't want a "reputation," so they don't seek help.

Not surprisingly, research shows that being sexually harassed causes intense psychological stress and lower self-esteem, and girls who are assaulted or raped face even greater emotional consequences. Sexual violence is known to lead to health problems such as depression, anxiety, eating disorders, post-traumatic stress disorder, and suicidal ideation (in addition to injury, sexually transmitted infections, and chronic illness). In addition, college students who have been sexually assaulted are more likely to engage in risky behaviors, such as binge drinking and drug use, and tend to have lowered academic achievement.

How Parents Can Help

Our teens need to know that we care deeply if they are being treated in a way that feels degrading. Psychologist Lisa Damour, who has worked with hundreds of girls who've been harassed and assaulted by boys or men, recommends that we say to our kids something like this: "Even if a guy is just giving you the creeps, I want you to take that feeling seriously and get some distance from him or get some help."

Moreover, we can emphasize with our kids that when people use vulgar language that feels degrading to them or to someone else—even if it is just in a text or social media post, and even if it is from someone they consider a friend, and even if that person is "joking"—they would do well to pay attention. Don't ignore it. That behavior is a sexualized form of bullying, and as with a bully, the intention is to intimidate and demean. It's not okay.

And our message to boys needs to be very clear: Not only do we expect them to refrain from sexual harassment and assault (obviously!), but we expect them to be protective of victims. This means that we expect them to leave chats and text threads that are demeaning or degrading to others. Moreover, we hope that they will be courageous enough to actively support victims by telling offenders to cut it out. We can talk to boys about what real support for a victim means (see page 153) and emphasize that it needs to go beyond sending a girl a text later that says, "That sucked."

One of the most difficult things for teenagers dealing with sexual harassment or sexual assault is telling their parents. I was sexually assaulted on a graduation trip after high school, and for weeks I didn't tell anyone. I had never spoken to my parents about my previous sexual experiences (I was a virgin, but I'd had boyfriends who I'd fooled around with). I was close to my parents emotionally, and generally shared with them a lot about my life, but I didn't want my first real conversation with my parents about sex to be about a traumatic experience.

So the first thing we parents can do is to talk to them about sex in general and with some regularity. Beyond that, we can talk to them specifically about harassment and assault, letting them know that we know that it happens a lot. We will always help them if they experience sexual harassment and assault, and we will not, under any circumstances, blame them for what happened, even if they were doing other things that they know we wouldn't approve of (such as drinking).

One way to approach this hard conversation with both boys and girls is to talk to them about what they can do if they have a friend who is being harassed or has been assaulted. This is an indirect way of showing them that we are going to be supportive if something happens to them. We can tell them that if one of their friends is being harassed or is sexually assaulted that we want them to be supportive as a friend. Here is what your kids can do if something happens to one of their friends:

- Emphasize that they believe their friend, support them, and are not judging them. False reports of sexual assault are significantly lower than the public perceives and are no higher than false reports for most other crimes. Tell them repeatedly, "It's not your fault." This fact is not negotiable. Rapists cause rape. Bullies cause sexual harassment. Nothing they did makes what happened justifiable.

- Encourage a victim to reach out to someone they trust, like a parent or teacher. Volunteer to be that person for their friends, and say explicitly that you will reserve judgment and can connect them or their friends with helpful resources. Let them know that it's okay if they are confused or don't know what to do next. They can lean on their trusted person to help them make decisions.

- Explain that they have no more reason to be ashamed than if they were the target of any other crime, like theft.

Sexual assault and harassment are crimes about power and control as much as they are about sex. For this reason, it is important for us as supporters to help victims regain a sense of personal power and control. This means letting them make their own decisions about what to do next.

Sexy Selfies

Parents frequently ask me what to do about their teenager's sexy social media posts. I think most of us parents of daughters have cringed deep, horrified cringes upon seeing our teens (and their friends) take very sexy selfies in bathing suits or low-cut shirts or tight short-shorts.

Teenage girls do this because these sorts of posts—as well as milder selfies—reward our girls for something our culture has long taught them to value: looking both beautiful and sexy. "With a simple tap," writes Rachel Simmons, author of *The Curse of the Good Girl,* "your daughter can offer herself up to the 'gram in exchange for attention, validation, and valuable social currency."

As the likes and comments on their sexy photos accrue, our daughters have a concrete and publicly visible—if inaccurate—measurement of their worth. They know exactly how many people think they are beautiful, and they can watch the number climb. When a girl posts selfies, especially sexy ones, we parents do well to be curious without being judgy, just as we do when we raise other difficult topics with our teens (see chapter four). We can ask her about posts that seem to be only about her appearance, perhaps remembering out loud how much we wanted to be thought of as beautiful when we were teenagers or how much we want that now, if we do. My girls were shocked to learn that even though I was an awkward and cerebral teenager, I still read loads of fashion magazines and even tried out to be a model (they think this is hilarious).

You can tell your daughter that while what she is doing is 100 percent understandable, it is your responsibility to protect her from harm, and that you need her to hear what you see when she posts sexy selfies. The problem, we can explain, is not so much with *her* as it is with the people who see her posts. Girls often forget that they are exposing themselves to a world that objectifies and sexualizes girls and young women. Simmons explains further:

> So, while your daughter may see herself as a student, athlete, friend, daughter, sister, and so on, her Instagram viewers—and that includes some of the people she may know and go to school with—may focus only on the body that she is showing. They may not see her as a whole person. **And they may take her less seriously as a person as a result.**

Although girls often feel empowered in the short term by the attention and validation they receive from their sexy selfies, in the long run they are reducing their own power. This is true both in the eyes of others and literally, as research shows that a single, simple comment on a young woman's appearance can measurably (if temporarily) reduce her intellectual capacity.

We can talk to our girls about how sometimes short-term feelings of being attractive and liked on social media don't translate into a true source of power in the world. People won't actually respect them or like them or love them more because of a sexy selfie. It's tricky, but we can help girls see that by posting objectifying and sexualized photos of themselves, they are participating in their own *dis*-empowerment by fostering cultural norms that reduce girls' value to their bodies.

Most teens will make mistakes with the selfies they post. This is why when they are younger, it is important to monitor their social media feeds and have regular discussions with them about it. As with everything else they are learning to do, they will need you to guide them, setting limits where necessary (see chapter two). "Maybe together you can decide that cropping her face out of a photo is not okay, because it's a way of reducing herself to an object instead of a real person," Simmons advises. Or "perhaps you'll suggest she not highlight certain parts of her body."

Simmons outlines some great guidelines for girls for their social media posting in her most recent book *Enough As She Is*:

- Use social media to say something about herself, rather than prove something about herself to others.

- Refrain from using social media as a tool to compete, and instead use it to connect.

- Don't use social media to ask a question about what others think of her, but instead use it to make a statement about what she thinks: about the world, the issues she cares about, or herself.

- Ask herself, before she posts content, a direct question: Why am I doing this? What is my intention? How am I feeling right now? And then be willing to answer that question honestly. If I am looking to be filled up with affirmation from others, is this the right way to do it?

Remember the Goal

If you are feeling overwhelmed, remember that you don't have to teach your teens everything there is to know about sex. Even if they make mistakes, which they will, and even if bad things happen, which they might, they will in all likelihood be okay if they have the resources and support that they need to recover. Perhaps you, like me, know this to be true from your own experience.

When in doubt, try to ask lots of open-ended questions. This is because the goal isn't for us to impart our infinite wisdom to our kids in lecture form. It's to be a resource and support for our kids as they develop healthy sexualities. We want to encourage our teens to share with us what they are afraid of or what they are curious about so that we can weigh in when asked.

To do this, we can phrase our questions in nonjudgmental ways that will prompt them to elaborate. These conversations about sex are difficult for many parents—they are for me—and they require courage, but it's better to suffer through the discomfort now than to regret later not having had a handful of awkward conversations.

Just as parents need to teach kids how to take care of their physical and emotional health, we need to teach our teens how to be healthy sexually. It's hard to talk about sex with kids. It's also the right thing to do. If you feel like you're going to chicken out, simply take a deep breath. Feel your feet on the floor. You can do it.

CHAPTER NINE

Drinking and Drugs

Here is what I wish all teens and their parents knew about
adolescent brain development and addiction.

In every age and culture, human beings have parties and celebrations—for big events like weddings, for holidays, or just for the weekend. Parties give us a chance to play, to not be so serious all the time. We humans need to feel accepted and loved and embraced by a group, and celebrations allow us to feel like we are a part of something larger than ourselves. In Western cultures, inebriation is often a central part of group celebrations. It loosens some people up and helps them express themselves without worry about what other people think.

Today more than ever, we need time to rejoice with our people or to just be present with them, and we need time when we can set aside our worries and responsibilities. Life is stressful, and we need to be able to let off steam or we will implode. And sometimes life is so painful that we just need a break from difficult feelings. Perhaps most of all, we need time to relax in the company of our friends.

Parties where we drink alcohol (and increasingly, use marijuana) give us a way to do all of these things—for us as parents and also for our teenagers. There are, of course, loads of other ways to relax, manage stress, express ourselves, celebrate, and cope with difficulty, but the *easiest* way is often to have a drink. It's so easy, and so normal, that personally I've found it harder *not* to drink in many social situations than it is to just accept the lovely glass of chardonnay that someone just handed me.

The cultural ubiquity of alcohol (and now, in many places, marijuana) puts many parents in a sticky spot when it comes to their teenagers' drug and alcohol use. "Do as I say, not as I do" doesn't fly with teenagers—hypocrisy is never a good coaching strategy, even when there's a law to justify it. And I've found that little is as divisive among the parents of high schoolers as the issue of whether or not to allow kids to drink at parties.

Parents who let their teenagers drink, host parties where alcohol is served, or use marijuana—or those who simply look the other way while they do these things—often make convincing arguments to justify their actions. Here are some common ones in my neck of the woods:

- Teenagers are going to party anyway, so I'd rather that they do it at home, where I can keep an eye on them.

- I'd really rather they drink the light beer I bought them than straight vodka out of a water bottle.

- I talked to the parents and they are going to be home. They'll be safe.

- Kids today are so busy and their lives are so intense. As long as they keep doing well in school, I'm fine if they go out on the weekends and party a little. Work hard, play hard.

- It's completely delusional to think that kids aren't going to party. Do you really want your kids to be the ones who get left out of all the high school fun? Or lie to you and sneak around behind your back? I'd rather my kids be open about what they are doing.

- There are a lot of medicinal properties to marijuana. I think it's healthier than drinking, anyway.

- I just want my kids to be able to handle alcohol like a European.

- *If you don't let them party in high school, they'll go wild in college. Remember so-and-so's kid? Her parents were always so strict, and she overdosed her freshman year at Yale.*

(That last one is the one I hear the most.)

This is a hard issue for parents, and it's a battle that many are electing not to fight. Even though two-thirds of parents don't actually condone teenage drinking, research shows that many make a lot of "exceptions" anyway. Why? Many say they look the other way because teen drinking is "inevitable." In an interesting twist on peer pressure, some parents feel pressured to let their kids drink by other *parents*. Some report worry that if they *don't* let their kids party, it will harm their parent-child relationship, or cause their children to rebel. And some parents just don't *know* what to do. They recall their own teen experiences but have little guidance or understanding about how things are different now or how to set limits with their teens.

The Research

Teenagers have been partying since the beginning of time. How harmful could it really be?

There is a lot of research out there about this, and some of it is surprising. Every year, excessive drinking causes more than 4,300 deaths among under-twenty-one-year-olds and sends 120,000 kids to the emergency room. In addition to increased risk of death, alcohol-related car crashes, and other injuries (like burns and falls), research shows that teenage drinkers are more likely to struggle:

- academically (they have more absences and worse grades)
- intellectually (they have more memory and learning problems)
- socially (they get into more fights and participate in fewer extra-curricular activities)
- physically (they get sick more often, and normal physical growth is more likely to be disrupted)
- sexually (they have more unwanted, unplanned, and unprotected sex)

Teens who use alcohol are also more likely to abuse other drugs, and the earlier they start drinking, the more likely it is that they will develop a "substance use disorder," or addiction, to alcohol or another drug later in life.

All these risks are greater for teens who binge drink. Defined as having more than four drinks (for girls) or five drinks (for boys) within two hours, binge drinking changes teen brains in visible ways—namely, by shrinking them. Recent binge drinking predicts smaller gray and white matter in both brain hemispheres. (White matter is the part of the brain that connects brain regions and affects processing speed; gray matter refers to the actual neurons and other brain cells.) This brain shrinkage causes poorer neurocognitive performance—in other words, binge drinking hinders teenagers' intellectual ability.

Fortunately, teenage drinking is not at all an inevitability. Although alcohol remains the substance most widely used by today's teenagers, fewer teens are drinking in high school. In 2016, nearly 40 percent of high school seniors and almost 60 percent of tenth graders had *never* tried alcohol at all (beyond a sip here or there). The number of eighth graders who have tried alcohol is half what it was in the 1990s. This may be, in part, because they aren't going out and seeing their friends in person as much as they used to, as we saw in chapter five. It may also be because they're using marijuana instead, as we'll see in the next section.

Whatever the reason, **the fact that teens aren't drinking as much is important for teens themselves to know**. Most teenagers have a high need to be a part of "normal" teen culture. These days, if they aren't drinking at all in high school, they are with the *majority*.

Still, a lot of teens do drink. Underage drinking accounts for about 11 percent of all alcohol consumed nationwide. For high school students, the highest drinking rates are among twelfth graders, and about one-third of high school seniors reported drinking alcohol within the last thirty days, with one in five reporting binge drinking.

So what predicts whether teens do or don't drink, especially in high school? Research shows that parents, and parenting, makes an enormous difference.

There is a lot that we can do—detailed below. But before I get to some research-backed strategies for reducing underage drinking, there are a few other things I'd love for you to know about substance abuse.

What I Wish Parents Knew About Pot

Today's teens may be drinking less than previous generations, but they are smoking weed (and vaping it, dabbing it, and eating it) more. I live in California, where marijuana is now legal for recreational use. My four teens report that pot was already very easy to come by before legalization and that now "everyone" uses it.

Fortunately, my kids are wrong. **A large majority of high schoolers have never tried pot at all**, not even in super-permissive California, and marijuana use is actually down a little, not up, over the last few years, because fewer teens are partying. (That very recent decline is a bit deceiving, though, because on the whole, Gen Z uses marijuana more than millennials did as teenagers.)

Attitudes about marijuana are changing, and not for the better. What worries me is that fewer and fewer teens think regular marijuana use is harmful. Fewer than one-third of high school seniors believe that regular marijuana use poses great risk of harm. This is *half* what it was twenty years ago.

Unfortunately, **perceived risk of harm is a very strong indicator of whether or not a teen will eventually use marijuana**. Though most teens don't smoke pot or ingest edibles, a solid 41 percent of American twelfth graders report having used marijuana or synthetic cannabinoids in the past year. That's a very large minority, and as more and more teens no longer understand that regular marijuana use is harmful to them, we can expect to see usage rates go up.

I am not surprised that marijuana is no longer being perceived as harmful. Here in California, the pro-weed movement is huge. We are all now subject to tons of billboards advertising happy, chill marijuana vendors. More than that, kids see (and smell) the adults around them getting stoned at concerts, at trailheads before a hike, and now, just walking down the street—and they assume that marijuana use is harmless and fun.

But nothing could be further from the truth.

Marijuana Slows Brain Development in Adolescence

Brain development is more significant during adolescence than during any other developmental stage (except in the womb). The transition from childhood to adulthood is a critical period of brain growth, and the brain's natural endocannabinoid system—which is affected by marijuana use—plays a very important role in this development.

The unique brain growth that we see only during adolescence is temporarily halted by marijuana use. How? Delta-9-tetrahydrocannabinol (THC), the ingredient in marijuana that produces a high, binds with the brain's cannabinoid (CB1) receptors. This blocks their normal function.

It also makes kids really high. Teenagers have more CB1 receptors than adults do for THC to bind to, and THC also stays in the CB1 receptor for longer than it would in an adult. According to neuroscientist Frances Jensen, author of *The Teenage Brain*, "[THC] locks on longer than in the adult brain. For instance, if [a teen] were to get high over a weekend, the effects may still be there on Thursday and Friday later that week. An adult wouldn't have that same long-term effect."

This is the effect I want parents and teens to understand: While THC is in the CB1 receptor, it **blocks the process of learning and memory and slows, or stops, adolescent brain development**.

Because of this, exposure to marijuana during adolescence "can dramatically alter brain maturation and cause long-lasting neurobiological changes that ultimately affect the function and behavior of the adult brain." This is according to a 2014 review of research published in academic journals that examined the consequences of marijuana use during adolescence, particularly the effects on cognitive functioning, emotional behavior, and the risk of developing a psychiatric disorder in adulthood. **The damage is irreversible.**

I think this bears repeating because, in my experience, parents consistently resist the notion that "a little pot smoking is harmful" by insisting that what I've written here is controversial. You don't have to trust *me* on this. According to Judith Grisel, an internationally recognized neuroscientist and expert on addiction at Bucknell University:

The world's best science now indicates that the long-term consequences of adolescent drug use, acting upon a very plastic brain that is highly tuned to news and pleasure while at the same time a bit retarded in terms of self-control, may be grim. . . . Chronic THC users have an increased tendency to feel blue, show more difficulty with complex reasoning, and suffer from things like anxiety, depression, and social problems. . . . For *adults*, the neural changes caused by marijuana . . . would likely recover with abstinence. However, consequences are more likely to be permanent when exposure occurs during adolescence. In addition to dampening reward sensitivity, THC acts in pathways that ascribe value or import to our experiences, and if these are muted, especially for a lifetime, the impacts are likely to be broad and deep. The heart of the matter is that the brain adapts to any drug that alters its activity and it appears to do this permanently when exposure occurs during development.

It's not controversial that marijuana causes brain damage in adolescence. It's a well-understood phenomenon.

Marijuana Use Is Associated with Severe Mental Illness

In addition to having long-lasting consequences on IQ and intelligence, early marijuana use is also associated with a two-fold increase in the risk of developing a psychotic disorder, like schizophrenia or bipolar disorder.

Many parents I know find this extremely difficult to believe, as do my own teenagers. Collectively, we really have been led to believe that pot is fairly harmless, but again, the limited medical research we do have on marijuana use in teenagers and adults demonstrates otherwise. In early 2017, the National Academy of Medicine released a comprehensive five-hundred-page report summarizing the scientific literature on the effects of cannabis use. Their conclusions related to mental illness were surprising—and conclusive.

The report clearly states that **there is "substantial scientific evidence" that cannabis use increases the risk of developing**

schizophrenia or other psychoses. The risk is highest among the most frequent users. In addition, the report states that there is clear evidence in the scientific literature that cannabis use increases risk for:

- the development of depressive disorders
- the incidence of suicidal ideation and suicide attempts and increases incidence of suicide completion
- the incidence of social anxiety disorder

In other words, contrary to popular belief, marijuana use doesn't make people feel happier or less anxious in social situations across the board—it also often increases depression, anxiety, and suicidality.

Moreover, it isn't the case that people who already struggle with depression, anxiety, or other mental illnesses are self-medicating with cannabis. The report found that anxiety, personality disorders, and bipolar disorders are not risk factors for the development of problem cannabis use—it's the other way around. Cannabis use, especially early cannabis use, is a risk factor for these mental and emotional disorders.

Still, 71 percent of high school seniors do not view "regular marijuana usage" to be harmful to their health. Most wouldn't smoke a cigarette because they understand that smoking is unhealthy. **It's time for us adults to be clearer with teens that marijuana is not a healthier choice.**

Marijuana Today Can Be Very Addictive, Especially for Teens

Most people think marijuana is "healthier" than alcohol or tobacco in part because they believe it isn't addictive. But pot can be very habit-forming. Surprisingly, marijuana use is associated with higher rates of behavioral problems than alcohol, including addiction. In 2016, 21 percent of current adult marijuana users met diagnostic criteria for dependence. Studies indicate that as many as 33 percent of users develop a diagnosable addiction, especially with strains of marijuana that have a higher THC content.

Teenagers are especially susceptible to addiction—to alcohol, to social media, to pornography, and, yes, to marijuana. In the same way that teens learn faster than adults do, it is also easier for their brains to "learn" an addiction. Learning stimulates and enhances the brain. Substances like marijuana do the same thing, but during adolescence, teen brains "build a reward circuit around that substance to a much stronger, harder, longer addiction," according to Jensen. "**The effects of substances are more permanent on the teen brain**," Jensen told National Public Radio. "They have more deleterious effects and can be more toxic to the teen than the adult."

Pot Today Is a Different Drug Than It Was a Generation Ago

I think a lot of parents in my generation believe that marijuana isn't harmful or addictive because it probably *wasn't* back in the day. **THC concentrations have skyrocketed upward in recent years, and growers have bred the antipsychotic properties out of today's marijuana.**

Reports differ depending on where marijuana is sourced, but studies of THC concentration in cannabis show that before 1980, concentration of THC averaged around 1.5 percent. Potency rose to about 3 percent in the early 1980s and stayed there until about 1992, when it began to rise steadily. In the last decade, samples have averaged about 11 percent THC; currently, specific breeding techniques are yielding strains that are 27 to 33 percent THC. Experts believe that this is likely now the norm in states where recreational marijuana is legal because higher THC concentration yields a more lucrative product.

Edibles: These Ain't Your Mama's Brownies

Teens who might hesitate to smoke or vape marijuana often feel less fearful about eating food made with cannabis, like a chocolate bar or gummy bear. There's no unfamiliar bong, dangerous smoke, or vape pen battery that needs to be charged. But edibles are a dicey way to get high, because the risk of overdose is much greater.

Why? Because it is difficult to know how much THC a user is actually ingesting, even if the edible is not homemade and the THC concentration is clearly labeled on the package. Edible THC is absorbed through the digestive system and metabolized by the liver into a more potent compound called 11-hydroxy-THC. This metabolite crosses the blood-brain barrier more efficiently and usually produces more intense effects. It also has a longer half-life and can be very sedating.

It can take up to three hours for a user to metabolize THC they've ingested, though it more commonly takes about forty-five minutes. While it is possible to feel some effect of the drug as early as twenty minutes after consumption, the concentration in a user's bloodstream will gradually increase for several hours. The effects of edible marijuana generally last four to six hours. Because the effects of *smoking* marijuana generally take only a minute or so to feel, teenagers often think the drug isn't working when they eat it, and they end up consuming much larger amounts—and getting much higher—than they would if they'd smoked or vaped marijuana.

Among online edible sellers, the generally agreed-upon starter dose for beginners (basically anyone who hasn't built up a THC tolerance) is 1 to 2.5 mg of THC. Most small edible cannabis chocolate bars contain 50 mg of THC and are scored into 12 squares, each barely larger than a raisin. This means that a single dose would be a quarter to a half of a *single small square*. But get this: Marijuana gummy bears generally contain 10 mg of THC. So it's not surprising that many new users end up curled up in a hallucinatory state for eight or more hours after just a couple of bites. If you aren't convinced that this is a common outcome, read the *New York Times* reporter Maureen Dowd's harrowing account of her first edible experience in Colorado. She ended up paralyzed and hallucinating on a hotel bed, with the paranoid delusion that she had died but no one had told her.

There are a lot of other factors that can affect how a teenager's body might interact with the cannabinoids found in edibles. If the user has other medications in their system, for example, their body may metabolize more or less of the THC they ingest. This is why overdose symptoms from eating marijuana—such as psychotic episodes, hallucinations, paranoia, temporary paralysis, and panic attacks—are often more severe than symptoms of an overdose from smoking marijuana.

Dabbing

You've probably seen your kids dabbing—a dance move where they throw their elbow across their face like they are covering a sneeze. The dab dance started with a rap group and exploded in popularity in 2015 when NFL players started doing it to celebrate touchdowns. What a lot of parents don't know, though, is that "the dab" is so-named because it looks like what people do when they inhale super-potent marijuana concentrates, sometimes referred to as honey oil, wax, budder, sugar, or shatter. They cough and collapse back a little. This is called "dabbing," and it is like smoking crack cocaine in that it delivers upwards of 80 percent THC.

The high, as you might imagine, is huge, and so are the side effects. They include, according to Emily Feinstein, the executive vice president of the Center on Addiction, "a rapid heartbeat, blackouts, psychosis, paranoia, and hallucinations that cause people to end up in psychiatric facilities."

But wait, there's more: Twenty years ago, marijuana had higher levels of cannabidiol (CBD), a nonpsychoactive cannabinoid. Although CBD may have medicinal benefits, growers are breeding CBD out of marijuana intended for recreational use. Why? Because it keeps users from getting as high as they would without the CBD.

Higher THC concentrations and lower CBD produces a higher high—and also a higher potential for overdose. A THC overdose won't kill a kid, but it can produce hallucinations, panic attacks, and extreme paranoia, and an overdose can cause psychotic disorders that can be hard for a teenager to ever recover from.

All of this is to say that marijuana use is not harmless for kids today, by any stretch of the imagination.

And Then Came JUUL

New technologies for using marijuana and nicotine have recently appeared and become widespread among teenagers. In 2017, the big national surveys started measuring the scores of kids who vape marijuana and nicotine, and at the time I'm writing this, JUUL is by far the most popular brand of vape pens and cartridges. Using one is called "JUULing" (pronounced "jeweling").

The skinny on vaping: Vape devices (also known as e-cigs, mods, vape pens, vapes, tank systems, and JUULs), contain a tank to hold e-liquid (or e-juice or vape sauce), a heating element (or atomizer), a battery, and a mouthpiece. Some vape devices look like regular cigarettes, cigars, or pipes, while others, like JUULs, resemble USB sticks. Tank systems are larger and look more like small cell phones. Some devices can be recharged using a computer USB port. The user either fills a chamber with the e-liquid or uses a disposable, self-contained pod.

Vaping isn't technically smoking because it doesn't involve burning anything. Instead, e-cigarettes release an aerosol that is inhaled and leaves so little trace (no smoke, no smell) that kids can easily vape at school or at home and not get caught.

Fewer and fewer teens regularly smoke cigarettes—less than 6 percent now, compared to 29 percent in the 1970s—but by their senior year of high school, more than one-third of teenagers have vaped, and one-quarter do it regularly. Vaping is appealing to many kids because it's often candy- or fruit-flavored (e-liquids come in thousands of flavors, including bubble gum, cotton candy, and grape, but also hot dog, banana bread, and king crab legs—which makes this adult's stomach turn).

Both marijuana and nicotine can be vaped, but many kids don't actually know what they are vaping. Of the twelfth graders who report vaping, for example, only one-quarter said they vaped nicotine. While many admit to vaping marijuana, one-third said that they vaped "only flavoring." But 99 percent of commercial products that can be vaped (like those sold in supermarkets and convenience stores) contain nicotine. Another study found that 63 percent of JUUL users did not know that the JUUL products they were using *always* contain nicotine. Not only that, but JUUL pods contain almost *double* the nicotine compared to other e-cigarette cartridges.

This means that kids who are JUULing are at an extremely high risk for addiction. Nicotine is as addictive as a drug gets, far more addictive than cocaine or opioids. And the earlier the developing brain is exposed to nicotine, the more rapidly kids become addicted—and the harder it will be for them to quit.

Most kids believe vaping nicotine isn't as harmful as smoking. But given that smoking is still the leading cause of preventable disease and death in the United States, there are a lot of activities that aren't as harmful as smoking but are still quite dangerous.

The truth is that vaping is far from harmless. At the time I'm writing this, the CDC has just started tracking and reporting the thousands of lung injuries and more than two dozen deaths caused by vaping. Like smoke, the aerosol that is inhaled consists of toxic chemicals, many of which are Group I carcinogens, the most potent and harmful carcinogens known. The chemicals, ultrafine particles, and heavy metals (such as nickel, tin, and lead) that are inhaled when vaping are known to cause cancer and lung disease.

Moreover, **vaping often leads to smoking tobacco**. We are already seeing that youth who vape are more than four times as likely as those who do not vape to begin smoking tobacco within eighteen months.

Finally, the greatest risk, in my mind, is what addiction to nicotine at a young age does to the developing brain. Nicotine addiction changes adolescents' threshold for addiction to other behaviors and substances. This means that **kids who regularly vape nicotine in high school (or younger) become especially prone to substance abuse, eating disorders, and addiction later in life**.

The Opioid Crisis and Other Illicit Drugs

The good news is that other than marijuana, illegal drug use is down relative to previous generations. The bad news is that the proportion of teenagers today who have used any illicit drug other than marijuana is still pretty high. About one in five twelfth graders report having used illicit drugs such as LSD or other hallucinogens, MDMA (also called E, ecstasy, or molly), cocaine, crack, heroin, ketamine, phencyclidine (PCP), amphetamines, methamphetamine (crystal meth), synthetics (Spice/K2 or Kratom), or steroids.

As a parent, my biggest concern is opioid use, because, surprisingly, opioid use often starts right at home. Most problematic teenage opioid use begins with a legitimate prescription painkiller. As a sociologist, my biggest concern is how heroin and other opioids are destroying American communities. More Americans die from opioid overdoses than car crashes these days, a trend driven by prescription painkillers.

Up to 80 percent of heroin users begin by misusing prescription painkillers. Many teens get hooked on opioids that were prescribed by a doctor after an injury or medical procedure (like having their wisdom teeth out). Although 95 percent of parents believe their child has never taken a prescription painkiller for a reason other than its intended use, 10 percent of teens report having abused or misused prescription drugs. More than half of those teens got the drugs at home, from family members, or from friends.

Research shows that legitimate teen opioid use during high school—taking pain medicines prescribed specifically for them by their doctor—is associated with a 33 percent increase in the risk of opioid abuse *after* high school. This increase in risk is concentrated among teenagers who have little to no history of drug use and, most surprisingly, have a strong disapproval of illegal drug use in high school.

We Americans hate to feel any sort of pain, and we parents definitely cannot stand to see our children in pain, but our inability to tolerate pain can have dire consequences. There are two ways that I believe that we parents can help reverse the opioid crisis. First, we can help our kids learn that they are actually strong enough to handle some pain. This does not, of course, mean that we let them suffer excessively, or that we inflict pain on them so that they might "toughen up." It does mean that we approach pain without panic. Pain sucks, but it is a part of life. There will be times, like when we get hurt or when we have surgery, that we need to withstand a little pain as a part of the healing process, and sometimes the drawbacks of pain medications are greater than the benefits. Sometimes we will actually *choose*, for our own health and well-being, to feel a little pain instead of taking medication to dull it.

Second, we can teach kids strategies to manage pain, both physical and emotional, without drugs. And we can give teens drug-free ways to cope with the stressors that make prescription painkillers more appealing, like those listed below.

So What's a Parent to Do?

Sadly, it's not enough for us to just talk to our kids about the risks related to underage drinking, vaping, or drug use—or to hand them this chapter to read. It would be *so much easier* if we could just load up our kids with information and then trust them to make rational decisions based on our helpful warnings. But telling kids what they need to know doesn't tend to change their behavior. Instead, we need to address the underlying causes of their drinking and drugging behaviors.

Teenagers are famously bad at understanding that the risks apply to *them*, too. The teenage brain isn't yet developed enough to be able to

IS ECSTASY HELPFUL OR HARMFUL?

Where I live in the San Francisco Bay Area, a large and well-respected organization called the Multidisciplinary Association for Psychedelic Studies is doing research on the ways that MDMA (also known as E, ecstasy, or molly) can be used to help people with life-threatening diseases like cancer deal with crippling anxiety and fear of dying.

Preliminary results of other research show that MDMA, typically a party drug, might be a promising new treatment for combat veterans with post-traumatic stress disorder. Studies like these had led me to believe that MDMA was pretty harmless, but according to neuroscientist Judith Grisel, "the dark side of this drug is truly awful. Many regular users look to be headed for a lifetime of depression and anxiety."

Why? Research shows that MDMA can damage nerve terminals, perhaps permanently. Primates given ecstasy four days in a row showed reductions in their serotonergic neurons *seven years later.* The serotonergic neurons influence our sense of well-being profoundly, and they are what prescription antidepressant medications like Prozac and Lexapro affect. Even more concerning, a large study accessing long-term effects of MDMA on humans showed similar results. Both current recreational MDMA users and those who'd been *abstinent for four to nine years* showed "significantly more clinically relevant levels of depression, impulsiveness, poor sleep, and memory impairment."

accurately predict the cause and effect of their actions—or to reason maturely, given their natural tendencies toward risk-taking and impulsiveness. And as we've seen in previous chapters, we can't just legislate the limits and expect our kids not to rebel. Each family is different, of course, but here are three research-based strategies for reducing teenage drug and alcohol abuse.

1. Ask Questions and Listen

While it's true that just giving our kids information doesn't work, that doesn't mean that we can't have a conversation with our kids about all this. Research shows that for a conversation to make a difference, however, it can't be all scare tactics and horror stories. And it needs to be a two-sided conversation where *teens* do most of the talking.

We can begin the conversation by acknowledging that kids get drunk and high for reasons that make some sense given their individual or social contexts. They want to feel accepted by a peer group, for example, and drug and alcohol use is a low barrier to entry. Or they are really curious about what it feels like to get stoned, and they don't really believe that marijuana is harmful. Or they are stressed and scattered, and nicotine makes them more focused.

There are dozens of reasons that kids drink and do drugs. But research indicates that **most kids aren't getting drunk or high because of peer pressure or just because they feel like getting high, but rather as a way to counter stress and anxiety**. Drinking and using drugs can temporarily help a lonely, isolated, or socially anxious teen feel included and accepted. Teens who are struggling with depression—perhaps because of family conflicts, school stress, or social awkwardness—might feel good only when they are using. In cases like these, it's entirely pointless for parents (or teachers) to wax on about the dangers of early addiction and the brain damage that can come from binge drinking and drug use.

To find out *why* our kids might be tempted to use drugs and alcohol, we use the tactics outlined in chapter three. We begin with empathy (rather than that place of fear that comes so naturally to me). First, we ask them what they are dealing with—whether that is peer pressure, curiosity, or unmanaged stress and anxiety. Our goal is to listen, to really see them, without judgment.

In our household, it has helped to begin by talking about why some *adults* use drugs and alcohol—to relax, blow off steam, feel less anxious and more accepted, or even just feel happy—and then ask our kids why they think *teenagers* drink. How are teens like adults? How are they different?

We can help our teens clarify for themselves not just the dangers, but the *upsides* to drug and alcohol use. What are they (or their peers) looking for when they use? What do they find or experience that they like? Once we know this—and *they* know this—healthier alternatives can become more apparent, and more appealing.

Stress and Anxiety

The reality is that drugs and alcohol *can* help teens relax and provide some relief from social anxiety and the other stresses and pressures they are facing. But this method of stress relief can quickly backfire. **Drugs and alcohol don't *eliminate* anxiety and other difficult emotions, they *mask* them.** And research shows that self-medication with drugs or alcohol can actually amplify underlying emotional problems, making things worse in the long run.

Most teens know that alcohol, for example, makes them feel less inhibited, which is why they call it "liquid courage." But they don't realize that drugs and alcohol also act on parts of the brain that ultimately make them feel flat, unmotivated, and depressed. This, in turn, can make them feel *more* anxious and/or depressed in their everyday lives. Similarly, many kids don't realize that a common side effect of marijuana use is anxiety, panic, and paranoia.

We need to teach teens that drug and alcohol use affects the balance of chemicals in their brain in ways that often make daily stressors harder to deal with. (See chapter six for more about inhibited dopamine function.) It also leaves them more prone to serious bouts of anxiety and depression.

All of this is fodder for further conversations with your teens, particularly if you know your teens are already using or if they have friends who are using regularly. Ask them to think about the role that drugs and/or alcohol are playing in their friends' (or their own) stress and anxiety management. Are they using to numb difficult emotions or forget about their problems? If so, what would be more constructive ways to deal with their stress, anxiety, or problems?

Academic Pressure

Depression and anxiety usually originate with what researchers call a "dysregulated stress response." This means that the parts of the brain that signal threats become hyperactive, making teens feel bombarded with worrying thoughts and anxious feelings. Anxiety can balloon on kids, so that they have larger and larger stress responses to smaller and smaller stimuli. Many teens' drug and alcohol use is an attempt to damp down that dysregulated stress response. This is why teens who are under chronic stress are more likely to turn to marijuana and alcohol to relax.

Teens who go to school in highly competitive or rigorous academic environments can face a specific form of stress and anxiety that often leads to a different type of drug abuse. Stimulant drugs such as caffeine, nicotine, prescription amphetamines like Adderall, and prescription methylphenidates like Ritalin and Concerta all act on the reward center in teenagers' brains, causing them to release more dopamine. This makes them feel more alert, focused, and motivated. Because of this, stimulants tend to improve academic performance in the short term, while worsening their already inhibited dopamine function over time.

Here again we can ask questions and listen. Are our kids under too much pressure at school? Where does that pressure originate? Does it make them feel tempted to use stimulants? If so, which ones?

2. Bulk Up on Protective Factors

Twenty years ago, Icelandic teens were among the heaviest-drinking in Europe. Then, in the late 1990s, psychologists from around the world teamed up with the Icelandic government to address Iceland's underage drinking problem. The results? Today Iceland boasts Europe's soberest teens. In 1998, 42 percent of Icelandic fifteen- and sixteen-year-olds reported getting drunk in the previous month. In 2016, only 5 percent did. The percentage who use marijuana is down from 17 percent to 7 percent. In 1998, nearly one-quarter smoked cigarettes daily, but by 2016 that percentage had plummeted to just 3 percent.

How did Iceland do this? Simply by providing healthier options to partying. Iceland's program was "designed around the idea of giving kids better things to do" than get high and drunk, explains Harvey Milkman, an American research psychologist who was an architect of Iceland's plan.

Iceland's goal was not necessarily to treat kids with drinking and drug problems as much as it was to prevent kids from starting in the first place. To find out what would help with prevention, they did some research and identified four main factors that seemed to be protecting teens:

1. participation in organized activities, especially athletics, three or four times a week
2. total time spent with parents during the week
3. feeling cared about at school
4. not being outdoors in the late evenings

So Iceland massively expanded access to after-school sports, music, dance, and arts programs, to give all kids lots of ways to feel included in a larger social group. The government launched a national campaign that encouraged parents to spend more time with their teens, educating them about the importance of "quantity time" with teens, especially during the week. The parent education campaign also directly recommended that parents not let minors drink or go to unsupervised parties, encouraging parents to watch out for their own kids and also to care about the well-being of other teens in their neighborhoods. Finally, Iceland passed laws prohibiting teens sixteen and under from being outside after 10:00 PM.

What I love about Iceland's list of protective factors is that it is all so commonsensical. It is easily replicable anywhere in the world. While we might not be able to control how cared-for our kids feel in their schools, many parents can influence their teens' extracurricular activities, the time they spend with us (their parents), and how late they are outdoors.

Healthier Ways to Cope

Like Iceland, we can help prevent drug and alcohol abuse (as well as anxiety and depression) by giving teens alternatives that address the underlying causes of their desire to use drugs and alcohol. Here are the most effective, research-based strategies:

- Many teens drink and do drugs because partying offers relatively easy entry and **acceptance into a social group**—something that all teens (all human beings, for that matter) long for. Iceland addressed this underlying cause by supporting and encouraging after-school sports and arts participation, which are more positive ways to feel a connection to something larger than yourself. It's harder to make a team, audition for a play, or muster the courage to create art than it is to go to a party and get drunk, but the sense of belonging and accomplishment that comes from these activities is usually far more profound.

In addition, extracurricular activities are protective because they address the underlying cause of increased risk-taking in teenagers. Drugs and alcohol are often included in the risks some teens are tempted to take. But many extracurricular activities require risk-taking as well. For example, the prospect of public failure is always a possibility with most sports and performing arts. This is the type of positive risk that we *want* our teens to take regularly.

- Encourage teens to get out into **nature** regularly. Support regular camping trips and outdoor excursions. A mountain of research (pun intended) shows that being in the natural world— even a leafy park—can stimulate the relaxation response. Exposure to nature has also been shown to reduce stress and improve focus, concentration, and motivation.

- **Exercise** is nonnegotiable for today's teenagers. Even moderate exercise has been shown to:

  — reduce stress and anxiety

  — give more energy

  — increase happiness and emotional well-being

  — improve ability to focus, resist temptations, and make good decisions

  — improve memory and learning

- **Practice gratitude.** As with exercise, gratitude practitioners reap loads of benefits. For example, people who jotted down something they were grateful for every day for just two weeks showed higher stress resilience and greater satisfaction with life. In addition, they reported fewer headaches and a reduction in stomach pain, coughs, and sore throats!

People practicing gratitude even report sleeping better and getting more exercise. Gratitude is associated with more effective learning strategies, more helpfulness toward others, raised self-confidence, a better work attitude, strengthened resiliency, less physical pain, and improved health.

But what if your teen leans more toward the grouchy or cynical rather than the grateful? Gratitude is still a skill they can learn, just as they would a new language or sport. Teens need only to regularly count the things in their lives that they feel thankful for.

The bad news is that it can't be forced. Cynical teens can be encouraged, but don't ask them to share what they are grateful for with you. Research shows that expressing gratitude can make teenagers feel more beholden to their parents at a time when they need more independence.

- **Meditation** is a terrifically effective antidote for stressed or scattered teens. Scores of studies have shown the benefits of meditation to be broad and profound: Meditation lowers stress and anxiety, improves focus, and makes teens more productive.

  These days, many schools receive funding from private foundations to teach kids Transcendental Meditation (TM), which research suggests is fantastic for the mental health of our youth. In fact, compared to other mindfulness and relaxation techniques, TM is the most effective for stress and anxiety reduction.

- Support their **sleep**! Sleep affects virtually every aspect of our lives, including teens' ability to cope with stress and academic pressure. Even 20 minutes of sleep deprivation three days in a row can dramatically lower teens' IQ. This increases their stress and academic pressure while decreasing their ability to *cope* with the stress.

  Sleep deprivation can also in and of itself be an underlying cause of drug and alcohol abuse. As discussed in chapter seven, sleep deprivation is extremely stressful to the adolescent brain and body. This makes it unsurprising that teens who don't get enough sleep have more drinking-related problems. In one study, teenagers who had trouble falling or staying asleep were 47 percent more likely to binge drink than their well-rested peers. They also were more likely to have serious drinking-related problems later in life. Another large study of teenagers showed that in addition to binge drinking, being short on sleep significantly predicted alcohol-related interpersonal problems, driving drunk, getting into a sexual situation that they later regretted due to drinking, and ever using any illicit drugs.

Fortunately, the effects were reversible. In one study, each extra hour of sleep teenagers got corresponded with a 10 percent decrease in binge drinking. As a reminder, the American Sleep Association—as well as other experts, like the prominent sleep researcher Matthew Walker—recommend that teenagers get 9 hours and 20 minutes of sleep per night.

This is not an exhaustive list of all the things that we parents can do to address the underlying causes of teen drug and alcohol abuse. The takeaway here is that teens don't need us to remind them to "make good choices" as much as they need good choices as an option—and the structure and support to point them toward healthier ways to cope.

3. Draw a Bright Line

My husband and I have taken what is, in our neck of the woods, a controversial stance. We are so clear about our expectation that our teens not use marijuana (or other drugs, including nicotine) that we drug test them using inexpensive tests from our local drugstore. We aren't doing this because we believe our children have used or will use drugs, or because we don't trust them to tell us if they do. (So far, no tests have ever turned up positive.) We do it because it gives them a solid excuse to abstain. They can say to their friends, "My parents are so crazy about this issue that they drug test me."

Teenagers need us to draw a super clear, bright line about our expectations. They don't do well with mixed messages from parents, especially around drug and alcohol use, and especially when they believe use might not be harmful to them. **So, as parents, we need to be crystal clear with our teenagers about our expectations that they not drink or do drugs.** When your kids tell you that "everyone is doing it," show them the data: Actually, a majority of kids *aren't* doing it. If you know that all their particular friends actually *are* drinking or doing drugs, this is a hard thing for teens to be left out of. Acknowledge that and make sure your kids understand that you understand how hard it is—and that you still expect them to abstain. That may mean that they need to find a healthier friend group.

Interestingly, our kids have never protested being drug tested, and they seem genuinely glad that we are so black and white about all this. They know that they will be making their own choices soon, when they are adults. For now, they seem happy that we are making the choice for them.

Many parents hesitate to draw a bright line because they have in the back of their minds that kids who abstain in high school will go wild in college—that when they are finally "free," they will overindulge in the forbidden fruit. But **there is no evidence that high school drinking and drug use "readies" kids to be more moderate users in college**. On the contrary, there is plenty of evidence that the earlier kids start using, the more likely it is that their drinking or drug use will be more extreme in college. Don't kid yourself: Teens don't need to "practice" addictive behavior in high school. **Early use is not protective . . . it's a risk factor.**

Parents often unintentionally send kids a mixed message about their expectations by *funding* kids' participation in drug- and alcohol-fueled experiences like fraternities and sororities, graduation trips, and "beach week." In some families and communities, these are long-standing traditions, and since parents themselves survived, say, fraternity hazing, it is easier to see them as harmless. But just because something is an old tradition does not mean that it is a good tradition. The world is radically different now, and it's hugely important that we parents not normalize bad behavior, or self-harm.

As parents, it is our job to construct speed bumps for our teens' risky behaviors (rather than enable them). **Money, or lack thereof, can be a fantastic speed bump.** With older kids, this is a good way to allow teens and college students to make their own choices. If they want to go on an alcohol- and weed-infused spring break trip, you don't have to pay for it. If that is how they want to spend their hard-earned minimum-wage savings, that's their call. As parents, we send a crystal-clear message about our values and our hopes for our kids by choosing not to fund underage binge drinking and other unhealthy behaviors.

In privileged communities, not-enabling might require an extra dose of empathy for our teens. (Cue the tiny violins.) We can acknowledge that it is hard not to be given everything that "everyone else" is given. We can accept that it is hard, even painful, for them to feel left out. That not being able to join a fraternity because your parents won't pay for it can be a distressing blow to their social status. It may force them to find a different—and, dare I say it, healthier—source of status and inclusion. Fortunately, they are strong enough to handle these things.

And by the same token, we can choose to fund healthier alternatives if we have the means. (If we don't have the means, we can support our kids in seeking scholarship funding.) Outdoor experiences and abroad programs make great alternatives to alcohol-centric Greek life on college campuses. And while these sorts of programs can be similarly expensive, they are a great investment in our kids' healthy behavior.

Knowing What They Are Consuming

Here's what drawing a bright line does *not* mean: withholding information about drugs and drinking that might reduce harm from use. We can say to our kids, "I do not condone underage drinking, marijuana or nicotine use, the use of any illicit drugs, or the abuse of prescription painkillers or prescription stimulants. And at the same time, if you or your friends are going to do it anyway, I want you to understand some ways that you can reduce harm and injury to yourself and others."

After we draw that bright line, we can make sure that teens understand what they or their friends are consuming, so they know when they are getting into a danger zone. For starters, in order to understand what binge drinking is, teenagers need to know what constitutes one standard drink:

- **12 ounces of regular beer** (4.5 percent alcohol). This means that a typical 16-ounce Solo cup filled three times from a keg of regular beer equals four and a half drinks. A 40-ounce bottle of beer equals more than three and a half drinks.

- **7 ounces of an IPA or darker beer, or malt liquor** (7 percent alcohol). A 22-ounce bottle of malt liquor equals three drinks. Three ale-type beers out of a Solo cup equals about seven drinks.

- **5 ounces of wine** (12 percent alcohol). A 12-ounce glass of wine is almost three drinks.

- **1½ ounces (1 "shot," or just 3 tablespoons) of hard liquor** (40 percent alcohol). A Solo cup or water bottle filled with half hard alcohol and half juice or mixer is equal to six drinks.

- **½ ounce of Everclear** (95 percent alcohol). A single shot of Everclear—one-third of a shot glass—is equal to three standard drinks.

Here are some other things you might want to discuss with your teens that fall into the "harm reduction" category:

- Hard alcohol and energy drinks are a bad concoction. Caffeine makes alcohol more addictive; moreover, the combination of caffeine and alcohol makes people feel more alert when they are drunk, and this keeps drinkers from realizing how drunk they truly are. Caffeine disarms the body's natural response to alcohol—drowsiness—which encourages us to stop drinking and go to bed. All of this can worsen the problems associated with binge drinking.

- Not all marijuana is the same. Make sure kids know that THC concentrations matter a lot, so if they are going to use marijuana, it's important for them to know what they are using.

- Ecstasy and other drugs that teens might take at music festivals or rave-type parties are often laced with other dangerous drugs. So too with opioids. Here in the San Francisco Bay Area, three youths have recently overdosed on what they thought were prescription opioids but were actually counterfeit and laced with the opioid fentanyl. For that reason, as parents, we might decide to have at-home testing kits (widely available online) so that teens can test street drugs to see what is in them. Kids who are interested in a hallucinogen, for example, might not want to take it once they know it is laced with meth or heroin. By providing such testing kits at home (perhaps "for their friends"), we can raise kids' awareness of the dangers of taking street drugs.

In our family, we do let our older teens go to parties where some kids will likely be drinking and vaping. And we don't track our kids' whereabouts on their phones, because we want them to feel independent and responsible for their own behaviors. But we also recognize that sometimes we need to support them in getting out of a situation they can no longer handle. We use our version of an "X-plan." If they text us a code word, we immediately call and tell them something serious has come up, and they need to get home right away (or that we are on our way to get them).

We're so clear that we will support them if they get into trouble that we put it in writing (see Appendix):

> If for any reason you feel uncomfortable in a given situation, you may call us and we will retrieve you—no questions asked— from any circumstance at any time of the day or night. We understand that you will make mistakes and misjudge situations, and we'd like you to correct your mistakes before they become dangerous. Err on the side of caution. You can probably expect to have a conversation with us over breakfast the next morning about how, perhaps, you found yourself at a strange party fifteen miles from home, but we want to be clear: **We will never give you a reason to regret asking for help.**

I'm hopeful that our kids don't now and won't later abuse drugs or alcohol. Even so, I know that they all have an active interest in protecting their friends who *do* use from harm. For that reason, even if they aren't using drugs themselves, they may need all this information. Hopefully, they will put it to good use.

In the end, one of the most important things that we can do as parents is model healthy behavior. We need to show kids that we can enjoy alcohol-free parties and that we don't need to drink or use drugs to have fun or to relax. Sometimes, modeling is hard. It's also probably the most important thing we can do for our kids.

CHAPTER TEN

Money

*Want to raise a teen who doesn't act spoiled, doesn't spend money
irresponsibly, and can distinguish between debit and credit? Me too.*

What stresses you out?

If you are like many Americans, money does. Two-thirds of
adults in America say that money is a significant stressor, and 30 percent say they worry about money constantly. This is not surprising—
according to the Federal Reserve, the average American household
with any kind of debt carries $135,768 in debt (this includes mort-
gages), and yet the median household income is just $59,039.

Nor is it surprising that Americans are carrying more debt than
in previous generations. Medical costs, for example, have increased
33 percent, and takeout meals and restaurant prices have increased 27
percent since 2008—but the median income has grown only 22 percent. Similarly, auto loan balances have risen by 42 percent in the last
decade, and, incredibly, student loan debt has increased by a whop-
ping 144 percent in the past decade, thanks to skyrocketing college
tuition rates.

While many parents think that financial stress is for adults, teens
worry about money, too. The annual Stress in America survey revealed
that *one-third* of Gen Z is already stressed about their personal debt—
what they owe on their credit cards, car payments, and student loans.

While we parents might not be able to do much about the increasing cost of living or the climbing price of college tuition, there is a lot
that we can teach our kids so that they know how to manage their

money—whether they have a lot or a little—wisely. Consciously or not, parents tend to teach their children "the value of the dollar." We pass down to our children our emotional relationship with money—what it means to us, how much we value it, and how we feel about it—as well as the practical aspects of how to earn, save, invest, and manage it.

Once again, the world has changed, and so has our teens' relationship with money. Because more and more things that used to be considered luxuries are now considered necessities, the siren song of consumption is much stronger for some teens than it used to be. And as social media has made us all more status-aware, more and more of our kids are taking on materialistic values that put money front and center.

Even if our kids don't have more materialistic values than they did in previous generations, or if they aren't with the 82 percent of freshman college students who currently say that being "very well off financially" is important to them (an all-time high for a survey that began in 1967), they will likely have more stuff—more clothing, more technology, and more consumer goods—than any generation before them. Simply owning more stuff will require greater stewardship of those material belongings, which will take more time and attention.

Teens and Money

Most teens aren't naturally skillful with their money. A few years ago, I heard a radio interview that has stuck with me. The interview, which went viral, was a cautionary tale of a privileged young woman named Kim who blew her college fund. Her grandparents, Kim said, had given her $90,000 to attend a school that would cost her $20,000 a year. But the summer before her senior year, the money was gone, so she had no way of finishing her degree. Kim said she spent the money on clothes and other goodies not related to tuition. "I probably should have not done that. I took a trip to Europe."

Kim blamed her parents. "Maybe they should have taught me to budget or something," she said. "They never sat me down and had a real serious talk about it."

The issue Kim's interview raised is real. Most kids won't be able to teach themselves how to be financially responsible adults. Financial

WHAT DO YOUR KIDS OVERHEAR
YOU SAY ABOUT MONEY?

Some children grow up anxious about money because they hear their parents fight about it, complain about it, and worry out loud about whether or not they have enough. My dear friend Rona Renner, author of *Is That Me Yelling?*, was one of those children. She started to work at a young age because her family was very poor, but even though she was earning real money and helping to pay for her family's expenses, she never had a good sense about how to manage the money she was earning or the positive power that it was giving her and her family.

Renner advises parents not to burden kids with money problems. This doesn't mean that you can't tell your children what you can and can't afford. It's important to be able to tell a child, "We can't take that trip until we have more money saved for it." But it does mean that as parents, we do well not to let them overhear us worrying about our worst money fears.

Money does not have to be the conversational third rail our culture has deemed it to be. There is a big difference between overhearing your parents arguing about money and hearing them have a calm and deliberative conversation about it. This also goes for when there is a change to a family's financial situation (like a divorce or job loss): be honest, but manage the stress outside of your teen's earshot.

literacy is something that is taught, usually by parents (who may need to do a little financial skill-building themselves) or a financially savvy grandparent.

The goal, in my mind, is for my children to graduate from college having already managed their own money (with me and their other parents supervising). I want them to have a working budget and to have paid every type of bill that they will need to pay out there in the real world. I want them to know the difference between savings and checking accounts, between credit and debit cards. I want them to have some experience paying down a debt, for them to understand how interest compounds—and how interest can leave them either more deeply in debt or, in the case of investments, wealthier.

I want my kids to understand that money will not appear in relationship to their desire or even their need. I want them to experience the joy and the positive power that comes from giving their money away to people and causes they believe in, and the joy of spending money on other people. And more than anything, I want them to understand that money is nothing to fear, nor is it anything to worship.

The Foundations of Materialism

Many parents I know worry that if they talk to their teens about money a lot, their kids will become more materialistic. Fortunately, this worry is unfounded. Research shows that there are two things that influence how materialistic kids are. The first is obvious: Consciously or not, we adults socialize kids to be materialistic. When parents—as well as peers and celebrities—model materialism, kids care more about wealth and luxury. So when parents are materialistic, kids are likely to follow suit. Same thing with media use: The more TV, social media, YouTube, etc. that kids use, the more likely they are to be materialistic (see page 78).

The less obvious factor behind materialism has to do with the degree to which teens' needs are being filled. When people feel insecure or unfulfilled—because of poverty or because a basic psychological need like safety, competence, connectedness, or autonomy isn't being met—they often try to quell their insecurity by striving for wealth and a lot of fancy stuff. Because of this, less nurturing and more emotionally cold parents tend to have more materialistic offspring.

Materialism and the behaviors that go with it—desiring and buying brand-name clothes and luxury items—can be symptoms of insecurity and a coping strategy used to alleviate feelings of self-doubt or bolster a poor self-image. If what kids are really seeking is greater happiness and fulfillment, materialism is a terrible coping method. At best, it will provide only short-term relief, and in the long run research shows materialism is likely to actually deepen feelings of insecurity. Furthermore, trying to find satisfaction through material purchases can leave our teens in debt, which will likely only add to their feelings of fear and insecurity.

The good news, then, is that if we want our kids to be less materialistic, virtually all the strategies and tactics for increasing connection and limiting media use outlined in part two of this book will help with that. The goal is both to curb teens' exposure to media and to help them learn to fill their emotional needs, not their material ones, when they feel anxious or uncomfortable.

DOES MONEY BUY HAPPINESS?

I hear a lot of complaints from other parents about "that one rich kid" and wealthy families in their community who seem to have an unlimited budget for fancy things and status symbols. They are often seen on social media or at school showing off their wealth. Flashy, materialistic people are always going to be out there, and they offer us a great opportunity to talk with our teens about money and happiness. Here are some talking points.

- Plenty of people pursue money for its own sake, not realizing that they will never feel like they have enough. Money alone does not bring meaning, fulfillment, or purpose, and those are the things that make life worth living. You don't have to believe me on this, just look to your own experience. What makes you feel most deeply satisfied in your life? What makes you feel loved? Did money buy that?

- Money does buy fleeting pleasure, instant gratification, and loads and loads of stuff. And these things always leave us wanting more. Remember that the things that trigger the reward system in the brain are different from the things that foster positive emotions, like hope, curiosity, contentment, and inspiration.

- Money does buy social status and therefore a certain type of power, but it doesn't buy security. Because money is easily lost, the status that comes from money (and fame, for that matter) can also easily be lost. People who gain status based on their material possessions need to constantly demonstrate their wealth in order to keep up their status. It's less exhausting and more fulfilling to earn respect from others based on qualities that are within you (like your kindness or hard work or curiosity). Because you can always control how kind you are, how hard you work, how you express interest, and so on, these are things that you won't easily lose.

- Money does buy a lot of great things that can lay a foundation for well-being and lasting joy. For example, money can pay for a good education, health care, a safe neighborhood, time with people you love, and the type of travel that exposes us to new ideas and places. While you don't always have to have a lot of money to experience these things, it really helps. For that reason, we can make an effort to save money regularly so we can spend it on the things that count.

Allowance

Kids who get an allowance tend to be more financially savvy than those who don't. They score higher on a test of pricing knowledge, and they are less likely to mistake credit as a limitless form of currency. I am a huge believer in giving children and younger teens allowances until they are fifteen or sixteen years old. At that point, the kids in our household are expected to get paying jobs so that they can gain hands-on financial experience.

An allowance gives kids a chance to manage money that they see as their own, and it prevents us parents from being tempted to just give them money every time they need it (or really want something). When kids experience money "appearing" whenever they want or need to buy something, it can be really difficult for them to adjust later.

Allowance works best when it is *not* tied to regular household responsibilities or weekly chores. I know this is counterintuitive, and most parents want kids to understand that in the real world they only get paid when they work. But in households, this just isn't true: Parents don't get paid for the household chores they do. Families are built on mutual obligations—the ways that we help and nurture each other—not paid work.

Kids need to feel like they are a part of something larger than themselves. Giving them real responsibilities in our households fuels this intrinsic sense of place and belonging. Research shows that kids who do unpaid chores are happier and have a higher sense of self-worth. But when we *pay* kids to play a role in the family, we unwittingly kill their intrinsic motivation by providing a flashy external motivator: money. They often start to see themselves more like household employees and "quit their jobs" when their allowance is no longer enough to motivate them.

Building a Budget

As you are setting your kids up with an allowance, talk about why you are doing what you are doing, and what you hope they will learn. Make it clear that kids are still expected to consult with you about major purchases, but as long as they are managing their money well, it's theirs to spend on whatever they wish, to save, and to give to charity.

Perhaps the most important thing is to be very clear about what they are expected to pay for with their allowance. Set up a budget with them. This can be a very simple spreadsheet with a list of expenses and the anticipated monthly (or weekly) cost of those items.

In fifth grade, my kids started paying for their own clothes, school supplies, personal items like toiletries, gifts for their friends and family members' birthdays, and sports equipment. Eventually, this list grew to include the monthly cost of their smartphones and their phone bills, including their share of the data, and pitching in to put gas in the family car our kids share. Once we built this budget, we set their allowance based on what they would need each month for these necessities, plus savings and charitable giving.

Charitable Giving

We budget money for our kids to make a small monthly (or a larger annual) donation to charitable causes that are near and dear to their

ARE WE RICH?

Kids often wonder where their families stand in the income hierarchy. It's important to me that my kids understand that we are not *better* than people who have less money than we do, nor are we less than people who have more. I want them to understand that we've had more opportunities than a lot of other people have had. For example, my parents paid for my undergraduate education, and I never had any student loan debt. This has made it a lot easier for me financially. To be sure, I took advantage of the many opportunities I was offered; still, I know that I am not more deserving than those around me who are less well off financially.

We live in what we often perceive to be a meritocracy, where social mobility and wealth are dependent only on an individual's personal qualities, like intelligence and hard work. When we believe too deeply in this meritocracy, we can easily forget to see the gifts we've been given. We think we've *earned* everything we've been given. At Fiona's graduation, Blossom Beatty Pidduck, head of the Thacher School, read this fitting passage from Deuteronomy 6:10–11:

> You have been brought into the land . . . to live in great and goodly cities, which you built not, and houses full of all good things, which you filled not, and wells dug, which you digged not, vineyards and olive trees, which you planted not; when you shall have eaten and be full.

She went on to explain:

> Each of you has received gifts, gifts born of the foresight, generosity, sacrifice, and work of others. You've had access to experiences and resources that the vast majority of young people on this planet will never know. There is no shame in these gifts. Shame over what you have been given will only prevent you from doing the one thing you must, which is to see your gifts and recognize them for what they are.
> In so doing you will receive an even greater gift: The capacity to share what's been given to you with others. The

ability to dig wells, to plant trees, to build communities
filled with all good things, so that others can have eaten
and be full.

There is no shame in how much money we have—whether it is a lot
or a little. There is only responsibility. We must recognize what we
have been given, and we must not hoard our good fortune. Instead,
we must share it.

hearts. This is arguably the most important budget item. It teaches
them that their relationship with money need not be one of hoarding
or scarcity, and that they actually do have enough to give to those in
need. Learning to give their money away—something a lot of people
need to practice to feel comfortable doing—teaches them how positive
and powerful money can be.

Charitable giving is also the best way for kids to experience the
ways that money *can* buy happiness. Even though people typically
believe that they will be happier spending money on themselves, it
turns out that people tend to find greater happiness by spending it on
others. In one study, participants were given either $5 or $20 and told
either to buy something for themselves or to spend it on someone else.
Even though most participants predicted that they'd be happier if they
spent it on themselves, in reality they were measurably happier when
they gave the money away.

Other studies have shown that when people give to charities, brain
regions associated with pleasure, social connection, and trust are activated, something researchers call a "warm glow effect." And altruistic
behavior releases endorphins in the brain and body, which produce
positive feelings sometimes called a "helper's high."

Savings

Finally, my kids' dad and I add a little bit to their monthly budget
(which, when totaled, becomes the amount of their allowance) for
savings, to get them into the habit of paying themselves first. Stuff

happens, and they need to plan for it. As adults, their savings could be for those years when, God forbid, their medical expenses are higher than usual or when they need to pay an unexpected insurance deductible or repair the car. For our kids, their savings are mostly to pay for repairs when their phone smashes on the ground or they spill a drink on their laptop. The bonus here is that when kids are responsible for their own replacement costs or repairs, they tend to be better stewards of their belongings.

Having some savings also gives kids some leeway to make mistakes and feel the consequences. Kids need to own their money, and all the miseries or victories that follow. One of my kids once spent her entire school supplies budget on locker decorations for middle school . . . before she'd purchased the necessities. She cried and begged for more money. She didn't want to bring *used* pens to school. She wanted a *new* thumb drive. In the end, she resourcefully prepared for school without our help by borrowing from her savings until the next month's allowance arrived. We love it when our kids make mistakes like this, as these sorts of lessons are much better learned with school supplies than, say, college tuition.

And, yes, my kids have total freedom to spend their own money on whatever they wish, as long as it doesn't create a liability for us. For example, we wouldn't let our daughter buy an old car that she technically had the money for, because she didn't fully understand the cost of repairs, maintenance, insurance, etc.

Once our kids' savings include a substantial cushion for mistakes and other unanticipated expenses, they can start saving for travel and other major purchases. For example, one of our kids took a trip to New York City by herself to visit some close friends the summer after her junior year in high school. She paid for this trip entirely herself with money she had saved, and to this day believes it was her best major purchase ever.

Paid Work

Because our kids' allowances don't cover entertainment like movies or a concert, when they were younger we gave them lots of optional opportunities to make money at home, beyond their regular household chores, until they were old enough to find a paying job outside the home. They learned to watch for opportunities to do work around the house and in our neighborhood. This had the added benefit of increasing their mindfulness about what needs to happen for a household (ours or a neighbor's) to run smoothly, whether it's yard work or arranging for pet care while on vacation.

When our kids turned fifteen and became old enough in California to get paying jobs, we ended what our kids now call the "free money" allowance program. Teens need to experience the power of their own initiative and the satisfaction of someone acknowledging the value of their work. Even though retail and restaurant jobs can often be boring or grueling, all of our kids have loved their jobs. Molly works at a coffee and ice cream shop. Tanner just landed a new summer job at the local lumber yard. Fiona spent last summer helping a local family-owned nursery get ready for the Christmas season—in July! And Macie, our equestrian, has worked at the barn where she has ridden for years, doing manual labor outside as well as administrative work in the office.

Holding a paying job is often a very positive source of self-esteem and power for teenagers, and it is a key life experience for them to have before they leave the nest—whether they need the money or not. It gives teens a sense of purpose and accomplishment. There is no other way to learn that while money doesn't just appear in relationship to desire (for 99.9 percent of the population, anyway), teens do have some control over making their own money "appear." For the vast majority of teens today, the only route to having money and the things they need and want to buy with their money will be for them to earn it. And having a sense of control is, as we saw in chapter two, essential for well-being.

While many teens from low-income families work throughout high school to help support the basic needs of their families, fewer and fewer middle- and upper-class teens have paying jobs these days. Why? Probably because paying jobs can be hard to manage for today's busy teens. More than that, they can be boring, something many teens can no longer tolerate.

Even if they *are* boring and hard to fit into an already busy schedule, paying jobs are a source of life skills teens cannot learn any other way. Finding after-school and summer jobs is a great way for kids to learn how to fill out a job application, to pull together a resume and cover letter, and to have an interview. Work helps kids learn how to get along well with what has turned out, for our kids, to be extremely diverse groups of coworkers. For one of our children, just learning how to manage her calendar and communicate to her manager when she can and cannot work has been an incredibly important, if challenging, opportunity. If teens can't find a paying job, I know some parents who have paid a small stipend for their teens to volunteer so they can learn some skills and also develop a work ethic. (The stipend is optional.)

Because our kids have not been able to reliably cover all of their expenses (and continue contributing to their savings) by working at their minimum-wage jobs over the summer and on weekends, we match what they earn in the world so that they still feel in control of their earnings and money. This matching is their new "allowance." We know that it is an incredible privilege to be able to do this for our children, and that it would be beyond the means of many families to do today. We are grateful for our privilege.

More Advanced Financial Skills

When our teens get their first paying jobs, we also insist that they start tracking and managing their budgets and accounts entirely themselves. They use apps on their phone for budgeting and managing their money. Although I do have concerns about security and privacy, I also think the benefits of being able to track purchases in real time against a budget can be game-changing for most people—teens as well as adults. Our teens always know where they stand and what they can afford because they track their money so precisely. If you don't manage a budget yourself, but you think it would be a good idea for your teens to do, I suggest that you download a budgeting app and use it yourself first. It's very easy these days, and your kids will feel less overwhelmed if you can walk them through creating a budget with confidence.

Online banking allows kids to easily set up automatic transfers to their savings accounts, so saving is not a monthly decision they make or something they need to remember to do. They also pay their individual phone bills automatically by making a monthly transfer to my account (because I pay our collective bill).

Once our kids start driving, we get them each credit cards (for safety reasons, so they don't need to use their debit cards to buy gas or carry around a lot of cash) and for emergencies. Before we hand the cards over, they've each sat down and met with our banker Amanda at Wells Fargo, who taught them how their credit cards worked and about their credit score. She explained to them the difference between paying off their credit card and just paying the minimum. She showed them how the interest they would owe if they didn't pay off their cards in full could make a $40 tank of gas cost closer to $50 over the course of a year. Most important, Amanda helped them set up their accounts so that their credit cards would automatically be paid off in full each month from their checking account.

I'm eternally grateful that Amanda was willing to do this sort of teaching, because I do think kids listen differently when it's someone other than their parents. I like that our kids get to work with an actual person that they know at our bank. That said, though, most families probably need to handle these sorts of lessons around credit cards themselves, and that's fine, too.

Credit Versus Debit

I've been surprised by how hard it has been for our kids to under-stand (in practice, not conceptually) the difference between credit and debit. It's one thing to track what you have in a checking account against your budget. It turns out it's quite another to track what you are going to have to pay at the end of the month on a credit card bill against your budget for the previous month—but that you don't actu-ally have to pay right now. Moreover, the concept of a credit limit is important to understand. At some point, they may try to charge on a credit card and the transaction will be denied because it would exceed the credit limit. This can happen a lot for kids who have low credit limits, as they prove their credit worthiness. It is important for teens to learn to keep any eye on their balance and also on what they have in their checking account, so they can make a payment prior to charging something if necessary.

Each of our kids has tested our "this credit card is for gas and emergencies only" limitations on their credit cards, and in so doing made mistakes managing their money. Running out of money to pay your credit card bill is a very valuable learning experience to have early on, when your parents are still involved enough to take the credit card out of play for a little while. Some kids need to use a cash-only system before they can take on the much more abstract tasks of managing their money online, using a debit card, setting up systems like Venmo or PayPal, or managing a credit card.

It's also incredibly important that kids understand the "revolving balance" on a credit card, or the unpaid balance that is carried from one month to the next; otherwise teens can get the impression that they can buy anything they want and still just pay that minimum balance. Furthermore, they need to understand how a high interest rate can make a debt harder and harder to pay off. Giving them more concrete examples—using their own spending and their own money—can really help. As mentioned, we have our kids' credit cards set up so that there is no unpaid balance at the end of the month, and thus no interest charged.

Learning about credit cards also sets teens up to understand the idea of debt and loans, particularly student loans. The average American household with student loan debt owes $47,671, and student loan debts are rising faster than any other form of debt. Teens need to understand the difference between their subsidized and unsubsidized student loans, and they need to have a plan for how to repay their student loans as soon as interest on them starts to accrue. If a college student starts having trouble repaying their loans, as many people do, they need to understand their options. For instance, skipping payments and student loan forbearance are not the best ones. Currently, student loan forbearance is adding considerably to America's $1.44 trillion student debt load.

Investing and Saving for Retirement

When our teens turn eighteen, we start teaching them about investing and saving for retirement. We add a new line item to their budgets: investments. For now, this means that they make a $10 contribution each month to an IRA (individual retirement account) that we opened in each of their names. We show them how to invest their money in an extremely low-cost index fund that will grow over time to provide for their retirement. This requires us to explain some pretty complex concepts:

- what an interest rate is
- how interest compounds over time
- what stocks and bonds are
- how mutual funds, ETFs (exchange-traded funds), and index funds work and how they are different from each other
- how and why $10,000 in savings in their twenties can effortlessly turn into $50,000 in retirement if they invest it in an index fund or ETF
- how Social Security works, the projected future of the program, and that they will be responsible for their own retirement
- how when they are older, they will use their annual budget to calculate how much they need to save for retirement
- how much they need to save for retirement if they start saving now versus how much they need to save if they wait until they are much older (another lesson in compounding interest)
- what an IRA is
- what a tax deduction is

And there's obviously so much more than that. None of our kids are all that interested in investing—and neither am I—so it's been one of those things that we don't love talking about but that we do anyway, because it is important.

This sort of financial education sets teens up to be financially savvy and responsible with their spending and saving. They learn to be good stewards of their belongings without being materialistic and to spend their money on others as well as on themselves. Finally, they learn *not* to stress about their finances—but rather to be comfortable thinking, talking, and working with their money.

Reconnecting to What Really Matters

When panic attacks and depression took over in the spring of Sayra's senior year, she began to doubt everything in her life. The ground fell out beneath her. The world lost its color. Her most pressing question became: "Why live?"

Adolescence—that "long decade" of massive development between the ages of eleven and twenty-five—has always been a time of questioning and change. But this *new* adolescence is exponentially so. We are at one of the greatest inflection points in human history, with more aspects of our societies, workplaces, and lifestyles being reshaped than ever before. It's an exciting time to live in, and also a risky one, because normal adolescent transformation is often going haywire.

Like many young people contemplating suicide, Sayra had lost the thread of meaning in her life. She was running faster and faster on a hamster wheel of achievement, increasingly disconnected from her peers, family, school, neighborhood, and church. She grew increasingly disconnected even from herself—from her exhaustion, from her emotions, from true fulfillment. Sayra was so good at everything that she was *literally* a poster child for her university: Her photo and story featured in all the marketing materials. But success and achievement were masking Sayra's isolation.

Overvaluing Accomplishment, Undervaluing Kindness

Adolescence is going haywire because, like Sayra, as a society we've lost the thread of meaning. Both directly and indirectly, our hyper-individualistic society teaches our kids to pursue achievement and status rather than altruism and equality. Teens today learn that they will earn our admiration through their accomplishments and not through their meaningful contribution to their community. They are pushed to strive for acceptance at elite universities, to compete for what seem like scarce resources.

So, it's not surprising that more than 80 percent of youth across a wide spectrum of race, culture, and social class value their success and personal happiness over their concern for others. We can blame social media all we want, but the truth is that teens today believe that this is what we parents also value. When the Harvard Graduate School of Education asked more than ten thousand students how they viewed their parents' child-raising priorities, nearly two-thirds reported that both their parents and peers would rank *achievement* above *kindness*. Moreover, students were three times more likely to agree than disagree with this statement: "My parents are prouder if I get good grades in my classes than if I'm a caring community member in class and school."

Most parents push their children's achievement as a means to an end. We just want our kids to be happy, and in a meritocracy like the US, achievement is seen as the golden key to financial security and success. High achievement, often at the expense of collaboration and community, is perceived as critical for our children's future security—and therefore their happiness.

Empty Promises

Unfortunately for our kids, the pleasure that comes from success will never bring them meaning, purpose, or fulfillment. As a society we tend to conflate gratification with happiness, but there's an enormous difference between fleeting pleasure and lasting joy. When we do something gratifying—say, shopping, checking our Instagram feed, playing video games, or indulging in processed foods—we stimulate the reward system in our brain, which releases dopamine and our brain's natural opiates. This does usually produce a short-lived hit of pleasure. For a moment, we may feel happy. More reliably, though, dopamine also produces a desire for *more*. And this longer-lasting craving is a state of suffering, not happiness.

But as we push our kids toward success and happiness, we don't tell them that these things will never be enough to fulfill their deep human needs for love and connection. That no achievement will ever be satisfying over the long run and that nothing rewarding will ever feel like enough. That no amount of money or sex or fame or power or prestige can fill the hole in their psyche left by isolation and loneliness. That no fancy degree or prestigious job can help them find meaning. Success and happiness turn out to be empty promises.

The happiness we are after is not actually pleasure or gratification. What we really need is the experience of a wide range of positive emotions like gratitude, inspiration, and love, but when we prioritize success and pleasure, real positive emotions fall to the wayside. These days, few teens are explicitly taught how to prioritize and foster positive emotions (in themselves and, perhaps more important, in others) as a way to reset their battered nervous systems and improve their mental health.

The Loneliness Crisis

The hyper-individualistic pursuit of success and happiness has led us headlong into a crisis of isolation. The average American adult has only one close confidant. Nearly one-quarter of adults in the US and the UK say they often or always feel lonely, that they lack companionship, that they feel left out, or that they feel isolated from others. The leading reason people seek counseling is loneliness.

And as we have seen, this crisis of isolation has hit our teenagers *hard*. The adolescent suicide rate has increased *70 percent* since 2006. While we tend to think that people who take their own lives are suffering from an *individual* mental illness, great social theorists like Émile Durkheim and Karl Marx long ago put forth the idea that isolation and alienation are at the root of most mental illness. Durkheim famously demonstrated more than a century ago that suicide is best understood as a *social* phenomenon, not an individual pathology.

Unfortunately, Gen Z is lonelier than any generation that has come before it. Teenagers today spend less time together, both in intimate settings, like on a date, and simply hanging out with each other casually. They feel more isolated and left out than we can imagine. They are disconnected from their peers, from nature, and from God. Fewer are affiliated with a religion, faith, or philosophy than at any other time in history.

Massive income inequality, the likes of which we haven't seen in this country since 1928, also keeps today's teenagers from feeling like they are a part of a larger community. They compete with their classmates intensely, often for the scarce resource of an elite education. They feel it acutely each time they lose even a tiny modicum of status in our elitist social hierarchy. And as our country becomes more and more politically extreme and divided, they detach rather than engage. Fewer college students are affiliated with a political party than ever before.

Today's teens have also become alienated from *themselves* and from how they are feeling. Social media rewards them for performance but not true expression. Posts that reveal how they are really feeling rarely deliver the likes and comments—the validation—they seek, especially compared to a post that hints at power or prestige, at sex, fame, or money. A photo of a fancy vacation, a sexy selfie, or even just a staged photo of themselves looking fun and carefree will more reliably bring them the attention that they long for than a post that reveals something authentic about their feelings. Performing on social media gives kids false hope of connection and love, but reliably delivers only the sense that they are being judged.

New technologies—smartphones and processed foods and a wide spectrum of pharmacologies—make it easier than ever for our teens to become totally numb to their own feelings. The second they feel bored, sad, or angry, they can look to a screen to distract themselves from their emotions. Or they can eat that whole bag of Takis Fuego, hot chili pepper and lime flavored, for that extra dopamine hit. Or they can numb their pain by vaping, binge drinking, or taking a pill. All of these widely available options distance them from themselves and their emotions.

These many layers of isolation separate today's teens from experiencing themselves as committed and connected. What meaningful role can they play in their community (or nation) while at home, alone in their rooms, obsessing about a class assignment, fixated on social media, or masturbating to porn? What purpose will they find while they pursue their own individual happiness and comfort?

Continuing to push today's adolescents to achieve, or even to just do what makes them happy, will not reverse Generation Z's skyrocketing suicide rate. Indeed, global happiness studies have shown again and again that neither poverty nor unhappiness predict a nation's suicide rate. The variable that *does* predict suicide is *meaning*. The more a nation's population lacks meaning, the higher that nation's suicide rate. Countries with the lowest rates of meaning, like Japan and the US, have the highest suicide rates.

Finding Meaning

It may be a social phenomenon, but Gen Z's tsunami of collective isolation is playing itself out one person at a time. It's been a year since Sayra hit her low and got into treatment for severe depression and anxiety. She is starting to see more clearly how her life started spiraling downward. Because she was able to hide behind a bright and enviable facade of social media posts and accomplishments that made it seem like she was thriving, no one—herself included—saw that she was exhausted and stressed to the breaking point. Keeping up with her internships, paid jobs, senior thesis, and regular coursework left her no time for rest or for real-life social connection. As graduation loomed, she could no longer focus. She began to spend more and more time scrolling through Instagram and Facebook, avoiding her rising panic and depressive thoughts—and further impairing the sleep she so badly needed.

The structure of Sayra's life crumbled. Threads of connection to herself, her friends and family, and her school community dissolved. She stayed up later and later to finish her schoolwork, and soon she was getting only three or four hours of sleep, night after night, for weeks on end. Even though she was surrounded by friends and family, our family included, she had become isolated. We were duped by her social media posts that made it seem like she was thriving, and by her cheerful, I'm-fine-I'm-just-busy facade when we saw her in person.

It is not possible, of course, for any human being to feel healthy and happy when they are as severely sleep-deprived as Sayra was. Nor is well-being possible when a person is isolated from real life. Sayra was putting immense pressure on herself to continue to achieve, even at the cost of her health and well-being. In addition, like young people everywhere, she felt despair about our divided nation. Sometimes she felt consumed by the unending bad news that came to her through her social media accounts. Weekly mass shootings and a reckless president—tearing her parents' immigrant community into shreds—left her shaken. Under these conditions, excruciating anxiety and depression is inevitable, even natural. It's the human body's way of protesting, of forcing major change.

The world needs young people like Sayra. We need the great tsunami of depression and anxiety and suicide now hitting Generation Z. As Johann Hari wisely wrote in *Lost Connections*:

> They are telling us something has gone wrong with the way we live. We need to stop trying to muffle or silence or pathologize that pain. Instead, we need to listen to it, and honor it. It is only when we listen to our pain that we can follow it back to its source—and only there, when we can see its true causes, can we begin to overcome it.

Sayra is finding meaning in her suffering. She feels hopeful that she can help others who might be experiencing something similar. By sharing her story, she can see on the page what's gone wrong. And because she can see the social causes of her pain, she is rising above it.

I believe that Sayra will find both fulfillment and success in her life. I don't think that she needs to lower her expectations for herself (for her future financial security, for example). But her success will come as a byproduct of her newfound meaning, and not from her original ambitions. Sayra is learning to follow psychologist Viktor Frankl's sage advice:

Don't aim at success. The more you aim at it and make it a target, the more you are going to miss it. For success, like happiness, cannot be pursued; it must ensue, and it only does so as the unintended side effect of one's dedication to a cause greater than oneself.

It's hard for us parents to think about pointing our children toward something different—to think about pointing them away from the success and happiness that we've been guiding them toward for their whole lives. It's difficult to imagine shifting away from pushing them toward ambitious goals so that we can help them commit themselves to causes greater than themselves. To do this, we worry, will require leaving too much on the table.

But ambition is not the holy grail. The belief that the most ambitious kids are the most likely to succeed is a false assumption. These days, it's just not true. More often than not, such striving leads to the kind of stress and anxiety that seem to be hamstringing our kids today. Too much ambition causes kids to focus on themselves even more than they're already prone to, and as much research has shown, this isn't a good strategy for getting ahead.

Fortunately, if our kids have the skills that are outlined in this book, they will not also need ambition or a desire to achieve for the sake of achievement. **They will achieve as a by-product of their deep joy, their fulfillment, and their ability to focus deeply and rest when they need to.** They will rise to the top because of their willingness to make mistakes and their ability to make good choices, especially related to drugs and alcohol, their emerging sexualities, and their financial well-being. Most of all, they will succeed because of the opportunities that come their way from their deep and broad social connections.

And so, as a generation of parents, we must give our children more than the empty promises of fleeting happiness and financial success. Instead, we must give them the tools they need to thrive emotionally, socially, and intellectually. We must help them learn to weather this era's massive transformations without being pulled under by depression, anxiety, or addiction. We must help them find meaning, purpose, lasting joy, and deep fulfillment.

Adaptation

Here, finally, is the good news: We *understand* what is happening to our teenagers. Thankfully, we know what it takes for our kids to be joyful and fulfilled in this age of anxiety and distraction. And because we understand how it is possible for teenagers today to get off track—to lose their connection to themselves, to their friends and family, and to their larger communities—we can keep them from derailing in the first place. We can adapt our parenting.

In the end, the only thing that today's tweeners, teens, and college students need is reconnection. They need to reconnect to themselves, their peers, their families, their larger communities, and their purpose in the world. **All of the parenting strategies outlined in this book are tactics for reconnection.** As parents, we need to help our kids:

- **Feel seen, safe, and soothed.**

  Thriving teens have a loving and affectionate adult in their lives. This means that they've got someone who really sees them—a person who can truly listen without trying to fix, reassure, or problem-solve. Caring adults can best help teens learn how to care for themselves independently when the adults themselves practice and model for their teens self-care, self-soothing, and stress management.

- **Have a sense of control over their lives.**

  Connected teens have both freedom and structure. Family life provides a healthy and predictable rhythm to their day. Adults consistently hold them accountable to age-appropriate family and school rules—like expectations about drug and alcohol use—in a warm and engaged way. Teens have full agency to function independently within these limits.

- **Learn how to deal with discomfort.**

  Teens need to learn through their own experience that so-called negative emotions are not necessarily traumatic, scarring, unnatural—or to be avoided. They have solid strategies for dealing with stress. Because they are willing to experience tough emotions, such as disappointment, embarrassment, and frustration, these teens can persist toward their long-term goals in the face of difficulty. They are able to take risks, have difficult conversations, and stay true to what they know is right.

- **Foster their own positive emotions—not just perform them.**

  It's easy in adolescence to succumb to the coolness of cynicism. Joyful and fulfilled teens, however, understand that cynicism is a marker of fear, not intelligence. Kids who consciously cultivate gratitude, love, happiness, peace, awe, inspiration, optimism, and faith broaden their perception in the moment and build resources over time. Their ability to foster positive emotions allows them to access their most high-functioning, creative, and intelligent selves.

- **Feel connected to something larger than themselves.**

  Thriving teens have friends and family they see—face to face—regularly. They manage loneliness by reaching out to real people rather than by succumbing to social media use. Most important, they feel a sense of belonging and commitment to their families, friends, neighborhoods, schools, and other communities. They have begun the process of connecting to their purpose and are actively searching for a greater sense of meaning. They can see that the point is not what they expect from life or what will make them happy. Instead, they return again and again to the question: "What is life asking from me?"

- **Command their own attention.**

  Teens can't persist in pursuing their long-term goals if they can't remember what they're doing or why they're doing it. In a world where corporations pay per view to rule teens' concentration and interest, and where social media and gaming empires depend on their ability to command kids' attention, successful teens are still able to stay focused on the things that are important for their long-term well-being. They study when they need to study and sleep when they need to sleep. They cope effectively with the digital temptations that surround them. They use computers and smartphones strategically rather than compulsively, as tools that make them more efficient, effective, connected, and creative, instead of just being distracted and drained by electronics.

- **Follow natural rhythms of sleep and rest.**

  In today's striving culture of overwork, taking a break to stare out the window seems lazy. Sleep seems like a waste of time. *Not* checking your phone or social media while driving seems boring and unproductive. Despite all this, thriving teens are able to take meaningful breaks during the day, over the course of the week, and throughout each season from their devices and online activities. They find time for quiet and rest, often in nature, or a silent practice like yoga or meditation, or in artistic expression or spirituality. They can tolerate stillness and the feelings that come up within it. As a result, they know how they are feeling and what their next best step forward might be.

- **Engage with wise and reliable sources of information.**

  Teens may be able to google just about anything to find information about the forces that will color their lives, but they don't have the life experience they need to make sense of all that information coming at them. Adolescents with strong adult relationships have access to wisdom that only experience can bring, and when teens apply the wisdom of their elders to the dicier aspects of adolescence, they navigate more joyfully and more successfully.

The Great Reconnection

Together, we *can* pull our kids back from their alienation and isolation—or prevent it from happening in the first place. We can use the strategies and tactics outlined in this book to reconnect them to something larger than their individual strivings.

It's been humbling for me, as the author of *Raising Happiness*, to realize that happiness isn't the right goal, and it never has been. As George Vaillant wisely wrote, happiness is only the cart; love is the horse. And it's been humbling for me to fully realize that our children's success is also not the goal.

The goal has always been *connection*. To know ourselves well enough to connect our greatest longings to the great need of the world. To help our kids find the place, as writer and theologian Frederick Buechner put it, where their deep gladness and the world's deep hunger meet.

It's natural for teenagers to do some navel-gazing, to focus on themselves as they figure out who they are. They do need to carve out their own identities in order to make their way in the world. But ultimately, if they are to find lasting joy and fulfillment in life, we need to help them set their sights on a more awe-inspiring view. We need to help them, as one of my favorite authors, Greg Boyle, writes, "shift from the cramped world of self-preoccupation into a more expansive place of fellowship, of true kinship."

I believe that together we are up to this task.

Appendix: Sample Teen Contracts

Sometimes it helps to be super explicit with your kids about your expectations—this is a part of the scaffolding discussed in chapter two. Even though it will likely annoy them to no end, creating a contract with your kids can be a way to be really, really clear about your family rules and your own expectations.

Here are two sample contracts that people often ask me for. Feel free to make them your own. You can find electronic versions that you can copy and edit at christinecarter.com/resources.

And, for the record, they aren't even really mine. Many years ago, I started collecting contracts like these from other parents. What you see below is my patchwork of excerpts from things that other parents wrote. The technology contract lifts heavily from Janell Burley Hofmann's iRules and her contract with her son—that is another good resource if you are looking for something more succinct (janellburleyhofmann .com/the-contract/). Consider these contracts crowdsourced from your village of fellow parents.

Driving Contract

For teens who are under eighteen or if you are helping them pay for a car, gas, and/or insurance.

Dear Sweet Child,

Congratulations on getting your driver's license!! We are so excited for you!! We already believe that you are an excellent driver, and we trust your judgment. At the same time, we want to be really clear about our expectations around the use of any car. When things go wrong, parents usually say that they wish they'd been clearer. Why?

- Driving is especially dangerous for teens because the human brain does not fully develop its *ability to assess risk* and danger until we reach the age of twenty-two to twenty-five. No amount of driver training can overcome this risk.
- In California (and most other states), a teen driver violating state laws who causes injury or death to people or damage to property can trigger criminal and civil penalties and financial liability for parents.
- On an average day in the US, more than eleven teens *die* in crashes. Even though you are a confident driver, you are still technically a beginner at a dangerous task. Having passed your driver's test is not the same thing as having a lot of experience under your belt.

Many of these requirements to use our cars are obvious, but here are our expectations:

- Your driving will be supervised by us. For the next year, we will decide, day by day, when and where it is safe for you to drive. This simply means that you will get permission from one of us before you drive, and we will agree on your destination, route (if need be, if it is far or difficult), time of departure and return, and, eventually, passengers.

- Always wear your seat belt and make sure that every passenger in your car, of any age, wears one. Of teens aged thirteen to nineteen who died in car crashes in 2012, **52 percent of drivers** and **59 percent of passengers** were not wearing seat belts.

- It goes without saying that we expect you to obey speed limits and the rules of the road. We expect you to reduce your speed when road conditions require (e.g., bad weather, darkness, sharp turns, hills, visibility, congestion, unfamiliar roads). **Speeding** is a factor in **one out of every three** fatal teen crashes.

- It is against California law for drivers under eighteen to use a phone while driving, even with a hands-free device. Unless your car is in park, never use any electronic device, whether hand-held, hands-free, or voice-activated, for any purpose not related to the safe operation of the vehicle. Specifically, no sending or reading texts, sending or viewing photos or videos, or making phone calls. Get in the habit of putting your phone in do-not-disturb mode while you drive so that you are not distracted by dings or vibrations, or so that you are not tempted to look.

  - One out of every four car accidents in the US is caused by texting and driving.

  - Texting while driving is six times more likely to cause an accident than driving drunk.

  - Answering a text takes away your attention for about five seconds. Traveling at 55 mph, that's enough time to travel the length of a football field.

  - Of fatal crashes among fifteen-to-nineteen-year-old drivers involving distractions, 21 percent were identified as using cell phones.

- Never give rides to hitchhikers.

- Never use headphones or earbuds to listen to music while you drive.

- Never eat or drink while driving, and for now, please don't change the music while the car is moving. Driver distractions, such as eating and changing music, were indicated for 16 percent of all drivers involved in **fatal crashes** for people under the age of twenty.

- For the next year, you may not drive unsupervised between the hours of 11:00 PM and 5:00 AM. (This is California law.) Teen motor vehicle crash deaths occur most frequently from 9:00 PM to midnight.

- For the next year, you may not carry passengers younger than twenty-one (again, this is a California law) except for your siblings. When there are no adults in the car, the risk of sixteen- or seventeen-year-old drivers being killed in a crash **increases 44 percent with one passenger under the age of 21, doubles with two young passengers, and quadruples with three or more young passengers.**

- We obviously expect that you won't be using drugs or alcohol, and certainly that you won't use drugs or alcohol and drive. We expect that you will never, ever drive under the influence of alcohol or impairing drugs. Among drivers aged sixteen to nineteen killed in car crashes last year, **23 percent** had blood alcohol concentrations of .08 percent or higher. And there are a lot of misconceptions about pot use and driving. **Driving while high is not safer than driving drunk or driving while texting.** It is estimated that in states where marijuana use is high, as it is in California, 20 percent of all fatal car crashes involve marijuana (not just with teens).

- Exhaustion can be as impairing as drugs, alcohol, and texting. Please don't drive when you are sleepy or very tired.

- If you get a ticket, it will be your responsibility to pay the full amount of the ticket, go to traffic school if necessary, and pay for the increase in the cost of insurance in the case of a moving violation.

- If you get into an accident, it will be your responsibility to pay for the insurance deductible and any repairs that are not covered by insurance.

If we find out that you've been breaking any laws or that you are not fulfilling our expectations, we will immediately revoke your right to drive. Driving is a privilege that comes with considerable responsibility.

Beyond basic safety, our expectation is that you will:

- Take good care of the car that you are driving, treating it as we would. Keep it clean, keep the gas tank full, and let us know when it needs maintenance so we can help you get it scheduled.

- Continue to be a wonderful and contributing member of our household in ways that include the car (driving your siblings to their events) and that don't (emptying the dishwasher and keeping your room clean).

- We expect that you will be a very safe *passenger* when driving with your friends, or with your siblings. In 2012, **54 percent of the deaths of teenage passengers** occurred in vehicles driven by another teen. When riding as a passenger in a car, you can help the driver get to the destination safely.

Finally, and this is important: If for any reason you feel uncomfortable driving in a given situation, you may call us for a safe ride to avoid a dangerous situation. We will retrieve you—no questions asked—from any circumstance at any time of the day or night. We understand that you will make mistakes and misjudge situations, and we'd like you to correct your mistakes *before* they become dangerous. Err on the side of caution. You can probably expect to have a conversation with us over breakfast the next morning about how, perhaps, you found yourself at a strange party fifteen miles from home, but we want to be clear: **We will never give you a reason to regret asking for help.**

We know that you appreciate how lucky you are to have a car to drive. We love you, and are so excited to see what an amazing young person you are growing up to be.

Love,

Your doting parents

Please sign here:

I agree to the following restrictions and understand that these restrictions will be modified by my parents as I get more driving experience and demonstrate that I am a responsible driver. I understand that you will impose penalties, including removal of my driving privileges, if I violate the agreement.

Signatures

Driver: _____   Date: _____

Parent promise: I also agree to drive safely and to be an excellent role model.

Mom: _____   Date: _____

Dad: _____   Date: _____

Technology Contract

Dear Sweet Child of Ours,

You are the very lucky user of technology we never dreamed of having when we were your age. You are a good and responsible kid and we *want* you to have these things. But also: Use of all these devices and technologies is a privilege, not an entitlement. Even when you pay for them out of your allowance, or from your job earnings, so long as you are living under our roof and are on our cell phone plan, they are not really yours to do absolutely anything you want with.

This document clearly states our expectations around your screen time and technology use. We know this list is long. It's that important. Learning to use technology appropriately is actually a lot like learning to drive: There are a lot of regulations to keep you safe. Just as we wouldn't let you drive without first teaching you the rules, giving you lessons, and letting you practice, we aren't just going to let you use smartphones, tablets, computers, the Xbox, etc., without establishing clear expectations and safety guidelines.

Because we lived through the dark ages before the internet, we have seen how fantastic all this great new technology is, and how it has changed our lives for the better. We have also noticed how this technology changes the way people communicate and, therefore, our relationships with one another. Old-fashioned communication is very important for your spirit and your social development. By the same token, too much new communication, through social media and messaging, has been definitively shown to make kids feel left out, lonely, irritable, anxious, and even depressed.

This long list of guidelines is no doubt irritating to you. You know many kids whose parents don't care as much as we do about these things. Some of these kids will learn to use technology in a healthy way on their own, but many of them won't, and it will likely affect their moods, their friendships, their relationships with family members, and their ability to learn and thrive.

Also, we know that you probably think that you already know all of this stuff, as we have been like broken records reminding you about it. At times, we know that you are utterly convinced that you know more than we do when it comes to your phone. That's normal, and often you are right! But it is our job to raise you to become a well-rounded, healthy, and happy individual who can function with technology, not be a slave to it, hence this contract and "training manual."

1. If you choose to put a password on your devices, we will have the password. If you want to have private communication with your friends, please do it in person, on the phone, or via letter. Nothing on the internet, including texts, emails, and DMs, is ever private.

2. Do not ever ignore a phone call if the screen reads "Mom" or "Dad." Ignoring our calls is disrespectful and irresponsible. (If you are driving, studying, sleeping, or in class or at work, we understand that you will not take our calls because your phone will be in do not disturb mode, off, or out of sight. In these cases, our expectation is that you will call us back as soon as you can.)

3. Do not let screen time interfere with your sleep, which you need to be happy and healthy. Turn your phone *off* (not just on silent) and plug it in at the charging station thirty minutes before bed. You may retrieve your phone the following morning when you are totally ready to leave for school.

4. Follow all school guidelines about phone use.

5. If your phone, tablet, or computer falls into the toilet, smashes on the ground, or vanishes into thin air, you are responsible for the cost of repair or replacement. Mow the lawn, do some filing, work extra hours at your job, babysit, or save your birthday money. It will happen, so be prepared.

6. Do not involve yourself in conversations that might be hurtful to others. Do not use technology to lie, fool, or deceive another human being. Do not text, email, or say anything digitally that you would not say in person, out loud. Do not confide something truly private to anyone else electronically; if someone confides in you this way, call them or speak to them face-to-face. If you find that you are in a conversation that you would feel ashamed, guilty, or embarrassed about if we knew, stop and ask yourself why. Be a good friend and family member first. Get in the habit of

excusing yourself from questionable conversations—it becomes easier with practice, and some things are better to miss out on. If you can't stop your peers from hurting others, ask an adult for help. Your parents and teachers take these things very seriously.

7. Similarly, do not take seductive, sexy, or inappropriate pictures of yourself or anyone else. This obviously includes pictures of your private parts. This might make you laugh now, but despite your good judgment and high intelligence (and how totally outrageous this seems), some of your peers will do this, and you may be tempted. Don't do it. It is risky and could ruin your teenage/college/adult life. It is always a bad idea. There are a lot of healthier ways to get attention if you are craving it.

8. The internet is vast and much more powerful than you. Be careful what you put out there. Anything you send as a text, email, or post to a website—even something you think you can take down or think is private—is actually *public* and *permanent*. It is hard to make most of what goes up on the internet disappear, especially bad reputations and hurt feelings. (We have had the experience of *not* hiring a very talented individual only because of something they posted on Facebook many years before they interviewed for the job. It was a devastating situation for everyone.)

9. [For a middle schooler] We reserve the right to be the only ones to give you license to download any new apps. Please let us know if you want something new and why. We love to discuss these things with you, and we mostly trust your judgment.

10. No pornography. If you have access to the web, search it only for information you would openly share with us. If you have a question about sex, ask an actual person (preferably us), not someone who makes a living selling pornography. We know a lot more than you might think we do.

11. Turn your phone off (or silence it, with the vibration off) in public, especially in restaurants, while you are walking in public, at movies, or while speaking with another human being. You are not rude, so don't allow your phone to change that.

12. Take a break from technology at some point every single day, and for an entire weekend at least once a month. Leave your phone at home sometimes and feel safe and secure in that decision. It is not an extension of you.

13. Engage in time-tested ways to have fun and be happy. Play board games and do puzzles. Keep your eyes up. See the world happening around you. Stare out the window. Listen to the birds. Take a walk or a run without your phone. Make eye contact with the people around you, and say hello. If you are curious about something, ask a person who knows about it rather than googling it.

14. Don't document everything you love in pictures and videos. When you take a picture, it hinders your ability to remember the event as it happened. There is no need to document everything. Live your life and let most of your experiences be stored in your memory.

15. When we are in the car, unless you have special permission, leave your phone in your purse or in the car seat pocket—somewhere that you can't see it. Do this even if you are in someone else's car.

16. All meals in our household are technology-free meals. Your phone or computer needs to be put away, out of sight. (You may need to help us with this one, too.)

17. Keep your phone out of the dining room, kitchen, and bathrooms.

18. If you would like to watch YouTube or other videos on your phone or computer, please do not do it while in bed. You may do so outside of your bedroom in common areas of the house.

19. If you choose to have social media on your phone, use the limits feature of Screen Time or another similar app. We will keep an eye on your screen time using this app as well.

20. Your first responsibility is to be a good family member. Please do not let your phone distract you from your household responsibilities. We expect you to do your homework, keep your bedroom and common areas clean, and do your chores before texting with your friends and using your devices. If we ask you

to do something and you don't do it, we will take your devices away so that you can pay better attention to your responsibilities. Similarly, if you are spending too much time on a device and this is affecting your mood or your relationships with your family, we will give you a little break from technology.

21. You will make mistakes, and that is okay. We will take away your phone. We will sit down and talk about it. We will start over again. We are all always learning. We are on your team, and we are in this together.

We hope that you can agree to these terms. Most of the lessons listed here do not apply only to phones or screen time, but to life in general. You are growing up fast in a rapidly changing world. It is exciting and enticing. Remember to trust your powerful mind and giant heart above any device or machine.

We love you forever and ever, no matter what.

Love,
Mom & Dad

❏ I have read and agree to these terms. Can I have my phone now?

❏ I have put my passwords in the Google document that we all have access to, and I agree to keep this up to date.

Signed _____

Parent promise: I also agree to live by these guidelines and to be an excellent role model.

Mom: _____   Date: _____

Dad: _____   Date: _____

Summary of Family Technology Rules

Places where phone, tablet, and computer use is not allowed:

- dining room
- kitchen
- bathroom
- in your bed

Times when phone, tablet, and computer use is not allowed:

- during meals, even if you are eating alone
  — Mindful eating is important for health and happiness.
- when we are in the car as a family (except, at times, on long road trips)
  — It's important to not start feeling like the car is automatically time for texting and catching up on social media.
  — It's important to look out the window and know where you are.
  — Car time can be quiet time to think and listen to music, and this stillness is really important for happiness.
- while you are studying (unless you are working over the phone with a friend or need your computer to do your homework)
  — It's important to be able to dedicate time to focus on your learning for about forty-five minutes at a time. Your phone should not be within reach or visible to you during this time.
- at night, starting thirty minutes before bedtime

Acknowledgments

I would not have written this book were it not for my amazing kids and loving husband. Mark, Macie, Fiona, Tanner, and Molly: *thank you* for being so patient with me. Extra special thanks goes to our youngest, who, through no fault of her own, has had to deal with me and all my great parenting ideas the most. Molly, you are truly hilarious when you imitate me; thanks for helping me lighten up and not take everything so seriously. Huge thanks also goes to Molly and Fiona's dad, Mike, who is a great co-parent. Mike, thank you for never making fun of me and for always taking my anxious phone calls seriously.

Sayra: Thank you for being so open with me about your struggles, and for all you've contributed to both this book and our family. We love you so much.

Thank you to Amy Rennert, Glenn Yeffeth, Leah Wilson, and the whole team at BenBella for believing in this project from the start. Thanks to Joe Rhatigan and Claire Schulz for their editing and unending positivity. Thank you to Karen Wise for fabulous copy editing, and to Lisa Story and Ashley Casteel for so carefully proofreading this book. Thanks to Chloe Kormos and Margaret Phipps for your research assistance. Jessika Rieck and Sarah Avinger, many thanks to you and your team for production, for the terrific cover and beautiful interior design. And although we didn't end up working together on this book, I'm also grateful to Marnie Cochran for forcing me to figure out what I really wanted this book to be.

I'm grateful to all those who helped this book find a wider stage, especially Jennifer Canzoneri, Adrienne Lang, Alicia Kania, Marielle

Reading, Michelle Fee Smith, Amy Rennert, and all the many, many people who championed this book before it even existed in print.

This book would not have been so fun to write were it not for all the people who read so much (or all!) of it and gave me comments—especially my friends Marie Lyons and Rona Renner. Thanks also to Marissa Harrison, Maureen Kelly, Candice Atherton, Richard Ryan, Susie Rinehart, Marielle Reading, Laura Beth Nielsen, and Sabina McMahon.

Special thanks to Marielle Reading: You make work fun, and you make everything I do possible. Thank you for being a great friend and colleague.

This book has been a few years in the making, and I'd be remiss to not thank Michael Mulligan for originally agreeing to write it with me! This turned out not to be our project together, MKM, but I look forward to the one that is. I miss working with you.

Many of the ideas in this book started as columns for *Greater Good Magazine*, and I'm so grateful for the crew at the Greater Good Science Center. Jason and Jeremy, thank you for your careful editing. Kira, Jesse, and Elise: Your support has made such a difference to me—thank you for keeping me around. Special thanks to Tom and Ruth Ann Hornaday and Dacher Keltner for their longtime support and friendship. I love my career, and I would not have it were it not for you three.

I am blessed to have such great friends, and I know that I couldn't have written this book without their love and support, both practical and emotional. You all have endured many, many hours listening to me think out loud about raising teenagers. Thanks to Claire Ferrari, Dan Mulhern, Jen Burke, Michael and Joy Sawyer Mulligan, Steve Wilde, Annie and Coley Cassidy, Susie Rinehart, Laura Beth Nielsen, Kelly Huber, Kendra Perry, Michelle Gale, Monique DeVane, Melissa Raymond, and Chris Boas. I'm extra grateful for the Turducken gang: You mean the world to me. Thank you especially to Alex Peterson for all of your help raising my teenagers, and for being so loving and loyal. I am so grateful and lucky to count each one of you as a dear friend.

Thank you to Richard Cuadra for providing support and insight to me personally, but also to so many of my friends and family members. You've been such a lifesaver, and I could not have written this book or raised my teenagers if you didn't have my back.

Thank you to my big, beautiful family. Thanks to the whole Bell-Carter gang for your unconditional love and ready fun. Amy, you are like a sister to me. Jeanne, thank you for always being such a great mentor, friend, and cousin. Uncle Jud and Aunt Judy, thanks for being Grammy and Grampy Snuggles to all my kids. Timmy, your love and support has meant everything; also, the fact that you turned out great despite your wild adolescence has been a great solace to me. Sammy, I really appreciate all the little ways you've supported both my kids and my work. A huge, raucous thanks to the Millstein Swartz clan for all the many ways you've loved and supported me during this project. Barbara, Alisa, and Brian: you've been the best role models I can imagine for raising amazing, well-adjusted teenagers.

Last but certainly not least: Nonie and Dadu, you are the *best*. Thank you for teaching me how to raise teenagers in a different era—thankfully, many of your lessons have been timeless. I love you both more than I can express.

Notes

Preface

xi   **Fewer than half**   "Stress in America: Generation Z," American Psychological Association, October 2018, https://www.apa.org/news/press/releases /stress/2018/stress-gen-z.pdf.

xi   **Last year, almost one-third**   L. Kann, T. McManus, W. A. Harris, et al., "Youth Risk Behavior Surveillance: United States 2017," Centers for Disease Control and Prevention *Surveillance Summaries* 67 (June 15, 2018): 1–114, doi:10.15585/mmwr.ss6708a1.

xi   **The number of American adolescents**   Brett Burstein, Holly Agostino, and Brian Greenfield, "Suicidal Attempts and Ideation Among Children and Adolescents in US Emergency Departments, 2007–2015," *JAMA Pediatrics* 173 (April 2019): 9–11, doi:10.1001/jamapediatrics.2019.0464.

xi   **Since 2008**   Burstein, Agostino, and Greenfield, "Suicidal Attempts and Ideation Among Children and Adolescents."

Introduction

xvi   **mental illness in teenagers**   I keep my eye on large nationally representative databases like Monitoring the Future (MtF), the Centers for Disease Control and Prevention's Youth Risk Behavior Surveillance System (YRBSS), the Higher Education Research Institute's American Freshman (AF) Survey, and the General Social Survey (GSS). A recent survey by the National Survey on Drug Use and Health, conducted by the US Department of Health and Human Services, shows that depressive episodes are up almost 60 percent compared to 2010.

xvi   **"It's a tsunami"**   Jean M. Twenge, *iGen: Why Today's Super-Connected Kids Are Growing Up Less Rebellious, More Tolerant, Less Happy—and Completely Unprepared for Adulthood—and What That Means for the Rest of Us* (New York: Simon and Schuster, 2017).

xvii   **More than 60 percent**   Twenge, *iGen*, "Appendix A: Sources, Methods, and Separating Cohorts and Time Periods," http://www.jeantwenge.com/wp -content/uploads/2017/08/igen-appendix.pdf/.

225

xviii **"In homes and classrooms"**   Vicki Abeles, *Beyond Measure: Rescuing an Overscheduled, Overtested, Underestimated Generation* (New York: Simon and Schuster, 2016).

xviii **the American Freshman Survey**   American College Health Association, "American College Health Association/National College Health Assessment II: Reference Group Executive Summary, Spring 2018" (Hanover, MD: American College Health Association, 2018).

xix   **In the late 1970s**   Twenge, *iGen.*

xix   **teens with lower socioeconomic status . . . tried to do it**   L. Kann, T. McManus, W. A. Harris, et al., "Youth Risk Behavior Surveillance: United States 2017," Centers for Disease Control and Prevention *Surveillance Summaries* 67 (June 15, 2018): 1–114, doi:10.15585/mmwr.ss6708a1.

xxi   **Eric "Astro" Teller**   Thomas L. Friedman, *Thank You for Being Late* (London: Penguin UK, 2016).

xxiii **40 percent of Americans today**   Board of Governors of the Federal Reserve System, "Report on the Economic Well-Being of US Households in 2017," May 2018, https://www.federalreserve.gov/publications/files/2017-report-economic-well-being-us-households-201805.pdf.

Chapter One

5   **An interesting study**   Robert Epstein, "What Makes a Good Parent?" *Scientific American Mind* 21, no. 5 (November 2010): 46–51, doi:10.1038/scientificamericanmind1110-46.

6   **this sort of self-focus is linked**   L. Scherwitz, K. Berton, and H. Leventhal, "Type A Behavior, Self-Involvement, and Cardiovascular Response," *Psychosomatic Medicine* 40, no. 8 (December 1978): 593–609, doi:10.1097/00006842-197812000-00002.

12   **Compared to those**   Sarah Whittle, Julian Simmons, Meg Dennison, et al., "Positive Parenting Predicts the Development of Adolescent Neural Reward Circuitry: A Longitudinal Study," *Frontiers in Human Neuroscience* 7 (March 2014), doi:10.3389/conf.fnhum.2013.212.00074.

12   **In one study**   Yang Qu, Andrew J. Fuligni, Adriana Galvan, et al., "Buffering Effect of Positive Parent-Child Relationships on Adolescent Risk Taking: A Longitudinal Neuroimaging Investigation," *Developmental Cognitive Neuroscience* 15 (October 2015): 26–34, doi:10.1016/j.dcn.2015.08.005.

12   **Research shows that**   Golan Shahar and Christopher C. Henrich, "Perceived Family Social Support Buffers Against the Effects of Exposure to Rocket Attacks on Adolescent Depression, Aggression, and Severe Violence." *Journal of Family Psychology* 30, no. 1 (2016): 163–68, doi:10.1037/fam0000179; Melissa A. Milkie, Kei M. Nomaguchi, and Kathleen E. Denny, "Does the Amount of Time Mothers Spend with Children or Adolescents Matter?" *Journal of Marriage and Family* 77, no. 2 (2015): 355–72, doi:10.1111/jomf.12170; M. Hojat

and M. D. Resnick, "Protecting Adolescents from Harm—Reply," *JAMA Journal of the American Medical Association* 279, no. 5 (1998): 353–54; Chun Bun Lamb, Susan M. McHale, and Ann C. Crouter, "Parent-Child Shared Time from Middle Childhood to Late Adolescence: Developmental Course and Adjustment Correlates," *Child Development* 83, no. 6 (2012): 2089–103, doi:10.1111/j.1467-8624.2012.01826.x.

Chapter Two

16   **A mountain of research**   David Scott Yeager, Rebecca Johnson, Brian James Spitzer, et al., "The Far-Reaching Effects of Believing People Can Change: Implicit Theories of Personality, Shape, Stress, Health, and Achievement During Adolescence." *Journal of Personality and Social Psychology* 106, no. 6 (June 2014): 867–84, doi:10.1037/a0036335; F. Petito and R. A. Cummins, "Quality of Life in Adolescence: The Role of Perceived Control, Parenting Style, and Social Support," *Behaviour Change* 17, no. 3 (2000): 196–207, doi:10.1375/bech.17.3.196; Jonathan Haidt and Judith Rodin, "Control and Efficacy as Interdisciplinary Bridges," *Review of General Psychology* 3, no. 4 (1999): 317–37, doi:10.1037/1089-2680.3.4.317.

17   **by one study's estimate**   Daniel Kindlon, *Too Much of a Good Thing: Raising Children of Character in an Indulgent Age* (New York: Hyperion, 2001).

24   **autonomy, competence, and relatedness**   Katie E. Gunnell, Peter R. E. Crocker, Philip M. Wilson, et al., "Psychological Need Satisfaction and Thwarting: A Test of Basic Psychological Needs Theory in Physical Activity Contexts." *Psychology of Sport and Exercise* 14, no. 5 (2013): 599–607, doi:10.1016/j.psychsport.2013.03.007.

26   **This not-making-a-plan thing**   Sarah Jayne Blakemore and Suparna Choudhury, "Development of the Adolescent Brain: Implications for Executive Function and Social Cognition," *Journal of Child Psychology and Psychiatry and Allied Disciplines* 47, no. 3–4 (March/April 2006): 296–312, doi:10.1111/j.1469-7610.2006.01611.x.

Chapter Three

34   **one in eight people struggle with hunger**   Nicholas Kristof, "3 TVs and No Food: Growing Up Poor in America," *New York Times,* Opinion, October 28, 2016, https://www.nytimes.com/2016/10/30/opinion/sunday/3-tvs-and-no-food-growing-up-poor-in-america.html.

34   **more than 12 percent**   Kayla R. Fontenot, Jessica L. Semega, and Melissa A. Kollar, United States Census Bureau, "Income and Poverty in the United States: 2017," September 12, 2018, https://www.census.gov/content/census/en/library/publications/2018/demo/p60-263.html.

34   **About 80 percent**   United States Census Bureau, "2017 American Housing Survey Data," September 6, 2018, https://www.census.gov/newsroom/press -releases/2018/ahs.html.

35   **A mountain of research shows**   Morley D. Glicken, "Understanding Resilience," in *Learning from Resilient People: Lessons We Can Apply to Counseling and Psychotherapy* (Thousand Oaks, CA: SAGE Publications, 2006).

37   **there is surprisingly little evidence**   For a full literature review, see Johann Hari, *Lost Connections: Uncovering the Real Causes of Depression—and the Unexpected Solutions* (New York: Bloomsbury USA, 2018).

37   **In 2017, 191 million**   Christine L. Mattson, Lyna Schieber, Lawrence Scholl, et al., "Annual Surveillance Report of Drug-Related Risks and Outcomes: United States, 2017," Centers for Disease Control and Prevention, https://www.cdc.gov/drugoverdose/pdf/pubs/2017-cdc-drug-surveillance -report.pdf.

41   **a convenient acronym, NUTS**   "N.U.T.S.: Understanding Stress," Heart-Mind Online, accessed June 24, 2019, https://heartmindonline.org/resources/ nuts-understanding-stress.

42   **Three-quarters of teenagers . . . do not yet have this ability**   "Stress in America: Generation Z," American Psychological Association, October 2018, https://www.apa.org/news/press/releases/stress/2018/stress-gen-z.pdf.

42   **nearly half say social media**   "Stress in America: Generation Z."

42   **the number of daily hassles**   Jeffrey G. Johnson and Martin F. Sherman, "Daily Hassles Mediate the Relationship Between Major Life Events and Psychiatric Symptomatology: Longitudinal Findings from an Adolescent Sample," *Journal of Social and Clinical Psychology* 16, no. 4 (1997): 389–404, doi:10.1521/ jscp.1997.16.4.389.

44   **Research psychologist Kristin Neff**   Kelley J. Robinson, Selina Mayer, Ashley Batts Allen, et al., "Resisting Self-Compassion: Why Are Some People Opposed to Being Kind to Themselves?" *Self and Identity* 15, no. 5 (2016): 505–24, doi:10 .1080/15298868.2016.1160952.

46   **the "undoing effect" of positive emotions**   Barbara L. Fredrickson, Roberta A Mancuso, Christine Branigan, et al., "The Undoing Effect of Positive Emotions." *Motivation and Emotion* 24, no. 4 (December 2000): 237–58, doi:10.1023/a:1010796329158.

51   **People who jotted down**   Emiliana R. Simon-Thomas, "A 'Thnx' a Day Keeps the Doctor Away," Greater Good Science Center, December 19, 2012, http:// greatergood.berkeley.edu/article/item/a_thnx_a_day_keeps_the_doctor_away.

51   **Researchers induce awe**   Patty Van Cappellen and Vasslis Saroglou, "Awe Activates Religious and Spiritual Feelings and Behavioral Intentions," *Psychology of Religion and Spirituality* 4, no. 3 (2012): 223–36, doi:10.1037/a0025986; Stacey Kennelly, "Can Awe Buy You More Time and Happiness?" *Greater Good Magazine*, August 17, 2012, http://greatergood.berkeley.edu/article/item/ can_awe_buy_you_more_time_and_happiness.

51   **It can make you feel**   Melanie Rudd, Kathleen D. Vohs, and Jennifer Aaker, "Psychological Science," *Psychological Science* (October 2012): 1–22, doi:10.1177/0956797612438731; Kennelly, "Can Awe Buy You More Time and Happiness?"

51   **One way to foster hope**   Laura A. King, "The Health Benefits of Writing About Life Goals," *Personality and Social Psychology Bulletin* 27, no. 7 (July 1, 2001): 798–807, doi:10.1177/0146167201277003.

51   **something that tends to motivate**   Kennon M. Sheldon and Sonja Lyubomirsky, "How to Increase and Sustain Positive Emotion: The Effects of Expressing Gratitude and Visualizing Best Possible Selves," *Journal of Positive Psychology* 1, no. 2 (2006): 73–82, doi:10.1080/17439760500510676.

52   **detailed instructions for this exercise**   "Best Possible Self," Greater Good in Action, accessed June 13, 2019, https://ggia.berkeley.edu/practice/best_possible_self.

53   **Scores of studies . . . makes people healthier**   Luke Fortney and Molly Taylor, "Meditation in Medical Practice: A Review of the Evidence and Practice," *Primary Care: Clinics in Office Practice* 37, no. 1 (March 2010): 81–90, doi:10.1016/j.pop.2009.09.004.

53   **After meditating daily**   Bruce Barrett, "Meditation or Exercise for Preventing Acute Respiratory Infection: A Randomized Controlled Trial," *Annals of Family Medicine* 10, no. 4 (2012): 337–46, doi:10.1370/afm.1376.

53   **listening to music reduces these signs**   Stephanie Khalfa, Simone Dalla Bella, Mathieu Roy, et al., "Effects of Relaxing Music on Salivary Cortisol Level after Psychological Stress," *Annals of the New York Academy of Sciences* 999, no. 1 (2003): 374–76, doi:10.1370/afm.1376.

53   **Exercise prepares our brains**   Thomas Stephens, "Physical Activity and Mental Health in the United States and Canada: Evidence from Four Population Surveys," *Preventive Medicine* 17, no. 1 (January 1988): 35–47, doi:10.1016/0091-7435(88)90070-9.

53   **Laughter lowers stress hormones**   Mary Payne Bennett and Cecile Lengacher, "Humor and Laughter May Influence Health III: Laughter and Health Outcomes." *Evidence-Based Complementary and Alternative Medicine (eCAM)* 5, no. 1 (March 2008): 37–40, doi:10.1093/ecam/nem041; Mary Payne Bennett and Cecile Lengacher, "Humor and Laughter May Influence Health IV: Humor and Immune Function," *Evidence-Based Complementary and Alternative Medicine (eCAM)* 6, no. 2 (June 2009): 159–64, doi:10.1093/ecam/nem149.

Chapter Four

56   **what is somewhat effective for elementary school children**   D. S. Yeager, R. E. Dahl, and C. S. Dweck, "Why Interventions to Influence Adolescent Behavior Often Fail but Could Succeed," *Perspectives on Psychological Science* 13, no. 1 (2018): 101–22, doi:10.1177/1745691617722620.

56   **motivational interviewing from Ron Dahl**   Melanie A. Gold and Ronald E. Dahl, "Using Motivational Interviewing to Facilitate Healthier Sleep-Related Behaviors in Adolescents," in *Behavioral Treatments for Sleep Disorders* (Cambridge, MA: Academic Press, 2011), 367–81.

70   **self-compassionate students**   Bianca Lorenz, "Self-Compassion for Freshmen," *Greater Good Magazine*, October 8, 2013, https://greatergood.berkeley.edu/article/item/self_compassion_for_freshmen.

Chapter Five

74   **Half of parents surveyed**   Association for Psychological Science, "Teens Unlikely to be Harmed by Moderate Digital Screen Use," January 13, 2017, accessed June 13, 2019, https://www.psychologicalscience.org/news/releases/teens-unlikely-to-be-harmed-by-moderate-digital-screen-use.html; Common Sense Media, "Common Sense Media/SurveyMonkey YouTube Poll Topline," accessed June 13, 2019, https://d2e111jq13me73.cloudfront.net/sites/default/files/uploads/pdfs/commonsense-surveymonkey-youtube-topline.pdf.

74   **American teens who spend more time online**   Jean M. Twenge, *iGen: Why Today's Super-Connected Kids Are Growing Up Less Rebellious, More Tolerant, Less Happy—and Completely Unprepared for Adulthood—and What That Means for the Rest of Us* (New York: Simon and Schuster, 2017).

74   **This is compared to 28 percent**   Twenge, *iGen.*

75   **study published in *Psychological Science***   Andrew K. Przybylski and Netta Weinstein, "A Large-Scale Test of the Goldilocks Hypothesis: Quantifying the Relations Between Digital-Screen Use and the Mental Well-Being of Adolescents," *Psychological Science* 28, no. 2 (2017): 204–15, doi:10.1177/0956797616678438.

76   **there are several studies**   Ethan Kross, Philippe Verduyn, Emre Demiralp, et al., "Facebook Use Predicts Declines in Subjective Well-Being in Young Adults." *PloS one* 8, no. 8 (2013): e69841, doi:10.1371/journal.pone.0069841; Holly B. Shakya and Nicholas A. Christakis, "Association of Facebook Use with Compromised Well-Being: A Longitudinal Study," *American Journal of Epidemiology* 185, no. 3 (2017): 203–11, doi:10.1093/aje/kww189; Morten Tromholt, "The Facebook Experiment: Quitting Facebook Leads to Higher Levels of Well-Being," *Cyberpsychology, Behavior, and Social Networking* 19, no. 11 (2016): 661–66, doi:10.1089/cyber.2016.0259.

77   **A surprising 48 percent**   Jean M. Twenge, A. Bell Cooper, Thomas E. Joiner, et al., "Age, Period, and Cohort Trends in Mood Disorder Indicators and Suicide-Related Outcomes in a Nationally Representative Dataset, 2005–2017," *Journal of Abnormal Psychology* 128, no. 3 (2019): 185–99, doi:10.1037/abn0000410.

78   **Brain studies show**   Naomi I. Eisenberger, Matthew D. Lieberman, and Kipling D. Williams, "Does Rejection Hurt? An fMRI Study of Social Exclusion," *Science* 302, no. 5643 (2003): 290–92, doi:10.1126/science.1089134; Geoff

MacDonald and Mark R. Leary, "Why Does Social Exclusion Hurt? The Relationship Between Social and Physical Pain," *Psychological Bulletin* 131, no. 2 (2005): 202, doi:10.1037/0033-2909.131.2.202.

78   **research documents that**   Twenge, *iGen*, "Appendix A: Sources, Methods, and Separating Cohorts and Time Periods," http://www.jeantwenge.com/wp-content/uploads/2017/08/igen-appendix.pdf.

78   **Experiments by neuroscientist John Cacioppo**   Louise C. Hawkley and John T. Cacioppo, "Loneliness Matters: A Theoretical and Empirical Review of Consequences and Mechanisms," *Annals of Behavioral Medicine* 40, no. 2 (2010): 218–27, doi:10.1007/s12160-010-9210-8.

78   **students entering college today**   Twenge,. *iGen*, "Appendix A: Sources, Methods, and Separating Cohorts and Time Periods," http://www.jeantwenge.com/wp-content/uploads/2017/08/igen-appendix.pdf.

79   **The data show**   Twenge et al., "Age, Period, and Cohort Trends."

79   **Psychologist Tim Kasser's work**   Tim Kasser, *The High Price of Materialism* (Cambridge, MA: MIT Press, 2002).

79   **spending a lot of time on smartphones**   Pengcheng Wang, Jia Nie, Xingchao Wang, et al., "How Are Smartphones Associated with Adolescent Materialism?," *Journal of Health Psychology* (September 2018), doi:1359105318801069.

80   **the median upper-income family . . . 90 percent** *combined*   "Income Inequality in the United States," Income Inequality, accessed June 9, 2019, https://inequality.org/facts/income-inequality/.

80   **In 2007, top earners**   Rakesh Kochhar and Anthony Cilluffo, "How Wealth Inequality Has Changed in the U.S. since the Great Recession, by Race, Ethnicity and Income," Pew Research Center, November 1, 2017, http://www.pewresearch.org/fact-tank/2017/11/01/how-wealth-inequality-has-changed-in-the-u-s-since-the-great-recession-by-race-ethnicity-and-income/.

81   **social awareness is heightened**   David S. Yeager, Ronald E. Dahl, and Carol S. Dweck, "Why Interventions to Influence Adolescent Behavior Often Fail but Could Succeed," *Perspectives on Psychological Science* 13, no. 1 (2018): 101–22, doi:10.1177/1745691617722620.

81   **Just a momentary shift**   Donald H. Edwards and Edward A. Kravitz, "Serotonin, Social Status and Aggression," *Current Opinion in Neurobiology* 7, no. 6 (1997): 812–19, doi:10.1016/S0959-4388(97)80140-7.

81   **It's having a large breadth**   George E. Vaillant, *Triumphs of Experience: The Men of the Harvard Grant Study* (Cambridge, MA: Harvard University Press, 2012).

82   **Preterm babies**   Tiffany Field, Miguel Diego, and Maria Hernandez-Reif "Preterm Infant Massage Therapy Research: A Review," *Infant Behavior and Development* 33, no. 2 (April 2010): 115–24, doi:10.1016/j.infbeh.2009.12.004.

82   **Touch promotes trust . . . love and compassion**   Dacher Keltner, "Hands On Research: The Science of Touch," *Greater Good Magazine*, September 29, 2010, https://greatergood.berkeley.edu/article/item/hands_on_research.

83   **There's a series of studies**   James A. Coan, Hillary S. Schaefer, and
      Richard J. Davidson, "Lending a Hand: Social Regulation of the Neu-
      ral Response to Threat," *Psychological Science* 17, no. 12 (2006): 1032–39,
      doi:10.1111/j.1467-9280.2006.01832.x.

83   **one study showed that the brief touches**   M. W. Kraus, C. Huang, and D.
      Keltner, "Tactile Communication, Cooperation, and Performance: An Etholog-
      ical Study of the NBA," *Emotion* 10, no. 5 (2010): 745–49, doi:10.1037/a0019382.

86   **Kids who eat dinner . . . being close-knit as a family**   Joseph A. Califano,
      "The Importance of Family Dinners VI," National Center on Addiction and Sub-
      stance Abuse at Columbia University, September 2010, https://www.centeron
      addiction.org/addiction-research/reports/importance-of-family-dinners-2010.

87   **people who focus on family or religion**   T. Kasser and Kennon M Sheldon,
      "What Makes for a Merry Christmas?" *Journal of Happiness Studies* 3 (August
      2002): 313–29, doi:10.1023/A:1021516410457.

89   **"If religion was once"**   Emily Esfahani Smith, *The Power of Meaning: Finding
      Fulfillment in a World Obsessed with Happiness* (New York: Broadway Books,
      2017).

90   **In the 1960s, the top priority**   John H. Pryor, Sylvia Hurtado, Victor B.
      Saenz, et al., "The American Freshman: Forty-Year Trends," *Los Angeles: Higher
      Education Research Institute* 3 (2007).

90   **But today, the top priority**   Kevin Eagen, Ellen Stolzenberg, Hilary Zimmer-
      man, et al., "The American Freshman: National Norms 2016," accessed June 13,
      2019 https://www.heri.ucla.edu/monographs/TheAmericanFreshman2016.pdf.

90   **People who find a reason for being**   The Purpose Challenge, accessed June
      13, 2019 http://purposechallenge.org/; Stacey Kennelly, "Can Awe Buy you
      More Time and Happiness?" *Greater Good Magazine*, August 17, 2012, https://
      greatergood.berkeley.edu/article/item/can_awe_buy_you_more_time_and
      _happiness; Neil Si-Jia Zhang, "Can Purpose Keep you Alive?" *Greater Good
      Magazine*, August 27, 2014, https://greatergood.berkeley.edu/article/item
      /can_purpose_keep_you_alive.

91   **Ask them: . . . difference in the world?**   The Purpose Challenge.

Chapter Six

94   **The prevalence of children diagnosed**   G. Xu, L. Strathearn, B. Liu, et al.,
      (2018). "Twenty-Year Trends in Diagnosed Attention-Deficit/Hyperactivity
      Disorder Among US Children and Adolescents, 1997–2016," *JAMA Network
      Open* 1, no, 4 (2018): e181471, doi:10.1001/jamanetworkopen.2018.1471.

95   **Currently more than 6 million**   Xu et al., "Twenty-Year Trends."

95   **there has also been a sharp rise**   WebMD, "ADHD Drug Use by Young
      Adults Doubled: Report," March 13, 2014, https://www.webmd.com/add-adhd
      /news/20140312/adhd-drugs-young-adults.

98   **By 2015, high school seniors**   Jean M. Twenge, *iGen: Why Today's Super-Connected Kids Are Growing Up Less Rebellious, More Tolerant, Less Happy—and Completely Unprepared for Adulthood—and What That Means for the Rest of Us* (New York: Simon and Schuster, 2017).

100   **In adults, multitasking slows**   Tony Schwartz and Catherine McCarthy, "Manage Your Energy, Not Your Time," *Harvard Business Review* 85, no. 10 (2007): 63.

101   **According to cognitive neuroscientist Daniel Levitin**   Daniel J. Levitin, *The Organized Mind: Thinking Straight in the Age of Information Overload* (New York: Penguin, 2014).

104   **On average, interruptions take**   Kermit Pattison, "Worker, Interrupted: The Cost of Task Switching," *Fast Company*, July 28, 2008, https://www.fastcompany.com/944128/worker-interrupted-cost-task-switching.

104   **A mountain of research**   Erik M. Altmann, J. Gregory Trafton, and David Z. Hambrick, "Momentary Interruptions Can Derail the Train of Thought," *Journal of Experimental Psychology: General* 143, no. 1 (2014): 215, doi:10.1037/a0030986.

104   **Just being in a work situation**   Martin Wainwright, "Emails 'Pose Threat to IQ,'" *Guardian*, April 22, 2005, https://www.theguardian.com/technology/2005/apr/22/money.workandcareers.

105   **People who've been interrupted**   Pattison, "Worker, Interrupted: The Cost of Task Switching."

105   **This makes a lot of people feel**   Brian P. Bailey and Joseph A. Konstan, "On the Need for Attention-Aware Systems: Measuring Effects of Interruption on Task Performance, Error Rate, and Affective State," *Computers in Human Behavior* 22, no. 4 (2006): 685–708, doi:10.1016/j.chb.2005.12.009.

107   **"That constant awareness"**   Nadia Goodman, "How to Achieve a State of Total Concentration," *Entrepreneur*, February 6, 2013, https://www.entrepreneur.com/article/225663.

107   **Research shows that proximity matters**   "The Mere Presence of Your Smartphone Reduces Brain Power, Study Shows," *UT News*, June 26, 2017, https://news.utexas.edu/2017/06/26/the-mere-presence-of-your-smartphone-reduces-brain-power/.

Chapter Seven

109   **Nearly half of male college students**   American College Health Association, "American College Health Association/National College Health Assessment II: Reference Group Executive Summary, Fall 2018" (Silver Spring, MD: American College Health Association; 2018), https://www.acha.org/documents/ncha/NCHA-II_Fall_2018_Reference_Group_Executive_Summary.pdf.

110   **This trouble with busyness**   Mihaly Csikszentmihalyi and Isabella Selega Csikszentmihalyi, eds., *Optimal Experience: Psychological Studies of Flow in Consciousness* (Cambridge, UK: Cambridge University Press, 1992).

112   **This state of feeling overwhelmed**   Daniel Goleman, *Focus: The Hidden Driver of Excellence* (New York: Harper, 2013).

112   **We have two primary attentional networks**   Daniel J. Levitin, *The Organized Mind: Thinking Straight in the Age of Information Overload* (New York: Penguin, 2014).

113   **Many people (67 percent**   Timothy D. Wilson, David A. Reinhard, Erin C. Westgate, et al., "Just Think: The Challenges of the Disengaged Mind," *Science* 345, no. 6192 (2014): 75–77, doi:10.1126/science.1250830.

113   **All those neurons start making connections**   All of this explains other research that shows that conscious, effortful thinking does nothing to improve creativity, or to help people come up with innovative solutions to problems. For example, when researchers give people a task that requires creativity (such as instructions to come up with a list of ways to use a brick), people don't generate longer or more creative lists if they have a few extra minutes to think before they start. See, for example, Mathias Benedek, Caterina Mühlmann, Emanuel Jauk, et al., "Assessment of Divergent Thinking by Means of the Subjective Top-Scoring Method: Effects of the Number of Top-Ideas and Time-on-Task on Reliability and Validity," *Psychology of Aesthetics, Creativity, and the Arts* 7, no. 4 (2013): 341, doi:10.1037/a0033644.

114   **research shows that close to half**   Jean M. Twenge, Zlatan Krizan, and Garrett Hisler, "Decreases in Self-Reported Sleep Duration Among US Adolescents, 2009–2015, and Association with New Media Screen Time," *Sleep Medicine* 9 (November 2017): 47–53, doi:10.1016/j.sleep.2017.08.013.

115   **Teens who regularly get less**   Jean M. Twenge, *iGen: Why Today's Super-Connected Kids Are Growing Up Less Rebellious, More Tolerant, Less Happy—and Completely Unprepared for Adulthood—and What That Means for the Rest of Us* (New York: Simon and Schuster, 2017).

115   **sleep-deprived people are less inclined**   E. Ben Simon and M. P. Walker, "Sleep Loss Causes Social Withdrawal and Loneliness," *Nature Communications* 9, no. 1 (August 14, 2018): 3146, doi:10.1038/s41467-018-05377-0.

121   **A mountain of research supports this claim**   Matthew Walker, *Why We Sleep: Unlocking the Power of Sleep and Dreams* (New York: Simon and Schuster, 2017).

Chapter Eight

131   **Justin Garcia, the research director**   Nancy Jo Sales, "Tinder and the Dawn of the 'Dating Apocalypse,'" *Vanity Fair*, August 5, 2015, https://www.vanityfair.com/culture/2015/08/tinder-hook-up-culture-end-of-dating; Chris ChoGlueck, "Sexual Science: An Interview with Justin Garcia," *Indiana*

University Bloomington, May 29, 2018, https://blogs.iu.edu/sciu/2018/05/29/sexual-science-justin-garcia/.

131 **"Sex has become so easy"** Sales, "Tinder."

132 **"I'll get a text that says"** Sales, "Tinder."

132 **Tinder users, for example** Sindy R. Sumter, Laura Vandenbosch, and Loes Ligtenberg, "Love Me Tinder: Untangling Emerging Adults' Motivations for Using the Dating Application Tinder," *Telematics and Informatics* 34, no. 1 (2017): 67–78, doi:10.1016/j.tele.2016.04.009.

132 **research by the Japanese government** Tracy McVeigh, "For Japan's 'Stranded Singles,' Virtual Love Beats the Real Thing," *Guardian*, November 20, 2016, https://www.theguardian.com/world/2016/nov/20/japan-stranded-singles-virtual-love.

132 **12 percent of all...eleven years old** The D Infographics, "Internet Pornography Statistics," December 23, 2011, http://thedinfographics.com/2011/12/23/internet-pornography-statistics/.

133 **most experts believe** Cindy Pierce, *Sex, College, and Social Media: A Commonsense Guide to Navigating the Hookup Culture* (New York: Routledge, 2016).

133 **kids *younger than ten years old*** Russ Warner, "The Detrimental Effects of Pornography on Small Children," Net Nanny, December 19, 2017, https://www.netnanny.com/blog/the-detrimental-effects-of-pornography-on-small-children/.

133 **As late as 2006** Jean M. Twenge, *iGen: Why Today's Super-Connected Kids Are Growing Up Less Rebellious, More Tolerant, Less Happy—and Completely Unprepared for Adulthood—and What That Means for the Rest of Us* (New York: Simon and Schuster, 2017).

134 **But the research finds no significant gender differences** S. Madigan, A. Ly, C. L. Rash, et al., "Prevalence of Multiple Forms of Sexting Behavior Among Youth: A Systematic Review and Meta-analysis," *JAMA Pediatrics* 172, no. 4 (2018): 327–335, doi:10.1001/jamapediatrics.2017.5314.

134 **Today, the number of sexually active . . . 39 percent of girls** Centers for Disease Control, "Trends in the Prevalence of Sexual Behaviors and HIV Testing National YRBS: 1991–2017," 2017, https://www.cdc.gov/healthyyouth/data/yrbs/pdf/trends/2017_sexual_trend_yrbs.pdf.

135 **They are simply less sexually active** Child Trends, "Sexual Activity Among Teens," 2017, https://www.childtrends.org/indicators/sexual-activity-among-teens.

135 **they say they don't go on dates . . . 60 percent** Child Trends, "Dating Among Teens," 2019, https://www.childtrends.org/indicators/dating.

136 **Hookup culture promises** Peggy Orenstein, *Girls and Sex: Navigating the Complicated New Landscape* (New York: Oneworld Publications, 2016).

136 **teenage sexual activity can directly affect** B. Soller, D. L. Haynie, and A. Kuhlemeier, "Sexual Intercourse, Romantic Relationship Inauthenticity,

and Adolescent Mental Health, *Social Science Research* 64 (2017): 237–248, doi:10.1016/j.ssresearch.2016.10.002.

136 **teenage sexual activity is associated with** D. D. Hallfors, M. W. Waller, C. A. Ford, et al., "Adolescent Depression and Suicide Risk: Association with Sex and Drug Behavior," *American Journal of Preventive Medicine* 27, no. 3 (2004): 224–31, doi:10.1016/j.amepre.2004.06.001.

136 **sexual activity predicts later depression** D. D. Hallfors, M. W. Waller, D. Bauer, et al., "Which Comes First in Adolescence: Sex and Drugs or Depression?," *American Journal of Preventive Medicine* 29, no. 3 (2005): 163–170, doi:10.1016/j.amepre.2005.06.002.

137 **only twenty-one US states teach sex and HIV education** National Conference of State Legislatures, "State Policies on Sex Education in Schools," March 21, 2019, http://www.ncsl.org/research/health/state-policies-on-sex-education -in-schools.aspx.

141 **pornography use among adolescents** David L. Perry, "The Impact of Pornography on Children," American College of Pediatricians, June 2016, https://www.acpeds.org/the-college-speaks/position-statements /the-impact-of-pornography-on-children#_ednref11.

141 **In the UK, the ChildLine counseling service** Patrick Howse, "'Pornography Addiction Worry' for Tenth of 12- to 13-Year-Olds," *BBC News,* March 31, 2015, https://www.bbc.com/news/education-32115162.

141 **A Dutch study found** Valarie Voon, "Cambridge University Study: Internet Porn Addiction Mirrors Drug Addiction," Your Brain on Porn, July 2014, https://www.yourbrainonporn.com/relevant-research-and-articles-about-the -studies/porn-use-sex-addiction-studies/cambridge-university-study-internet -porn-addiction-mirrors-drug-addiction-voon-et-al-2014/.

142 **in 1991, about one in ten . . . more than one third had** Pierce, *Sex, College, and Social Media.*

146 **One-quarter of young women regret** Andrew Galperin, Martie G. Haselton, David A. Frederick, et al., "Sexual Regret: Evidence for Evolved Sex Differences," *Archives of Sexual Behavior* 42, no. 7 (2013): 1145–61, doi:10.1007 /s10508-012-0019-3.

147 **one study showed that nearly 90 percent** Ana J. Bridges, Robert Wosnitzer, Erica Scharrer, et al., "Aggression and Sexual Behavior in Best-Selling Pornography Videos: A Content Analysis Update," *Violence Against Women* 16, no. 10 (2010): 1065–85, doi:10.1177/1077801210382866.

147 **many college men believe** Pierce, *Sex, College, and Social Media.*

147 **According to Alexandra Katehakis** Pierce, *Sex, College, and Social Media.*

150 **A national survey from the Harvard Graduate School of Education** Richard Weissbourd, Trisha Ross Anderson, Alison Cashin, et al., "The Talk: How Adults Can Promote Young People's Healthy Relationships and Prevent Misogyny and Sexual Harassment," Making Caring Common Project, May 2017, https://mcc.gse.harvard.edu/reports/the-talk.

150 **research shows that more than 44 percent** Lisa Fedina, Jennifer Lynne Holmes, and Bethany L. Backes, "Campus Sexual Assault: A Systematic Review of Prevalence Research from 2000 to 2015" *Trauma, Violence & Abuse* 19, no. 1 (2018): 76–93, doi:10.1177/1524838016631129.

151 **Transgender youth are at the highest risk** Jaime M. Grant, Lisa Mottet, Justin Edward Tanis, et al., "Injustice at Every Turn: A Report of the National Transgender Discrimination Survey" (Washington: National Center for Transgender Equality and National Gay and Lesbian Task Force, 2011), https://www.transequality.org/sites/default/files/docs/resources/NTDS_Report.pdf.

151 **college students who have been** Fedina et al., "Campus Sexual Assault."

153 **False reports of sexual assault** Pierce, *Sex, College, and Social Media*.

154 **a single, simple comment** Rotem Kahalon, Nurit Shnabel, and Julia C. Becker, "'Don't Bother Your Pretty Little Head': Appearance Compliments Lead to Improved Mood but Impaired Cognitive Performance," *Psychology of Women Quarterly* 42, no. 2 (June 2018): 136–50, doi:10.1177/0361684318758596.

155 **Simmons outlines some great guidelines** Rachel Simmons, *Enough As She Is: How to Help Girls Move Beyond Impossible Standards of Success to Live Healthy, Happy, and Fulfilling Lives* (New York: HarperCollins, 2018).

Chapter Nine

159 **Even though two-thirds of parents . . . cause their children to rebel** Bettina Friese, Joel W. Grube, Roland S. Moore, et al., "Parents' Rules About Underage Drinking: A Qualitative Study of Why Parents Let Teens Drink," *Journal of Drug Education* 42, no. 4 (July 19, 2013), doi:10.2190/DE.42.4.a.

159 **There is a lot of research** Centers for Disease Control and Prevention, "Fact Sheets: Underage Drinking," modified August 2, 2018, https://www.cdc.gov/alcohol/fact-sheets/underage-drinking.htm.

160 **Teens who use alcohol are also more likely** US Department of Health and Human Services, "Report to Congress on the Prevention and Reduction of Underage Drinking" (Washington, DC: USDHHS, 2012).

160 **binge drinking changes teen brains in visible ways** Krista M. Lisdahl, Rachel Thayer, Lindsay M. Squeglia, et al., "Recent Binge Drinking Predicts Smaller Cerebellar Volumes in Adolescents," *Psychiatry Research: Neuroimaging* 211, no. 1 (2013): 17–23, doi:10.1016/j.pscychresns.2012.07.009.

160 **In 2016, nearly 40 percent** Lloyd D. Johnston, Patrick M. O'Malley, Richard A. Miech, et al., "Monitoring the Future National Survey Results on Drug Use, 1975–2016: Overview, Key Findings on Adolescent Drug Use" (Ann Arbor, MI: Institute for Social Research, University of Michigan, 2017), http://www.monitoringthefuture.org/pubs/monographs/mtf-overview2016.pdf.

161 **they are smoking weed . . . more** Jean M. Twenge, *iGen: Why Today's Super-Connected Kids Are Growing Up Less Rebellious, More Tolerant, Less*

Happy—and Completely Unprepared for Adulthood—and What That Means for the Rest of Us (New York: Simon and Schuster, 2017).

161   **A large majority of high schoolers**   G. Austin, J. Polik, T. Hanson, et al., "School Climate, Substance Use, and Student Well-Being in California, 2015–2017," Results of the Sixteenth Biennial Statewide Student Survey (San Francisco: WestEd, 2018).

161   **perceived risk of harm is a very strong indicator**   Richard Miech, Lloyd Johnston, and Patrick M. O'Malley, "Prevalence and Attitudes Regarding Marijuana Use Among Adolescents over the Past Decade," *Pediatrics* 140, no. 6 (2017), doi:10.1542/peds.2017-0982.

161   **a solid 41 percent**   Johnston et al., "Monitoring the Future."

162   **According to neuroscientist Frances Jensen**   Frances Jensen, interview by Terry Gross, "Why Teens Are Impulsive, Addiction-Prone, and Should Protect Their Brains," *Fresh Air*, National Public Radio, January 28, 2015.

162   **a 2014 review of research**   Justine Renard, Marie-Odile Krebs, Gwenaëlle Le Pen, et al., "Long-Term Consequences of Adolescent Cannabinoid Exposure in Adult Psychopathology," *Frontiers in Neuroscience* 8 (2014): 361, doi:10.3389/fnins.2014.00361.

162   **According to Judith Grisel**   Judith Grisel, *Never Enough: The Neuroscience and Experience of Addiction* (New York: Doubleday, 2019), 193.

163   **early marijuana use is also associated**   Renard, "Long-Term Consequences of Adolescent Cannabinoid Exposure."

163   **the National Academy of Medicine released**   National Academies of Sciences, Engineering, and Medicine, *The Health Effects of Cannabis and Cannabinoids: The Current State of Evidence and Recommendations for Research* (Washington, DC: National Academies Press, 2017), doi:10.17226/24625.

164   **The report found that anxiety**   National Academies of Sciences, Engineering, and Medicine, *The Health Effects of Cannabis and Cannabinoids*.

164   **71 percent of high school seniors**   National Institute on Drug Abuse, "Monitoring the Future Survey: High School and Youth Trends," December 2018, https://www.drugabuse.gov/publications/drugfacts/monitoring-future-survey-high-school-youth-trends.

164   **marijuana use is associated**   Substance Abuse and Mental Health Services Administration, "Key Substance Use and Mental Health Indicators in the United States: Results from the 2016 National Survey on Drug Use and Health (Rockville, MD: Center for Behavioral Health Statistics and Quality, 2017), https://www.samhsa.gov/data/sites/default/files/NSDUH-FFR1-2016/NSDUH-FFR1-2016.htm.

164   **In 2016, 21 percent**   Jonathan P. Caulkins, "The Real Dangers of Marijuana," *National Affairs* 40 (Summer 2019), https://www.nationalaffairs.com/publications/detail/the-real-dangers-of-marijuana.

164   **as many as 33 percent**   Stacey Colino, "Why Do People (Mistakenly) Think Marijuana Isn't Addictive?," Addiction.com, April 28, 2015, https://www.addiction.com/9283/why-do-people-mistakenly-think-marijuana-isnt-addictive/.

165 **teen brains "build a reward circuit"**   Jensen, "Why Teens Are Impulsive, Addiction-Prone, and Should Protect Their Brains."

165 **studies of THC concentration . . . 33 percent THC**   Mahmoud A. ElSohly, Zlatko Mehmedic, Susan Foster, et al., "Changes in Cannabis Potency over the Last 2 Decades (1995–2014): Analysis of Current Data in the United States," *Biological Psychiatry* 79, no. 7 (2016): 613–19, doi:10.1016/j.biopsych.2016.01.004.

166 **Maureen Dowd's harrowing account**   Maureen Dowd, "Don't Harsh Our Mellow, Dude," *New York Times*, Opinion, June 3, 2014, https://www.nytimes.com/2014/06/04/opinion/dowd-dont-harsh-our-mellow-dude.html.

167 **according to Emily Feinstein**   Sarah Maslin Nir, "Chasing Bigger High, Marijuana Users Turn to 'Dabbing,'" *New York Times*, May 12, 2016, https://www.nytimes.com/2016/05/13/nyregion/chasing-bigger-high-marijuana-users-turn-to-dabbing. html.

168 **more than one-third of teenagers have vaped**   Leah Campbell, "Juuling: The Addictive New Vaping Trend Teens Are Hiding," Healthline, modified May 2019, https://www.healthline.com/health-news/juuling-the-new-vaping-trend-thats-twice-as-addictive-as-cigarettes%235#1.

168 **Of the twelfth graders who report vaping**   Kristy L. Marynak, Doris G. Gammon, Todd Rogers, et al., "Sales of Nicotine-Containing Electronic Cigarette Products: United States, 2015," *American Journal of Public Health* 107, no. 5 (2017): 702–705, doi:10.2105/AJPH.2017.303660.

168 **63 percent of JUUL users did not know**   Truth Initative, "JUUL E-Cigarettes Gain Popularity Among Youth, but Awareness of Nicotine Presence Remains Low," April 18, 2018, https://truthinitiative.org/press/press-release/juul-e-cigarettes-gain-popularity-among-youth-awareness-nicotine-presence.

168 **JUUL pods contain almost *double***   Campbell, "Juuling."

169 **We are already seeing that youth who vape**   University of Pittsburgh Schools of the Health Sciences, "E-Cig Use Increases Risk of Beginning Tobacco Cigarette Use in Young Adults," ScienceDaily, December 11, 2017, https://www.sciencedaily.com/releases/2017/12/171211090733.htm.

169 **About one in five twelfth graders**   Johnston et al., "Monitoring the Future."

169 **More Americans die from opioid overdoses**   Partnership for Drug-Free Kids/Center on Addiction, "How Can Prescription Drugs Lead to Heroin Use?," accessed June 25, 2019, https://drugfree.org/article/rx-to-heroin/.

169 **Up to 80 percent . . . or from friends**   Partnership for Drug-Free Kids/Center on Addiction, "How Can Prescription Drugs Lead to Heroin Use?"

170 **Research shows that legitimate teen opioid use**   Kennon Heard, Richard Miech, Lloyd Johnston, et al., "Prescription Opioids in Adolescence and Future Opioid Misuse," *Pediatrics* 136, no. 5 (November 2015), doi:10.1542/peds.2015-1364.

171 **Research shows that MDMA**   Grisel, *Never Enough*; Lynn Taurah, Chris Chandler, and Geoff Sanders, "Depression, Impulsiveness, Sleep, and Memory in Past and Present Polydrug Users of 3,4-Methylenedioxymethamphetamine

(MDMA, Ecstasy)," *Psychopharmacology* 231, no. 4 (2019): 737–51, doi:10.1007
/s00213-013-3288-1.

174   **Stimulant drugs such as caffeine**   Partnership for Drug-Free Kids/Cen-
ter on Addiction, "Stress and Drug Use: What Every Parent Should Know,"
August 2, 2017, https://drugfree.org/parent-blog/stress-drug-use-every-parent
-should-know/.

174   **Twenty years ago, Icelandic teens**   Emma Young, "How Iceland Got Teens
to Say No to Drugs," *Atlantic*, January 19, 2017, https://www.theatlantic.com
/health/archive/2017/01/teens-drugs-iceland/513668/.

174   **Iceland's program was "designed**   Young, "How Iceland Got Teens to Say No
to Drugs."

177   **research suggests is fantastic**   David W. Orme-Johnson and Vernon
A. Barnes, "Effects of the Transcendental Meditation Technique on Trait
Anxiety: A Meta-Analysis of Randomized Controlled Trials," *Journal of Alternative and Complementary Medicine* 20, no. 5 (2014): 330–41, doi:10.1089
/acm.2013.0204.

178   **In one study, teenagers who had trouble falling or staying asleep**   M. M.
Wong, K. J. Brower, J. T. Nigg, et al., "Childhood Sleep Problems, Response
Inhibition, and Alcohol and Drug Outcomes in Adolescence and Young Adulthood," *Alcoholism: Clinical and Experimental Research* 34, no. 6 (June 2010):
1033–44, doi:10.1111/j.1530-0277.2010.01178.x.

178   **Another large study of teenagers**   M. M. Wong, G. C. Robertson, and
R. B. Dyson, "Prospective Relationship Between Poor Sleep and Substance-
Related Problems in a National Sample of Adolescents," *Alcoholism: Clinical and Experimental Research* 39, no. 2 (February 2015): 355–62, doi:10.1111
/acer.12618.

178   **prominent sleep researcher Matthew Walker**   Matthew Walker, *Why We
Sleep: Unlocking the Power of Sleep and Dreams* (New York: Simon and Schuster, 2017).

Chapter Ten

184   **Two-thirds of adults**   "Stress in America: Generation Z," American Psychological Association, October 2018, https://www.apa.org/news/press/releases
/stress/2018/stress-gen-z.pdf.

184   **30 percent say they worry**   Shawn M. Carter, "30% of Americans Are 'Constantly' Stressed Out About Money," CNBC, March 20, 2018, https://www.cnbc
.com/2018/03/19/30-percent-of-americans-are-stressed-out-about-money
-constantly.html.

184   **Medical costs, for example . . . 22 percent**   Claire Tsosie and Erin El Issa, "2018
American Household Credit Card Debt Study," *Nerdwallet*, December 10, 2018,
https://www.nerdwallet.com/blog/average-credit-card-debt-household/#foot.

184 **student loan debt has increased** Maurie Backman, "5 Shocking Student Loan Stats," *The Motley Fool*, July 28, 2018, https://www.fool.com /retirement/2018/07/28/5-shocking-student-loan-stats.aspx.

185 **The interview, which went viral** Mandy Woodruff, "22-Year-Old College Student Blows Her $90,000 College Fund and Blames Her Parents," *Yahoo Finance*, July 17, 2015, https://finance.yahoo.com/news/a-college-student -blows-inheritance-bert-show-205833329.html.

187 **there are two things that influence . . . more materialistic offspring** M. E. Goldberg, G. J. Gorn, L. A. Perrachio, et al., "Understanding Materialism Among Youth," *Journal of Consumer Psychology* 13 (2003); T. Kasser, *The High Price of Materialism* (Cambridge, MA: MIT Press, 2002); P. Rose and S. P. DeJesus, "A Model of Motivated Cognition to Account for the Link Between Self-Monitoring and Materialism," *Psychology & Marketing* 24, no. 2 (2007).

189 **Kids who get an allowance tend to** Rona Abramovitch, Jonathan L. Freedman, and Patricia Pliner, "Children and Money: Getting an Allowance, Credit Versus Cash, and Knowledge of Pricing," *Journal of Economic Psychology* 12, no. 1 (1991): 27–45.

190 **kids who do unpaid chores are happier** Joy S. Grazer, "All in the Family: Why Housework Might Make Kids Happier," *Greater Good Magazine*, June 8, 2010, https://greatergood.berkeley.edu/article/item/all_in_the_family/.

190 **when we *pay* kids to play a role** Christine Carter, "Wanna Piece of Chocolate?" *Greater Good Magazine*, January 5, 2011, https://greatergood.berkeley .edu/raising_happiness/post/wanna_piece_of_chocolate.

192 **In one study, participants were given** Elizabeth W. Dunn, Lara B. Aknin, and Michael I. Norton, "Prosocial Spending and Happiness: Using Money to Benefit Others Pays Off," *Current Directions in Psychological Science* 23, no. 1 (2014): 41–47.

197 **The average American household with student loan debt** Tsosie and El Issa, "2018 American Household Credit Card Debt Study."

Conclusion

200 **more than 80 percent of youth** Harvard Graduate School of Education, "The Children We Mean to Raise: The Real Messages Adults Are Sending About Values," Making Caring Common Project, July 2014, https://mcc.gse.harvard .edu/reports/children-mean-raise.

201 **The average American adult has only one close confidant** Miller McPherson, Lynn Smith-Lovin, and Matthew E. Brashears, "Social Isolation in America: Changes in Core Discussion Networks over Two Decades," *American Sociological Review* 71, no. 3 (2006): 353–75, doi:10.1177/000312240607100301.

201 **Nearly one-quarter of adults** B. DiJulio, L. Hamel, C. Muñana, et al., "Loneliness and Social Isolation in the United States, the United Kingdom, and Japan: An International Survey," Henry J. Kaiser Family Foundation, August 30, 2018.

201   **The leading reason**   Mark R. Leary and Roy F. Baumeister, "The Need to Belong: Desire for Interpersonal Attachments as a Fundamental Human Motivation" in *Interpersonal Development* (New York: Routledge, 2017), 57–89.

201   **The adolescent suicide rate has increased**   Carson Chambers, "CDC: Teen Suicide Rate up 70% from 2006 to 2016," *ABC Action News*, March 21, 2018, https://www.abcactionnews.com/news/region-tampa/cdc-teen-suicide-rate-up-70-from-2006-to-2016.

202   **Massive income inequality . . . than ever before**   Hayley Glatter, "The Most Polarized Freshman Class in Half a Century," *Atlantic*, May 2, 2017, https://www.theatlantic.com/education/archive/2017/05/the-most-polarized-freshman-class-in-half-a-century/525135/.

203   **global happiness studies have shown**   Shigehiro Oishi and Ed Diener, "Residents of Poor Nations Have a Greater Sense of Meaning in Life Than Residents of Wealthy Nations," *Psychological Science* 25, no. 2 (2014): 422–30, doi:10.1177/0956797613507286.

205   **Don't aim at success**   Viktor E. Frankl, *Man's Search for Meaning* (New York: Simon and Schuster, 1985).

205   **More often than not, such striving**   Adam Grant, *Give and Take: A Revolutionary Approach to Success* (New York: Penguin, 2013).

209   **"shift from the cramped world"**   Greg Boyle, *Tattoos on the Heart: The Power of Boundless Compassion* (New York: Simon and Schuster, 2011).

Index

About the Author

Christine Carter, PhD, is author of *The New Adolescence* (2020), *The Sweet Spot: How to Achieve More by Doing Less* (2017), and *Raising Happiness* (2011). Dr. Carter was a Senior Fellow at Dartmouth (her alma mater) before she began work in marketing management, and later, school administration.

After completing her masters and doctoral degrees in sociology at the University of California, Berkeley, Dr. Carter was recruited to lead the Greater Good Science Center (GGSC) as its executive director. In 2014, she hired a new executive director so that she could pursue her writing and speaking career full-time. Dr. Carter remains a sociologist and Senior Fellow at the GGSC and writes a monthly advice column for *Greater Good Magazine*, in which she draws on scientific research to help people lead their most courageous, joyful, meaningful, and productive lives.

An engaging and sought-after speaker, Dr. Carter loves to share her work in person. Combining scientific research and practical application, she offers audiences not only a way to *cope* with modern pressures but tactics to truly *thrive*. She regularly keynotes at large conferences and fundraisers and is a popular commencement speaker. She is a frequent contributor to executive, general-interest, and parenting programs with other leading scholars and teachers.

She lives with her husband, four teenagers, and dog in Marin County, California.